MW01519921

A CULTURAL HISTORY
OF MARRIAGE

VOLUME 5

A Cultural History of Marriage
General Editor: Joanne M. Ferraro

Volume 1
A Cultural History of Marriage in Antiquity
Edited by Karen Klaiber Hersch

Volume 2
A Cultural History of Marriage in the Medieval Age
Edited by Joanne M. Ferraro and Frederik Pedersen

Volume 3
A Cultural History of Marriage in the Renaissance and Early Modern Age
Edited by Joanne M. Ferraro

Volume 4
A Cultural History of Marriage in the Age of Enlightenment
Edited by Edward Behrend-Martínez

Volume 5
A Cultural History of Marriage in the Age of Empires
Edited by Paul Puschmann

Volume 6
A Cultural History of Marriage in the Modern Age
Edited by Christina Simmons

A CULTURAL HISTORY OF MARRIAGE

IN THE AGE OF EMPIRES

Edited by Paul Puschmann

BLOOMSBURY ACADEMIC
LONDON • NEW YORK • OXFORD • NEW DELHI • SYDNEY

BLOOMSBURY ACADEMIC
Bloomsbury Publishing Plc
50 Bedford Square, London, WC1B 3DP, UK
1385 Broadway, New York, NY 10018, USA

BLOOMSBURY, BLOOMSBURY ACADEMIC and the Diana logo are
trademarks of Bloomsbury Publishing Plc

First published in Great Britain 2020

ISBN: HB: 978-1-3500-0189-3
          Set: 978-1-3500-0191-6

Series: The Cultural Histories Series

Typeset by Integra Software Services Pvt. Ltd.
Printed and bound in Great Britain

To find out more about our authors and books visit www.bloomsbury.com
and sign up for our newsletters.

CONTENTS

LIST OF FIGURES

INTRODUCTION

COURTSHIP AND RITUAL

RELIGION

STATE AND LAW

THE TIES THAT BIND

THE FAMILY ECONOMY

LOVE, SEX, AND SEXUALITY

BREAKING VOWS

REPRESENTATIONS

CONTRIBUTORS

Angélique Janssens is an endowed professor of historical demography at Maastricht University and associate professor at Radboud University, Nijmegen, the Netherlands. She is a member of the Radboud Group for Historical Demography and Family History and scientific director of the N.W. Posthumus Institute, the Research School for Economic and Social History in the Netherlands and Flanders. She is the author of *Family and Social Change: The Household as a Process in an Industrializing Community* (2002) and of *Labouring Lives: Women, Work and the Demographic Transition in the Netherlands, 1880–1960* (2014). She has published widely in international journals and is co-editor of *The History of the Family. An International Quarterly*.

Karl Kaser is a full professor of Southeastern European history and anthropology at the University of Graz, Austria. His most recent monographs are *Patriarchy after Patriarchy: Gender Relations in Turkey and in the Balkans* (2008); *The Balkans and the Near East: Introduction to a Shared History* (2011); and *Hollywood auf dem Balkan. Die visuelle Moderne an der europäischen Peripherie (1900–70)* (2017). Currently he is working on a monographic book project, "Visual Representations of Femininities and Masculinities: The Balkans and South Caucasia in the Digital Era." He is coordinator of the research and exchange project "Knowledge Exchange and Academic Cultures in the Humanities: Europe and the Black Sea Region, late 18th—21st Centuries."

Jan Kok wrote his dissertation on the history of single mothers in the nineteenth-century Netherlands. He worked as a post-doc at the International Institute of Social History in Amsterdam, and was involved in the creation of the Historical Sample of the Netherlands. His subsequent research revolved around this database, and he has published widely on topics such as leaving home, celibacy, marriage, and fertility. In 2010, he was appointed professor of comparative history of the life course, and in 2013 he became chair of economic, social and demographic history at Radboud University Nijmegen. He is co-editor-in-chief of *The History of the Family. An International Quarterly*.

Karl Leydecker is senior vice-principal at the University of Aberdeen in Scotland. Prior to that he was professor of German and comparative literature and vice-principal learning and teaching at the University of Dundee. His main research areas include divorce in German, European, and American literature from the eighteenth to the twentieth century, German and Austrian drama and social history 1890–1930, censorship of the theater in Berlin 1890–1918, German Expressionism, and novelists of the Weimar Republic. His recent publications include co-editing volume 2 of the five-volume edition of Ernst Toller, *Sämtliche Werke: Kritische Ausgabe* (2014) and *After Marriage in the Long Eighteenth Century: Literature, Law and Society* (2018), co-edited with Jenny DiPlacidi.

Satomi Kurosu is professor of sociology at Reitaku University, Japan. As director of the Population and Family History Project (PFHP), she leads the construction and analysis of multigenerational data sets of early modern Japan. She works in the field of historical demography and family sociology. Her research focuses on marriage, adoption, and other demographic behaviors in Japan and in comparative perspective. She is the author of numerous articles in international journals, and one of the lead authors of *Similarity in Difference: Marriage in Europe and Asia, 1700–1900* (2014).

Rebecca Probert is professor of law at the University of Exeter. Her research focuses on the history of marriage, bigamy, divorce, and cohabitation and she is the author of numerous articles and books, including *Marriage Law and Practice in the Long Eighteenth Century: A Reassessment* (2009) and *The Legal Regulation of Cohabitation: From Fornicators to Family, 1600–2010* (2012).

Paul Puschmann is an assistant professor of economic, social, and demographic history at Radboud University, Nijmegen, the Netherlands. He is affiliated with the Radboud Group for Historical Demography and Family History. Prior to his current position, he was a postdoctoral researcher at Family and Population Studies, KU Leuven, Belgium, where he also earned his Ph.D. Paul specializes in historical demography and has published on different aspects of migration, partner choice, and marriage in Europe, the Middle East, and North Africa. He is research program director of the Life-Courses, Family and Labour Network of the N.W. Posthumus Institute, the Research School for Economic and Social History in the Netherlands and Flanders, and he is co-editor of *Historical Life Course Studies*.

K. Dilhani Wijesinghe is a doctoral student at Reitaku University, Japan. She is the author of "Factors Associated with Teenage Pregnancies in Sri Lanka: A Study of Colombo Municipal Council," *Sri Lanka Journal of Population Studies* (forthcoming), and the co-author of "Projections of Population, Labour Force and its Female Component in Sri Lanka," *Economic Review* (2013), Research Division, Peoples' Bank.

Marja van Tilburg has been affiliated with the Department of History of the University of Groningen, the Netherlands, since 1986. She contributed to the interdisciplinary minor of Gender Studies and served on the board of the Centre for Gender Studies of the Faculty of Arts. Her thesis *Hoe hoorde het? Seksualiteit en partnerkeuze in de Nederlandse adviesliteratuur 1780–1890* (1998) explores the diffusion of Enlightenment pedagogy in conduct books for adolescents. She has explored the circuitous reception of the concept of "adolescence" in the education of young women, most recently in the anthology *A History of the Girl* (2018). In addition she has published on lifecycles and gender in European culture, including in *The Journal of Family History*.

GENERAL EDITOR'S PREFACE

JOANNE M. FERRARO

The six-volume Bloomsbury Academic Cultural History of Marriage series is designed for both students and scholars of history, gender and cultural studies, anthropology, sociology, and related disciplines. Its chronological boundaries and periodization are in accordance with the various other Bloomsbury Academic history series. While the volumes are implicitly Western and European in chronological perspective, the contributors have made strenuous efforts to make world comparisons where appropriate; to be mindful of religious differences where possible; and to reach across the disciplines. Together they offer a set of peer-reviewed original works of synthesis and interpretation that engage recent scholarship and use representative primary sources.

With a uniform set of themes in mind, each of the six volumes contains the same chapter titles so that readers can explore a particular topic across the entire series. Each chapter offers an overview of a theme as well as a wide range of case material derived from original research. There are eight common areas of investigation. The volumes open with a chapter on the preludes to marriage in the way of courtship and rites. Two chapters follow, covering the evolution of law and practice in both the religious and secular spheres, respectively; examining how authorities made marital consent binding; and exploring the ways in which clerics and secular officials attempted to regulate the behavior of wives and husbands. The fourth chapter, "The Ties that Bind," encompasses a broad spectrum of behavior, situating marital unions within the context of kinship groups and social networks as well as amidst alliances of property and power. Marriage as an economic contract and unit of production and reproduction is the general theme of the fifth chapter, "The Family Economy," and includes the subjects of dowry and estate management as well as the role of wives and husbands in income-producing activities and child rearing. While marriage legitimized sexual relations, whether or not it included love in times past continues to be the subject of vigorous debate, particularly for the period preceding the eighteenth century. In the sixth chapter, "Love, Sex, and Sexuality," historians tread cautiously, examining the quality of marriage and sexual relations on a case by case basis as well as reviewing expected, albeit ideal, norms in contrast to practice. Extramarital sex is also treated under this rubric and connects well with the theme of the seventh chapter, "Breaking Vows" through separation and divorce. Finally, the eighth chapter explores the myriad ways in which marriage was represented in art, material culture, theater, and literature.

The contributors have availed themselves of a wide array of both prescriptive and descriptive sources. Among the former are biblical, classical, and religious texts; legal treatises and legislation; and an assortment of mythological, literary, and artistic works. These documents and visual materials often represent the ideal templates of an age, such as the cloistered maiden, the faithful wife, or the successful husband. Among the descriptive sources are letters and diaries as well as court testimonies from archival repositories; ledgers and account books; ecclesiastical records of marriage and marital litigation; and for the Modern age, film as well as digital media. Their descriptions often transcend the ideal templates offered in prescriptive writings and afford insights into the realities of social experience. They shed light on human behavior and the ways in which women and men negotiated and contested the enforcement of formal laws and parental authority. It is important to note, however, that there are fewer such sources for the classical period, wherein scholars often must rely more heavily on artifacts, while the number of available textual sources steadily increases over time.

In tracing the evolution of marriage over the long term, the series highlights no less than sweeping changes in its significance to religious and secular institutions, to family status and estate management, and to the affective desires of women and men. Marriage was not available to everyone; opportunities were heavily dependent on financial means. Further, gender and social class were important determinants of marital experience and thus are important categories of analysis throughout the series. In principle men enjoyed more freedom within the conjugal bond than women, and free people had more flexibility than slaves or serfs. Yet it remains important to nuance such generalities by devoting close attention to regional differences as well as to the social and political status of individuals. Contributors in Volume 1, covering Antiquity, for example, have found that in contrast to Greece or Rome slaves in Ptolemaic Egypt could marry. These scholars have also determined that consent to marry was important in the Greco-Roman world, but nonetheless elite men as well as elite women were obliged to respect the priorities of their families and given little choice in the selection of spouses. Their marriages were arranged without a period of courtship, an experience that might possibly evolve within the union over time. It was not a sacrament but, rather, a legal transaction that provided for the transfer of property and the reproduction of the male line. Beyond family interests, marriage was of central importance to both community and state; the primary means of creating new households and citizens. It was fundamentally a patriarchal institution. However, scholars in Volume 1 suggest that the happiest marriages were in feminine hands.

The period between 500 and 1450, termed broadly the Medieval Age in Volume 2, witnessed a dramatic change in perceptions of the institution of marriage in Christian communities. The transformation was in large part a product of the growth of the Christian church both as an institution and as a primary organizing principle for European society. Between roughly the sixth and eleventh centuries prelates gradually converted the pagan tribes of the West to Christianity. Irish monks, with reinforcement from the Franks, fostered and defended the spread of the new creed in the face of non-Christian invaders, making it the majority religion. Religious men preserved classical scholarship and oversaw the administration of secular government. Importantly, they were the dominant sponsors of cultural advancement in art, philosophy, and political ideology, all infused with Christian themes. In the social sphere they slowly but persistently regulated marital life, insisting on free will, even for serfs, and that a valid marriage require the mutual consent of the couple. The philosophical, theological, and legal developments that unfolded between the twelfth and fifteenth centuries solidified the church's position as a dominant force in social life, influencing sexual norms, family economy, relations between the state and the individual and transforming both liturgy and iconography. Insofar as marriage was concerned several developments stand out: the establishment of incest restrictions that set the kinship boundaries for marriage; the insistence on free will; and the declaration that marriage was a sacrament, where the consent of the couple rendered it legally and spiritually binding before God. The twelfth and thirteenth centuries in particular witnessed changes in theologians' understanding of canon law and with them the conjugal union became central to discussions about salvation. Marriage was both a spiritual and physical state of mind. Spiritually it was to reflect Christ's loving relationship with the church, something that both the various members of the clergy and the laity could experience. However, while the clergy were bound by vows of celibacy, the laity were taught that monogamous marriage was the only place for sexual activity, and its sole purpose was for procreation. In the West a further proviso was established that veered away from the Gospels and the teachings of St. Paul: marriage could not be dissolved. This remained in stark contrast to both Greek Orthodox, Judaic, and Muslim traditions.

The economic, intellectual, and religious reorganization of Western European society that took place between 1450 and 1650, described generally in Volume 3 as the Renaissance and Early Modern Age, brought the parameters of marriage instituted by the medieval church under scrutiny. The period witnessed a commercial revolution that gave rise to a more literate and secular-minded professional class in Europe's urban centers; the expansion of Europe to the Americas, Africa, and Asia; and a new approach to education termed humanism that, together with the scientific revolution, challenged medieval scholastic epistemology. With the rise of secularism both materially and intellectually, theologians and jurists debated over whether marriage was a sacrament or a contract. For many families it was a means of guarding or improving their social and political positions as well as their financial status. Thus parental control over the choice of their children's spouses was tantamount, making notarial contracts essential. This more secular model of marriage challenged the church's jurisdictional claims of primacy and conflicted with the religious mandate that only the verbal consent of bride and groom was required in order to make the union valid. For young couples, privileging the contract over the sacrament exacerbated the conflict over free choice and parental control. These tensions were particularly high among the classes of economic substance, such as the nobility or the commercial and juridical elites.

The Protestant Reformation introduced a second challenge to the medieval parameters of marriage: the possibility of divorce. The practice was largely limited during the sixteenth and seventeenth centuries but nonetheless a dramatic conceptual break with the medieval past. Divorce in Protestant areas of Europe recognized the possibility of failed marriage. It was not necessarily under the sole jurisdiction of the ecclesiastical courts. In some places secular consistories also heard petitions to dissolve marital unions. In Catholic areas, on the other hand, ecclesiastical tribunals sometimes granted a separation of bed and board, but the institution of marriage remained permanent in the eyes of God. Ecclesiastical courts also judged whether marital unions were legally valid and binding. Betrothals, promises to marry, and the marriage rite itself had unfolded throughout the Middle Ages in a variety of ways, reflecting both regional and confessional differences but also the urgency in some cases to have sexual relations prior to wedlock. When one partner, generally the man, reneged on the promise the litigation reached the ecclesiastical court. The flood of breech of promise suits and general confusion over whether couples were in a binding relationship led Catholic theologians to regularize the form of marriage at the Council of Trent in 1563. Prelates laid down some basic requirements: publication of the banns three times in the parish where the marriage would take place; the presence of a prelate and witnesses at the service; and the couple's verbal expression of mutual consent.

The marriage also had to be consummated and registered. Ironically, the regularization of marriage rites also led to a proliferation of petitions to annul unions, ostensibly because couples had not followed the prescribed form.

The conflict between religious and secular models of marriage and between free will and parental control remained unresolved throughout the Renaissance and Early Modern Age and continued into the Age of Enlightenment, 1650–1800. The main issue, treated in detail in Volume 4, became whether marriage could be an affective bond and the fruit of love rather than an arranged match. Historians of that period are still debating whether marriage was a cold, business affair or filled with love and affection. Obviously no one model applies. However, the contributors in Volume 4 find that by the late eighteenth century there was greater emphasis on marrying for love, a trend that intertwined with historic economic developments and new Enlightenment ideals. Europe was expanding both economically and territorially, and there was a growing trend to allow free choice away from paternal authority. This did not break the religious stranglehold on marriage but it did attenuate it in some areas of the European continent.

The Age of Empires, 1800–1900, also witnessed several changes in the domain of marriage. Generally, government and secular law took on greater influence in the regulation of conjugal unions than in the past. The introduction of civil marriage made registration by the state compulsory, a development that encouraged the practice of civil ceremonies. In some areas, however, common law marriage prevailed over unions concluded under government supervision, while in others the influence of religion and religious rites remained substantial. The idea of romantic love, introduced in earlier times, featured prominently during this "Age of Romanticism," particularly in literature and theater. Novel plots where lovers played a leading role more often than not ended happily. Nonetheless, in some parts of the world marriage was still arranged by the parents of the couple, keeping in mind the exchange and extension of wealth and labor power as well as the future of the family lines. The opportunities for premarital sex varied from place to place. Where individuals married young there was no room for romance or sexuality prior to the wedding. Southeast Asia, Japan, Polynesia, and parts of Africa, North American, and Europe afforded some ritualized opportunities for sexual experience before marriage in the form of "night courting." Peers of the unmarried couple would supervise the activities in hopes of preventing unwanted pregnancies. In Western societies experiencing greater rural-to-urban migration and urbanization, the incidence of out-of-wedlock fertility rose, reaching its peak in the latter half of the nineteenth century with the introduction of birth control. The stigma of such pregnancies, however, prevailed and contributed to the spread of sexually repressive codes both in Europe and its colonies. The later nineteenth century also witnessed an increase in divorce, signaling a weakening of marriage as an institution and presaging what was to come in the twentieth century.

Perhaps the most sweeping change in the institution of marriage during the twentieth and twenty-first centuries, featured in the scholarship of Volume 6, The Modern Age, is that it was no longer the central organizing principle of social life. With the increasing autonomy of individuals, many people have chosen not to marry, living life as singles or simply cohabiting with a partner. It is not uncommon for individuals to have multiple sexual relationships over their life cycles or for childbearing to take place outside of marriage. A variety of factors have undermined both marriage and close connections with kin. Among them, globalization, improved means of long-distance transportation, and shifting labor opportunities, developments that have resulted in people leaving their natal villages, towns, and cities to settle in other far-off places, where family bonds are less accessible and there is less social pressure to conform to tradition. In this context kinship groups have become less cohesive, and the extended family has given way to nuclear units or individual autonomy. Increasing opportunities for women in the labor force, especially during the twenty-first century, have also contributed to changes in the nature or necessity of marriage. Women are less dependent on having husbands and are more reluctant to subscribe to the rigid gender roles of times past. The second-wave feminist movement of the late twentieth century has been critical in challenging patriarchal authority and in defining new roles for women in family and society. More women are obtaining advanced degrees and participating in the labor force. Finally, the twentieth and twenty-first centuries have also witnessed no less than a revolution in the recognition of the complexities of human sexuality. The LGBTQ movements have liberated individuals to have sexual relationships and bear children with preferred partners, and in many countries same-sex marriage has become legal. These dramatic changes have not come without turmoil, and religious leaders, politicians, civic authorities, the media, communities, and individuals continue to question the origins and meaning of marriage and to attempt to define its parameters and purpose. Thus Bloomsbury Academic's Cultural History of Marriage constitutes a timely and important body of scholarship addressing the ongoing debates of a broad segment of society today.

Introduction

During the Age of Empires (1800–1900) marriage was a key transition in the life course worldwide, and everywhere it was a rite of passage with major cultural significance. Marriage marked the transition into adulthood, and in nuclear family systems it also signified the passage into an independent life from parents with the establishment of an autonomous household. Marriage was the only institution that gave access to sexual intercourse that was socially, legally, and religiously accepted, and it was also the exclusive framework within which legal offspring were born and raised. Legitimate children were eligible for the inheritance of family property, could succeed their parents in public functions, and could take over the family business. The institution of marriage was important for all layers of society but especially for elite and farm-owning families, as marriage enabled them to keep their land, wealth, power, and prerogatives in the family. Marriage was also a potential gateway to improve one's position in society and to move up the social ladder.

FIGURE I.1 Currier & Ives Illustration 19th century, *The Marriage*, 1840. World History Archive. Alamy Stock Photo. Image ID:DYEMFM.

Marriage united two individuals of the opposite sex, but it was also a way to create or strengthen an alliance between the kin groups of the bride and groom, who often pooled land, capital, and labor and cooperated intensively.[1] Marriage was indeed economic in nature and went hand in hand with the transfer of property in the form of dowries and bride prices. The marriage of an heir also usually consisted of some kind of arrangement between the generations, whereby for instance a workshop or farm was transferred from the parents to the children in return for care and accommodation of the parents during old age.[2] In this sense marriage went hand in hand with obligations, but it also came along with essential rights and securities.

Married individuals had advantages over single people, as they could turn not only to their own families but also to their partners and their families in times of need. As a result, married people had a larger social network and more resources at their disposal, and this was essential to their existence. After all, individuals could appeal to family members for employment and housing and they could ask them for assistance in productive—for example in farmer's families during sowing and harvesting periods—and reproductive tasks—for example grandmothers who took care of infants and young children. In case of conflict, family members were asked to act as mediators and in times of war and violence the family could act as a protective shield. Last, but not least, the family might be a source of credit, goods, and food.

Since the economic, social, and cultural capital varied significantly among families, some were able to move the world, while others were merely able to offer basic assistance.

FIGURE I.2 *A Nineteenth Century Family Enjoying a Get Together and Feast on the Day of the Epiphany, L'Univers Illustre* published in Paris, January 6, 1868. Classic Image. Alamy Stock Photo. Image ID: C5YHKE.

This had a huge impact on the life chances of the individuals involved.[3] In an age in which there did not exist a social security system as we know it today in Western countries, individuals relied heavily on their family in case of illness, poverty, and misfortune. Therefore, choosing a marriage partner was a decision with far-reaching implications. Marrying a spouse from a wealthy and powerful family meant protection and security, while marrying someone from a poor family could lead to lifelong struggles to get by. Poverty was a serious threat; even in nineteenth-century-industrializing Europe, between 25 percent and 50 percent of the population was poor.[4] It is therefore understandable that economic considerations usually prevailed over romantic and emotional motives regarding the choice of a partner for life. Such economic considerations, however, did not necessarily prevent a happy family life nor did it imply that the relationship between spouses was cold and pragmatic.[5]

THE MANY FACES OF MARRIAGE

While marriage first of all served functional interests in the Age of Empires worldwide, the types of arrangements that were being made in terms of partner choice, number of partners, co-residence patterns, power relations, inheritance regulations, and divorce practices varied considerably across cultures, religions, family systems, social strata, and demographic regimes.[6] If we want to understand these differences, we have to look, first of all, at the power relations between men and women on one hand, and between parents and children, on the other.[7]

During the nineteenth and early twentieth century most societies were patriarchal.[8] Patriarchy is a system that determines power relations within households and families, favoring men over women, and parents over children. In practice it places husbands over wives, and fathers over sons and daughters, older brothers over younger brothers, but also mothers over daughters, mothers-in-law over daughters-in-law, and older sisters over younger sisters.[9] However, there was quite some variation in the authority men could exercise as husbands and fathers (and women as mothers and mothers-in-law), depending on the degree that patriarchy was supported by state, law, and religion and this translated into different marriage patterns and household formation systems.[10]

On one side of the spectrum there were societies—mainly Northwestern Europe and to a certain degree also North America, Australia, and New Zealand—where men only slightly overpowered women and parents exercised only minimal control over their children.[11] This weak form of patriarchy—what Arthur Wolf calls property patriarchy[12]— was linked to (semi-) free partner choice, late and non-universal marriage, small age differences between spouses, absolute monogamy, and nuclear families. As parents had only limited control over their children—only through inheritance in cases where they had wealth—the children stopped contributing to the parental budget at some time in their life, broke away from the family of orientation (in cases where there was no prospect of inheritance they did this early on)[13] and ultimately married a spouse of their own choice and formed an independent household. Men overpowered women, but men's power was mitigated by the fact that their partners were on average only slightly younger and could inherit property and earn an income. Premarital sex usually occurred in peer-controlled settings.[14] Next, marriages were monogamous, as the church had forbidden and punished polygamy ever since the Middle Ages, and late eighteenth- and nineteenth-century Western European states defined civil marriage exclusively as a union between one man and one woman.[15] Marriage was late and non-universal, partially as a result of the fact that children had to find an appropriate partner by themselves, which took more time than in arranged partner systems where parents started to search early on for a partner for their children.[16] Moreover, as parents could not force their children into marriage, children could choose to remain single if they did not want to take up the duties of married life or did not find a suitable marriage partner.[17]

Strong patriarchy—what Arthur Wolf calls state patriarchy in the context of China[18]— was by contrast mainly found in Islamic societies, in late-imperial China, India, and in many sub-Saharan African countries. This form of patriarchy was linked to arranged marriages, early and universal marriage among women, older husband–younger wife couples, the option of polygyny, and the cultural preference for extended households. Parental authority was absolute because it was backed up by state, law, and religion.[19] Gender relations were also highly asymmetrical, in the sense that husbands exercised strong power over their wives. This was translated into a strong requirement for women to remain virgins until marriage, female seclusion, women having to cover their hair in public areas in Islamic societies, foot breaking and foot-binding in the case of Chinese women, as well as violence against women, including female genital mutilation in various African and some Western-Asian societies.[20] In strong patriarchal societies male offspring were highly favored over female offspring, with girls facing a much higher risk of infanticide and a strongly disadvantaged life. As a result, in certain contexts and in certain age groups females had higher mortality rates.

In societies marked by strong patriarchy marriages were arranged and parents often started to search for a partner for their children during early childhood. This resulted in early and universal marriage among women, and in unequal relationships as parents chose on average significantly younger brides for their sons. Upon marriage, the couple usually moved into the extended household of the parents of the groom, where they kept working and contributing to the parental household budget, and they also remained under their authority. In most of these strong patriarchal societies it was easy for men to divorce, but they were usually also allowed to marry more than one wife and to have concubines, enhancing their sexual power.[21] However, the degree to which polygyny was put into practice varied significantly. In the Middle East and North Africa polygyny was, for instance, rare and mostly only practiced among the ruling families and the rich.[22] In Western Africa, by contrast, polygyny was widespread, and this was strengthened by the European slave trade, as more males than females were transported to the New World, distorting natural sex balances.[23]

Within strong patriarchal family systems a major dividing line can be drawn between families that preferred to arrange endogamous unions and those who favored exogamous marriages.[24] In the Middle East and North Africa strong preference was given to the former, especially in the form of cousin marriages, whereby daughters married a son of their father's brother. Marriage endogamy mitigated some of the extreme sides of patriarchy, as the bride belonged to the same blood line and could therefore not simply be mistreated and repudiated, as this would lead to family feuds.[25]

Of course there was a much larger diversity in marriage patterns and family systems than those found at the extreme ends of the patriarchy scale, as discussed above. We can think, for instance, about stem family societies, which were found in various regions of Europe and Asia.[26] Stem families took up an intermediate position between nuclear and extended family systems, as only one of the children acted as the heir and remained in the parental household. The heir was usually a male, but in certain regions, such as Japan, it could also be a daughter.[27] On the other hand, Latin American societies were characterized by strong parental authority and male dominance, but low marriage rates. In Southern Europe, family ties were strong and so was parental authority, but marriage ages were relatively high, access to marriage was restricted, and partner choice was semi-free like in Northwestern Europe and North America, but the requirement for women to enter marriage as a virgin was strong.[28]

Men did not rule over women everywhere in the world. There were also systems of matriarchy, such as in Negeri Sembilan on Malaya, in present-day Malaysia, where women exchanged men and could postulate their husband's sexual services as well as their productive power. Women could also claim exclusive rights over children, jointly acquired goods, land, dwellings, etc.[29] While in Negeri Sembilan each woman had only one husband at a time, there existed also systems of polyandry in which women were married to more than one man. This was, for instance, the case among part of the Sinhalese families in Ceylon, in present-day Sri Lanka. In this colonial society it was not uncommon for brothers to share one wife. In these polyandrous marriages in Ceylon, women did not rule over men, but gender relations were rather equal, as men and women kept their belongings and earnings separately. However, brothers who were married to the same wife did pool their possessions and earnings among each other.[30]

While marriage was one of the most universal institutions in the world, its ideology, meaning, organization, customs, and legal foundations varied considerably. In order to illustrate this further, we will provide a few examples. While in Jewish and Islamic societies marriage was a contract between two individuals of the opposite sex, in Catholic and Orthodox Christian societies it was a sacrament. In Western and Islamic societies

FIGURE I.3 *Sacrificing an Ox in Front of the Elmieh Palace, Celebrations for the Viceroy's Wedding, Cairo, Egypt*, illustration from *L'Illustration, Journal Universel*, vol. 61, no. 1565, February 22, 1873, DA Agostini Picture Library, via Getty Images.

entering marriage was a one-time event celebrated by a wedding, while in sub-Saharan African and in some Asian societies it was a process, which took many years and could include a range of festivities at various moments in time.[31] That marriage had many faces also becomes clear if we look at the large diversity of wedding-related customs, ranging from bridal showers, bachelor and bachelorette parties, to rice-throwing, the exchange of wedding rings, hand painting, the ritual cleaning of the bride, processions, the exchange of cattle, and divine sacrifices.

CONTINUITY AND CHANGE IN THE WAKE OF INDUSTRIALIZATION AND URBANIZATION

So far we have identified differences in marriage through geographical space. Now we will turn to changes over time. For a long time historians and social scientists alike have viewed changes in the domain of marriage and the family from a developmental perspective, whereby each world region was believed to go through the same stages of development but at different rates.[32] From this perspective, the West was believed to be a forerunner, while other parts of the world were following at their own pace. Urbanization and industrialization were seen as the big watersheds in social history, causing irreversible change.[33] These ideas went back to, amongst others, Frédéric Le Play, a French engineer, sociologist, and economist, who surveyed family types around the world, and the German sociologist Ferdinand Tönnies who made a distinction between what he called *Gemeinschaft* and *Gesellschaft*.[34] The former concept referred to pre-industrial societies, in which communities had maintained strong ties, and religion and local customs had guided social life. The concept of Gesellschaft referred to modern urban industrial societies, where life was faster, more chaotic and family ties had become weaker as a result of migration. Life had become more anonymous, impersonal, more secular, and driven more by economic incentives.

For much of the twentieth century scholars—theorizing further on the transition from Gemeinschaft to Gesellschaft—believed that in Western societies a shift from extended to nuclear households had taken place as a consequence of urbanization and industrialization, and that the rest of the world would witness the same trajectory. The married couple had intensified their ties at the expense of the larger kin group, a functional adaptation to societal change. Moreover, scholars from the Chicago School of Sociology believed that massive rural-to-urban migration—a key condition for urbanization and industrialization—had led to social disintegration, including rises in divorce, and that urban newcomers had become uprooted and had ended up at the edge of urban society.[35] Next, it was believed that the number of children in households had enormously decreased, as a result of a decline in fertility. Likewise, scholars thought that Western societies had transformed into meritocracies, where social status was no longer based on ascription (determined by the family in which one was born) but on achievement.[36] Last but not least, it was assumed that women had massively retreated from the labor market as a result of the rise of the male breadwinner model and that nuptiality had increased significantly as industrial labor had taken away Malthusian pressures.[37]

Empirical research over the last decades has relegated most of these propositions regarding the impacts of industrialization and urbanization on marriage and the family to the realm of myths. In Northwestern Europe, the nuclear family turned out to have been the dominant household type since the Middle Ages, and more recently it has been argued that the nuclear family was not so much a consequence but a cause of industrialization.[38] In the United States, the percentage of extended families doubled in the period 1750–1900, partially due to the decline in mortality, through which there was a larger pool of surviving relatives, but also because of the idealization of family life in the nineteenth century, to which we will return.[39] Average household size did not alter very much over time in Western Europe, as before the fertility transition many children had been born and many had died prematurely, keeping average family size relatively limited. When the fertility transition began, fewer children were born but more survived. Somewhat larger families were only produced during the phase in the demographic transition when mortality had declined but fertility rates remained steady.[40]

Research on the social inclusion of migrants shows that some newcomers to European cities indeed had difficulty becoming part of urban mainstream society, but others—those with human capital who migrated over longer distances—found their way easily as they moved within their own social network, including family.[41] These migrants were able to improve their position and on average even to reach higher positions than the native-born city dwellers.[42] Rural-to-urban migrants with limited human and social capital fared much worse. However, the marriage market remained highly segregated, and newcomers had a harder time getting access to marriage and reproduction, as research on port cities illustrates.[43] In addition, it was rather rare for single urban in-migrants who had moved over larger distances—either from abroad or from a different part of the country—to marry urban-born natives, signifying major cultural barriers.[44]

While certain groups of migrants managed to move up the social ladder, the idea of a meritocracy does not do justice to the rigid social class system of nineteenth- and early twentieth-century Western societies. The middle and higher classes managed to keep their positions mainly through an institution that became increasingly more important: higher education. They managed to do so as universities and university colleges remained highly inaccessible for the working classes.[45] Moreover, it seems that in large industrial and capital cities, such as Stockholm, natives managed to keep the jobs with higher social status for themselves and relegated urban in-migrants to the lower paid jobs that required fewer skills and offered fewer career prospects.[46]

But what were the effects of industrialization on gender relations and marriage patterns? For Flanders the Belgian historical demographer and sociologist Koen Matthijs observed what he called "a mimetic appetite for marriage" beginning with the middle of the nineteenth century, and since he observed declining ages at marriage first among women he linked it to the rise of the male breadwinner model, the retreat of a large part of the women from the labor market, the advent of the domesticity ideal, the increased appreciation for motherhood, and the new employment opportunities created for men as a result of industrialization.[47] Everywhere in the Western world the employment opportunities for women declined and marriage, family, motherhood, and domesticity were more valued during the latter half of the nineteenth century. Nevertheless, the results for Flanders cannot simply be extrapolated for other Western countries. In the United States, marriage ages were on the rise in the latter half of the nineteenth century, suggesting that industrialization did not facilitate the access to marriage everywhere.[48] Moreover, many women from laboring families in the Western world kept contributing to the family budget through paid labor, as they could not afford to stay at home.[49] While the breadwinner model became a social reality for the elite and the middle classes, it remained mainly a cultural ideal for the laboring classes.

Urbanization and industrialization went hand in hand with an intensification and idealization of family relations. The rise in importance of family ties in Western Europe is observable, for instance, in the increased participation of family members as marriage witnesses in civil marriage ceremonies. In the Netherlands this process started among the urban bourgeoisie in the western part of the country but was gradually transmitted to other regions. In the period 1830–1950, brides and grooms increasingly selected siblings, siblings-in-law, and cousins as their marriage witnesses, expanding the importance of lateral kin relations. This trend accelerated around 1890 when industrialization took off and urbanization increased.[50] Similar developments have been observed for Flanders during the nineteenth and early twentieth centuries.[51]

THE RISING IMPORTANCE OF MARRIAGE AND FAMILY

Although some of the nineteenth-century developments threatened the institution of marriage—for instance rising divorce rates in North America and Europe—marriage became in many ways even more anchored than it had been during previous centuries. In various parts of Latin America, where consensual unions had been the norm among the majority of the population, except for the indigenous population and the white elite, the general trend in marriage rates was upward from the end of the eighteenth century on, as the church—and later on also the state—campaigned against the sins of living together unmarried and having children out of wedlock.[52] Marriage was believed to secure the social order of the state as it made sure that social and racial inequalities were maintained. In order to stabilize society, those cohabiting couples who refused to marry were punished; men usually had to pay a fine and women went for limited amounts of time to prison.[53]

Notwithstanding the fact that the efforts by the state and church to formalize consensual unions and to legitimize children born out of wedlock were in the long run quite successful, both phenomena did not disappear in Latin America. One reason for this is that many Latin Americans lacked intrinsic incentives to formalize bonds. The lower social classes did not possess property that they had to secure for the next generation; at the same time women could act more independently when they remained unmarried. For others, marriage was no option as social status and/or racial differences between partners prevented them from obtaining permission to marry. Therefore, considerable numbers of couples continued to live in marriage-like unions without formalizing them. Nevertheless, marriage rates went up in the Age of Empires, and they continued to do so until the middle of the twentieth century, reaching a point when marriage became more widespread in Latin America than ever before or after.[54]

Australia and New Zealand witnessed quite comparable developments. At the start of the nineteenth century, these settler colonies had been marked by a very high prevalence of cohabitation, which was related to the high costs of marriage, the large excess of men among the settlers, and the fact that many of the new arrivals in Australia were convicts as well as the practical reasons involved in formalizing relationships between European men and indigenous women. In the course of the nineteenth century proportions of cohabiting couples declined in Australia and New Zealand as a result of efforts by the state and the church as well as the gradual decline in the imbalance of the sexes. Nevertheless, cohabitation remained more prevalent than in Europe.[55]

In the United States, the most noteworthy changes regarding the importance of marriage affected the black population. Unions of slaves had not been recognized by the state

FIGURE I.4 *Slavery, Unidentified Family Group in Southern USA, c.* 1860. Pictorial Press LTD. Alamy Stock Photo. Image ID: C3N0W8.

authorities and white slaveholders, but with the abolishment of slavery (1865) following the Civil War (1860–65), blacks reached a position where they could formalize existing unions and engage in new marital relationships. In practice, however, racism continued and new laws continued to discriminate against former slaves and their descendants. Consequently, in the Jim Crow era blacks still could not enter marriage under the same legal conditions as white Americans.[56] Nevertheless, from the 1870s on, proportions of never-married black women in the United States were very low, and considerably below that of white women, and their age at marriage was lower than for white women. For men the differences between whites and blacks were minor.[57]

In Western Europe, the institution of marriage also gained further importance. There it was not so much a decline in consensual unions and illegitimacy,[58] but a decline in singlehood. While singlehood had been a real alternative to marriage ever since the Middle Ages for European men and women, and was prized and encouraged by the Catholic Church, it became less so in the course of the nineteenth century. In the literature and art of the time older singles were represented in a negative way and lifetime singlehood was increasingly surrounded by suspicion. According to the French novelist Gustave Flaubert singles were perceived as egoistic and profligate; they were regarded as individuals who had created their own sadness in old age.[59]

FIGURE I.5 Emile Bayard (1837–91), *Husband and Wife with their Child,* drawing, *L'Illustration,* no. 2483, September 27, 1890. DEA/Biblioteca Ambrosiana/via Getty Images.

Marriage was increasingly regarded as the only pathway for men and women to reach happiness and self-fulfillment.

In most Asian and African societies, marriage remained as important as it had been in previous centuries. Marriage remained universal among women and took place early in the life cycle. European colonizers tried to change the marriage customs of indigenous populations—for instance regarding polygamy and arranged marriages—but sooner or later they had to content themselves with the fact that the indigenous population had other marriage customs, to which the colonial administration had to adapt its bureaucratic system in order to avoid major resistance.[60] In colonial populations where Christianity prevailed, marriage registration by the church usually became relatively well established, but in Islamic countries this was not the case. In French Morocco, for instance, the civil registration of marriage worked only for the European and Jewish populations, and this only changed gradually during independence.[61]

While globally marriage in the Age of Empires became even more widespread than it had been in previous centuries, the diversity in marriage patterns and household systems remained at least as large as it had been at the turn of the eighteenth century. Neither globalization and colonialism, nor migration, urbanization, and industrialization erased the cultural diversity in marriage practices around the world, but they did make marriage and the family even more important, attractive, and formal. The last was especially a result of efforts by the state and the church to formalize marriage bonds. In a world of turbulent political and economic change, marriage and the family remained safe havens, the linchpins of society that they had been for centuries.

FIGURE I.6 *Wealthy Family from Porto-Novo*, Benin illustration from *L'Illustration*, no. 2463, May 10, 1890. De Agostini/Biblioteca Ambrosiana via Getty Images.

ORGANIZATION OF THE VOLUME

This volume—just like the others in the series—consists of eight chapters. In the first chapter Jan Kok provides us with a broad overview of courtship and marriage rituals within the world's main family systems. The chapter makes clear that there were large differences in the degrees of freedom young people had regarding the choice of marriage partners and the degree to which they were allowed to meet and to get to know each other and to explore their sexuality before tying the marriage knot. In Europe and North America extensive periods of courtship existed, and in Southeast Asia there was also considerable freedom for singles to experiment before marriage. In the Western world, Japan, and various African societies, young people also enjoyed opportunities to have sexual contact before marriage in the form of night courting. This concept refers to ritualized sexual encounters in peer-controlled settings. Little or no courtship existed, by contrast, in societies where marriages were arranged by parents and the family, as was, for instance, the case in China, India, the Middle East, and North Africa. In such societies bride and groom met each other usually for the first time on their wedding night and premarital sex was strictly forbidden. Given the emphasis on the preservation of the bride's virginity, the chastity of daughters, was strictly controlled, and this often went hand in hand with female seclusion. However, large differences in "courtship space" also existed within family systems, according to gender, social status, caste, race, and the type of marriage arrangements. Generally speaking, women enjoyed less freedom than men as a result of sexual double standards, and the agency of young people from the higher classes was lower than that of the working classes, as there was more wealth and power to lose in these families in terms of marriage partner choice, while at the same time elite parents had the means to control their children. Diversity was not only found in terms of courtship space but also in terms of marriage rituals; many of them marked the transfer of the bride from the family of orientation to the family of procreation, but there were also rituals that signified the unity of the newly-wed couple and still others—like throwing rice at the couple—that aimed to enhance their fertility. In most cases, the consummation of the marriage itself was at the center of marriage rituals, especially in patriarchal societies—like in the Arab World—where the bride was supposed to enter marriage as a virgin, and a marriage was accompanied with a bride price.

In the second chapter Karl Kaser explores how the different world religions influenced marriage and marital life. In order to do so he differentiates between interventionist and noninterventionist religions and between primarily orthopractically oriented religions and primarily orthodoxly oriented religions, as well as between religions that fostered horizontal ties and religions that promoted a vertical orientation of family ties. This leads to a grand scheme in which the influence of the various world religions on marriage is linked to freedom of partner choice, the degree husbands and wives experienced gender equity, marriage intensity, marriage timing, and household formation. Kaser's contribution goes beyond an analysis of the age-old influence of religions on marriage by also discussing the changes that occurred during the nineteenth and early twentieth centuries as a consequence of secularization and the increasing power of the state in the realm of marriage, a realm in which religions had enjoyed a monopoly of power during premodern times. The expanding influence of state power during the nineteenth century caused confrontations of sacred and secular forces. In the long run the influence of religions declined, but this was not a linear process. Moreover, the transition of power met with more resistance in societies based on Islam, Confucianism, and Hinduism, as the new state's blueprint for marriage was formulated in a context of orthodoxy and horizontal family ties, while marriage in these religions had been characterized by orthopraxis and vertical family lines. Resistance against the secular blueprint also existed within (conservative) Judaism due to its orthopractical orientation as well as among Christian Orthodoxy and even Catholicism, although mainly in Europe. The separation of the sacred and secular spheres went most smoothly in the Protestant populations of the Atlantic geographical space. While the Catholic and Protestant churches were increasingly losing ground in the West, they started to intervene more in colonial societies in sub-Saharan Africa and Asia. In those areas the church collided not so much with secular forces but rather with the divergent views and practices concerning marriage among the indigenous population.

In the third chapter, Rebecca Probert analyzes the changing role of state and law regarding marriage affairs against the background of political revolutions, the rise of nation-states, colonization, industrialization, and urbanization. The analysis comprises various legal cultures and shows that states tried to obtain more influence on the institution of marriage almost everywhere in the world, but that the outcome could vary considerably and was often unpredictable for contemporaries. Moreover, in several societies developments toward more state intervention in marriage were temporary or more permanently reversed. In order to get more of a grip on the complex historical developments arising from the struggle between states and religious powers in the Age of Empires, Probert distinguishes four models of marriage regulations. The first model is mandatory civil marriages conducted by the state. The political entities that successfully applied this model put aside all other actors in the realm of marriage, such as the church or the parties involved, as it was the state alone that issued marriage licenses and decided who was and was not elegible for marriage, and it was the state that decided what constituted a legal marriage. In practice this meant that an official civil marriage ceremony had to take place. The second model constituted a compromise, as marriages were created both by the state and by religious institutions, but religious marriages had to comply with state legislation in order to be legally binding. The first and the second models operated mostly in the context of Western legal cultures, and in both models the role of religion was played down, although this was considerably less the case when the second model was being put into practice. In the third model, which was mostly found in Asian and African, and especially in Islamic legal cultures, entry into marriage continued to be regulated by religious institutions, and the influence of the state remained limited. In the fourth model it was the actions of individual historical actors alone that decided what constituted a marriage, and these actions were retroactively recognized by the state. A simple exchange of consent was often enough. The nineteenth-century common law marriage, which was adopted in many US states, fits this model. In this context law was directory and not mandatory, which meant that the choice of individual citizens was prioritized over state law.

In the fourth chapter, Satomi Kurosu and K. Dilhani Wijesinghe compare Asia and Europe in terms of marriage and kinship. They ask why couples married, when and how they married, and whom they married, and they search for systematic similarities and differences between European and Asian societies in this regard. Both in Europe and Asia, marriage was crucial for the survival of individuals, for old age provision, for legal reproduction, for the supply of labor, and for the formation of alliances. Everywhere in Eurasia dowries and bride prices were important, as they secured the bond between groom and bride and between their larger kin groups. However, in Asian societies parental involvement in marriage partner choice was large and also remained large during marriage, as the newly-wed couple moved into the parental household of the groom or the bride. In European societies, by contrast, there was more freedom for individuals to choose a marriage partner, and since the couple normally formed a new, independent household after the wedding, parental involvement was also more limited during the marriage. These differences account also for the fact that marriage was early and universal in Asia and late and non-universal in Europe. Another demographic difference to which this is related is the time interval between marriage and the onset of reproduction. This interval was considerably wider in the Asian context, and the authors explain this by referring to the different nature of marriage on both ends of the Eurasian continent.

In the fifth chapter Angélique Janssens focuses on the impact of industrialization, urbanization, and economic growth on work and family life as well as on the opportunities and the timing of marriage. In the first section she describes how industrialization in the course of the nineteenth century caused what Kenneth Pomeranz termed the *Great Divergence*: an ever-larger growing divide in terms of productivity and economic growth between mainly Western nations on the one hand and mainly non-Western nations on the other.[62] At the start of the Age of Empires the differences in economic performance among the various continents had been relatively small, but as industrialization took off in some countries and world regions but not (yet) in others, differences in economic performance grew larger and larger. After Janssens delineates these macroeconomic changes she outlines their impact on families and individuals. In this regard she pays attention to the shift from family economies to family wage economies. While in the former all or at least a majority of the household members engaged in productive tasks at home, i.e., in the family's artisanal workshop, farm, or cottage, in the latter family members earned a living outside of the home in factories by ways of wage work. This meant in principle that former barriers to marriage disappeared, as young people could earn an independent living early on thanks to the availability of factory work. Although marriage rates went up somewhat and ages at marriage declined in the long run, it did not lead to the expected large-scale dismantling of the European marriage pattern in the Age of Empires. Janssens explains this by referring to the fact that marrying later in the life course had over the centuries become a cultural norm, which did not simply disappear with industrialization. The idea that one should be well prepared for married life was maintained. Moreover, children also remained loyal to their parents in the sense that they stayed oriented for an extended period of time toward the family of orientation in order to pool wages with their parents and siblings. In the following two sections, Janssens details what industrialization meant for women and for children in the long and short run.

In the sixth chapter Paul Puschmann discusses developments in the domains of love, sex, and sexuality. The chapter starts with a short discussion of the key concepts and then focuses on the question of how much room there was for love regarding the choice of a partner for life. Worldwide economic and political considerations were key in this regard, but in Europe and North America the cultural ideal of romantic marriage started to take root and gradually love became a condition for marriage. The transition from instrumental toward romantic partner choice went hand in hand with a trend toward age-homogamy, signifying the fact that marriage partners became increasingly soul mates. However, economic motives regarding the choice of marriage partner did not disappear and marriage partners remained in many ways also partners in shared material interests. In most Asian and African societies marriages continued to be arranged, which meant that choice of partner had nothing to do with love. Nevertheless, in the Middle East and North Africa as well as in Latin America critics of this practice arose. In various Latin American countries this went together with protest among young couples by way of increasing numbers of elopements, but social criticism also led to legal changes, limiting the power of parents with regards to marriage affairs. The rise of the romantic marriage ideal in the West and critics of arranged marriages and the subordinate position of women in Latin America, the Middle East, and North Africa were also echoed in the fiction of the age. In North America and Europe the happy ending gradually became an acceptable way to terminate a love-story plot, signifying a shift toward a romantic marriage ideal. The presence or absence of love was not necessarily a good predictor of whether a marriage would become happy. Nevertheless, Western countries seem to have had better conditions for love marriages. On the other hand, the increase in divorces also raises the question of whether love-based marriages were more fragile than marriages based on economic incentives. The chapter closes with an overview of interventions in fertility and developments in the domains of sex and sexuality.

In the seventh chapter Karl Leydecker analyzes divorce as a topic in the European and North American fiction of the long nineteenth century, focusing mainly on Great Britain, France, Germany, and the United States. He shows that divorce in several Western countries became an important subject in the literature in the years following the French Revolution, when changes in the law made it much easier to obtain a divorce and, in fact, led to a substantial increase in divorces. This period, however, was short-lived, as during the Restoration it again became harder to obtain a divorce—especially for women— due to changes in the law. The changes in law and social reality were reflected in the fiction of the time in the sense that explicit depictions of divorce became very infrequent.

However, as Leydecker shows, divorce remained very much a narrative possibility in novels—for instance following adultery—throughout the nineteenth century. At the start of the twentieth century divorce had lost its revolutionary character in literature and became increasingly a banal phenomenon. Interestingly, many of the authors who wrote nineteenth-century fiction where divorce was a theme or a narrative possibility, were females, and a considerable number of them had experienced divorce themselves. Therefore, Leydecker connects the type of fiction in the literature on divorce with female emancipation.

In the eighth and last chapter, Marja van Tilburg discusses representations of marriages in Western Europe, with a particular focus on the bourgeois family, as it served increasingly as an example for other layers of societies in the long nineteenth century, following the French Revolution. The contribution deals with three subtopics. First of all, Van Tilburg examines marriage as an ideal institution, in the way it was represented in marriage manuals, which provided guidance to married and soon-to-wed couples about how to make a family work. She discusses continuities and changes in this ideal picture and compares them to eighteenth-century manuals, which focused very much on practical guidance in a religious, moralistic style about how to run a household. Thanks to the influence of the Enlightenment, marriage manuals not only became more popular than ever before, they also increasingly included aspects related to the societal responsibilities of the couple and echoed the idea that it was possible to create better individuals and a better society at large by improving the marital relationship through education. Marriage and family were thus seen as key aspects of societal organization, and the aim was to create happy couples through the joint responsibilities of husband and wife toward their family and society. From the marriage manuals and advice literature we get a good idea about family values and societal norms. Van Tilburg shows what was deemed important: choosing a partner consciously and mutual support and love between spouses. A strict division in tasks was deemed necessary to make the family adaptable to changes arising from urbanization and industrialization. And this brings us to the second subtopic of Van Tilburg's contribution: the separation of spheres and the prescribed gender roles of husband and wife. While husbands continued to concentrate on their role as providers, women became the guardians of the home, which turned into a new cultural space. The new gender identity of women was not only reflected in marriage advice literature but also in contemporary fiction. As the strict division of gender roles was increasingly put into practice, some precursors of their time started to criticize the institution of marriage because of its strict gender division and its disciplining nature. The third and last subtopic of this contribution is devoted to two of those influential critical voices, who produced both fiction and nonfiction: Mary Wollstonecraft and Magnus Hirschfeld.

Together these chapters provide us with a broad overview in differences and similarities in marriage across different cultures and world regions. However, the authors—who are specialist in the subtopics they deal with—also pay attention to changes in marriage and larger society in the Age of Empires and connect these to each other.

CHAPTER ONE

Courtship and Rites

A Survey of the World's Family Systems

JAN KOK

INTRODUCTION

Courtship has often been an exciting part of adolescent life. Finding and wooing a partner involves excitement, fun, and—for many—exploration of sexuality. But the experiences of the world's youths diverged widely in what their courtships looked like. On the one hand, for many youths, especially in East and Southern Asia, the possibilities to seek a partner themselves were extremely limited or nonexistent. On the other hand, for adolescents in Europe, for instance, courtships could be protracted almost interminably, as marriage prospects were dim for those without property. In a global overview of the history of courtship, the first step will be to chart the "space" for courtship in the lives of young men and women.

First, we need a workable definition. Merriam-Webster's dictionary describes *courtship* as "the act, process, or period of courting," and to *court* as "to seek the affections of; *especially*: to seek to win a pledge of marriage from."[1] This simple definition immediately raises—at least—four questions. First: who is doing the seeking? We need to understand the position of young adults, their opportunities to work, study, travel, and meet one another. It is also crucial to recognize that men and women had different interests in courtship and marriage, and certainly took different risks in premarital (sexual) relationships. In many societies, however, not the youths themselves but the parents, often through professional intermediaries, selected a marriage partner. Thus, we also have to go into the reasons, rites, and consequences of arranged marriages. Second: who were involved in the negotiations, activities, and supervision surrounding courtship? Even when prospective partners would have liked to keep their relationship secret, many parties held an active interest, such as parents, siblings, neighbors, peers, church and state officials. Third: who was considered a suitable partner? How important were age, looks and health, income (prospects), status, ethnicity, and religion? Apart from and beyond those factors; how important was love, or the passionate affection for the partner? According to many scholars, the nineteenth century was the era in which romantic love became a prime condition for marriage, at least in Europe and the Western offshoots. But others claim that the zest for marriage that was apparent in rising marriage rates was mainly caused by diminished employment opportunities for women.[2] Thus, to understand courtship, we also need to understand the motivation for marriage. Finally: what are the different steps in courtship perceived as "the process of courting"? When did one become active in courtship, when did a relation become serious enough to consult the parents, through what rites were marriage intentions communicated to the community? The stage of courtship ends with the wedding rituals; what did these signify?

Central in our discussion of "courtship space" is the question: how much freedom did youths have to find a partner who matched them emotionally and physically? In other words, what was the role for love? In his cross-cultural analysis, Goode rejected the simple dichotomy between romantic and non-romantic marriages, but proposed a continuum or range between polar types: "At one pole, a strong love attraction is socially viewed as a laughable or tragic aberration; at the other, it is mildly shameful to marry without being in love with one's intended spouse."[3] Whether love is perceived as "tragic," dangerous, or desirable depends on the role of marriage in a given society. When youths are married off to cement the alliances between dynasties or lineages, the emotions and choices of the partners themselves had better be kept out of the equation lest they endanger the transaction. Furthermore, when the young couple forms a subjugated unit in an extended household, their personal affection is, for the time being at least, of no importance or even potentially disruptive. Finally, when marriage is seen as a way of transmitting or joining estates or other forms of wealth, personal choices also take second place. In other words, (sexual) freedom and love within courtship depends on how marriages serve the political and economic interests of families at large.[4]

A useful approach for understanding the structural roles of courtship and marriage in different cultures is by looking at "family systems," which can be defined as "a cluster of norms informing family processes."[5] In this chapter, I follow the classification of family systems of Therborn[6] which he describes as "geocultures," or institutions or structures surrounding family life which are shaped by a (macro) region's traditions, religion, and ecology and have a lasting impact even after periods of rapid change.[7] Therborn discusses the role of sexuality and marriage in seven family systems, and in this chapter I follow his lead by discussing courtship in seven "families": the Confucian East Asian family, the South Asian Hindu family, the Islamic West Asian and North African family, the Christian (European and North American) family, the sub-Saharan African family, the Southeast Asian family, and the Latin American Creole family. These regional family systems are strong generalizations, but in this short space we simply cannot do justice to the huge intraregional variation existing within each system. Moreover, by approaching courtship from the perspective of norms and rules, we should not ignore the fact that these rules often did not apply to the landless and also that people, even when the rules did apply to them, could find ways to circumvent them. Lovers could elope or when marriage was still denied them, could live in some form of consensual union. We also have to be aware that the parental or societal pressure on finding the "right partner" could become so difficult that people eventually opted out of the marriage process altogether. Finally, the perspective of regional family systems offers insight into the path dependency of traditions, but this is not to deny the impact of globalizing forces already apparent in the nineteenth century. Scholars, missionaries, and colonizing governments across the globe were advocating the European family model—including if not free choice at least the spouses' consent to the marriage—as an essential step in becoming a modern, civilized, and prosperous society.[8]

In the following sections, we will look for the "structural space" for courtship in each regional family system, where possible keeping track of class differentials. The stage of courtship ends with the wedding rituals; what did these signify? In the words of Tambiah, a ritual is "a culturally constructed system of symbolic communication."[9] Marriage rituals convey important messages on the meanings of union formation, sexuality, and fertility in each family system. The concluding section will summarize the social and cultural variables that account for the variation in courtship across the globe.

THE CONFUCIAN EAST ASIAN FAMILY

The family types of China, Korea, and Japan have all been inspired by Confucian ideals on the hierarchical relations between family members and on the integration of the household in the state apparatus. However, there were strong differences between the three countries in the process of household formation and in the hierarchical position of new couples and, therefore, also in the "space" for courtship.

The ideal Chinese household consisted of a male head, his wife and possibly concubines, his married sons and their wives, and their children. The senior male would be a true patriarch, having absolute authority over his children, regardless of their age or marital status. Women married exogamously, thus into another family group in another village. Therefore, most women faced an early rupture with their own family. The family's property was to be held in joint ownership but could be divided (equally) by the sons after the father's death. Of course, this ideal could not be realized by small landowners. Among poor peasants often only one son could inherit, who had to compensate the others. Poverty also meant that girls were considered a heavy burden on the family budget. Thus, in poor families they were more likely to be killed or sold, to be given away as infants, or to be married later in exchange for gifts. Daughters in wealthy families, on the other hand, were pawns in strategies of forging alliances between clans and were given dowries. Their marriage tended to be at a somewhat later age.[10] In the household of their in-laws, young married women occupied the lowest position in the family hierarchy. Her husband did not offer her much consolation, as showing affection was considered a sign of male weakness.[11] The dowry asserted the status of her natal family, but it also guaranteed her some protection against ill-treatment.

Apart from this "major" marriage form, in which girls left the parental household in their teens, two other forms of marriage existed in China. In several regions, infant girls were raised by their parents-in-law. They would marry one of their sons (in a so-called "minor marriage") when the intended match promised to be a success. If not, they were passed on to another family. When no heir could be adopted, a girl stayed with her parents and married a man who was brought in temporarily, on the condition that the first child would be added to his wife's patrilineage.[12] The latter form is called an "uxorilocal marriage."

As will be clear from this brief description, there was virtually no room for courtship in China. Partners were often strangers to one another, and their preferences and emotions played no role in the calculations of their (grand)parents. Courtship "space" was also limited because many girls were kept indoors, which was made easy by the practice of foot-binding.[13] Until well into the twentieth century, girls hardly received any formal schooling.[14] However, women working in the fields or as servants had more chances to meet with men. Also festivals, such as New Year, were occasions to meet and possibly to fall in love. Running away with a lover was an option, but if caught the elopers were punished harshly. As a formal marriage was not possible, the girl would have to become a concubine, which gave her a lower status.

We can imagine the feelings of Chinese girls having to leave their family to live with a man they did not even know. A unique insight in their emotions is provided by the writings of women in southern Hunan province. During many centuries, women there had their own script, which men could not read. Women wrote (autobiographical) ballads to be recited to their friends, such as the "Complaint of the unmarried daughter," which talks of a girl being pushed out by her married brothers and of her secret love:

> My eldest brothers says over and over again that he wants to marry me off
> My second brother says over and over again that he will write the contract
> My third brother always shows a friendly character
> And has hidden the red paper for his older brothers
> My older brother accompanies me to the threshold of the gate
> My second brother accompanies me outside the gate
> Only my third brother has a friendly character
> And brings me even to the road to Jianghua
> Precisely there I meet Liuge going home!
> Why didn't he take me on his horse?
> Why in God's name didn't he saddle his horse for me?[15]

Practically all marriages, also among poorer classes, were arranged. For instance, field work in a Northern Chinese village showed that only 3 percent of marriages in 1949–59 were free-choice matches.[16] Partners were sought through the mediation of a professional go-between, mostly women. Organizing a marriage and selecting the partner was to be done by the mother. Not surprisingly, few Chinese brides were pregnant upon marriage. The exception were the girls marrying in the "minor" fashion. In early twentieth-century Taiwan about a quarter of these girls were pregnant at the time of marriage—five times as high as those marrying in the "major" fashion.[17] This resulted from the boys' parents wanting to test the future spouses' compatibility. As these youngsters who had grown up together were very reluctant to have sex, they had to be "pushed together."[18]

In Chinese society almost all women married, but due to a shortage of women (caused by female infanticide and concubinage) sizeable numbers of men remained unmatched. These poor, unmarried men (known as "bare sticks") were often associated with homosexuality, crime, and rape.[19] In Chinese ancestor worship, there was no ritual space for unmarried girls. Girls were meant to be part of their husband's family line, and their funeral tablets were to be worshipped by their children and in-laws. Thus, when women did not marry, special factors were at play. As developments in southern China show, female earning capacity increased the opportunities for some form of spinsterhood and relative autonomy. In the Canton area around 1900, the expanding silk industry made the female silk reelers much more valuable to their parents. Three days after their wedding, married girls would return already to their parents and visit their husbands only occasionally. This situation would last at least three years and only sooner if the girl became pregnant. This "delayed transfer marriage" went back to older customs in the region.[20] It began to transform to "compensation marriage" in which families negotiated the sum to be paid to the husband's family so they could buy a young girl to perform household tasks. The women would only join their husbands in old age or (in the form or their funeral tablet) death. Many women began to resist marriage altogether. By performing a specific ceremony, including wearing typical headgear, they became "sworn spinsters." The spinsters could live at home, but they could not die there, for fear that her spirit would not find peace. For this reason, "spinster houses" emerged, where these women could live together (often in homosexual relationships) and where after their death their funeral tablets could be placed. Another solution, also going back to ancient traditions, was to marry the spirit of a deceased man. This was an attractive solution to both families. The family of an unmarried daughter ("sworn spinster" or not) found a host for their daughter's spirit, and the family of the dead groom found him a wife and could adopt a grandson.[21]

Chinese marriage rituals symbolized the transfer of rights over a girl from her father to her husband's family. After the negotiations over the bride price or dowry were completed a ceremony (*sang-tia*) took place, in which the bride's mother-in-law placed rings on the middle finger of her left hand. The bride was seated facing away from the shrine in which her family's funeral tablets were placed. This symbolized her moving to another line of descent and thus another line of ancestors for worship.[22] The days before leaving were spent with "carefully structured sessions of ritualized sobbing involving the bride-to-be and her unmarried friends or younger sisters."[23] She was brought to her husband's home in a procession, seated in a palanquin, and followed by the palanquin of the matchmaker. Literally in-between the authority of her father and of her husband, she was "queen for an hour," wearing a special headdress styled after imperial consorts. But after arrival, she became the servants of her in-laws. This began true and proper after three days when the couple paid a ceremonial visit to her parents (*cue-kheq*, "to be a guest") in which she was treated as a guest.[24]

Although strongly affected by Chinese influences, the Japanese system differed in crucial aspects. The principle of patrilineal descent was much less important in the Japanese ancestral cult than in the Chinese. Thus, in contrast to China, blood ties from mother's and father's side were valued equally and there were no strict taboos on marriage within the group of agnatic kin.[25] The Japanese system is a stem family system, as all non-heirs leave upon marriage, and therefore only two married couples remain. During the Tokugawa period (1600–1867) the stem family or House (*ie*) held a central place in both religion and society. The ie formed a permanent social unit linking together deceased, current, and future members. One could only leave an ie to create a new one or to be adopted into one.[26] The ie was also the lowest, yet vital, level of government bureaucracy and control.

Farmers and artisans were much more flexible than elite families with the ie rules. Also non-elite women could work outside the home before marriage, for instance as servants.[27] Non-elite daughters married endogamous, without the mediation of a broker. In fact, there was a remarkable period of sexual freedom before marriage, including forms of collective night courtship. An interview with a hundred-year-old woman, born in 1903 on Kyushu island, provides a fascinating insight in the practice of *yobanashi* (night talk). Hatanaka Kamegiku recalled:

> When we were young, we'd sometimes spend the night at a friend's house ... The room where the friends slept and the room where the parents slept were separate ... And then men would come there too. If women were there, they would engage in some night play. If there was a girl he would like spending the night with, he would, you know, come alone. There would be two or three women sleeping, and he would tug at the one he liked. The women understood it too.[28]

Married men could also appear at this "night talk," and Kamegiku remembers the girls saying "that if you changed men three times in a month, altering men, you wouldn't have children." Of course, pregnancies did occur, but it was not considered a great problem.

The child could be given away to the men's family. The parents still decided on the marriage partner of their daughter, irrespective of her having (had) a child. Clearly, among poor Japanese, a compromise was found between courtship and arranged marriage.

In Korea, the Chinese Confucianist influence had a stronger impact in limiting women's freedom than in Japan.[29] But in late nineteenth-century Japan, patriarchy became stronger as well. The Meiji Restoration (1868) of the emperor ushered in a new era in Japan, in which the country tried to catch up with Western nations, yet retain its own identity. The Meiji Civil Code (1890) made the ie even more central in Japanese society. Samurai family ideals and practices became more pervasive in this period, including arranged marriage through go-betweens.[30] Marriage began with a temporary first phase, after which the wife could be sent away.[31]

THE SOUTH ASIAN HINDU FAMILY

In Hinduism, the concept of debt (to the Gods, the sages, and the ancestors) is central.[32] Marriage and procreation play a crucial role in paying off the debts toward one's ancestors. By marriage, the oldest son receives the home fire and becomes the householder who can perform the mourning rites. By having a son, he honors his ancestors properly. Marriage in Hinduism is a sacrament, a union of the mind, body, and soul, and as such perpetual and irrevocable. Therefore, Brahmin widows were supposed to follow their husband in death (sati), a practice outlawed by the British in the mid-nineteenth century.[33] In general, women were not allowed to divorce or to remarry. Women did not play a role in performing sacred duties; in fact, a wife's religious obligation was to worship her husband as if he were a god.[34] This also implied catering to his sexual desires, for which special guides (e.g., Kamasutra) were written. This focus on sexual contentment in marriage did not imply companionate conjugal relations. From the eighth century onwards, girls were even to be married before puberty.[35] By transferring daughters early there could be no doubt about their chastity and virtue. Early marriage was also favored because young girls were more malleable than older ones and they had more time to identify themselves with their new family.[36] At the end of the nineteenth century, the average age at marriage of women was thirteen, and for men.[37] But the family-in-law discouraged the consummation of the youngster's marriage until they could be responsible parents.[38] Therefore, girls' actual cohabitation with their husbands started later than the marriage (on average at age sixteen at the end of the nineteenth century).

Premarital contacts, let alone courtship, were almost impossible in this system. Female virtue was guaranteed by the seclusion (purdah) to which women were subjected. Christian women missionaries were appalled by the zenana, or women's quarters: "There must be as few windows as possible, and where they cannot be altogether avoided, care is taken that they do not open on a public street, or on a neighbour's house." As for the inmates: "Poor little girls! It is only till they are married that they are allowed to come to the door. After that event they are closely shut up. I could almost wish them to remain children."[39] A remarkable insight in the life of a nineteenth-century child bride is offered by the autobiography of a Bengali woman, Rashundari Debi (born around 1809) who was married at age twelve to a prosperous landowner. In a singular act of defiance, she taught herself in secret to read and write. Although her in-laws were kind enough, she felt trapped: "I was caged for life, in this life there will be no escape for me ... I was snatched away from my own people ... And was given a life sentence ... I would shed tears in secret but since I had to spend my life with these people, I eventually became a tame bird."[40] At age fourteen, she had to take care of the entire household of twenty-five people, without help.

"The" Indian family we have discussed so far, is in fact the ideal type of the upper-caste family. The middle and lower castes were more flexible in dealing with the rules, for instance, divorce and remarriage were possible.[41] In "lower" groups, households also tended to be more nuclear and women had relatively more freedom.[42] The utter hierarchical nature of Indian society has strong consequences for marriage. Although marrying within one's (sub)caste is obligatory, the ideal is also that women "marry up" in the hierarchy (hypergamy), thus bestowing status on the family (or village or clan) giving daughters in marriage. To emphasize this honorable transaction, families should give their daughters a dowry. We can understand that for families already at the top, few options were left. Either they had to amass excruciatingly high dowries to marry their daughter even higher up or they had to face loss of status because their daughters remained celibate or had to marry downwards. The frequent solution to this was (and still is) female infanticide. On the other side of the spectrum, hypergamy led to a shortage of

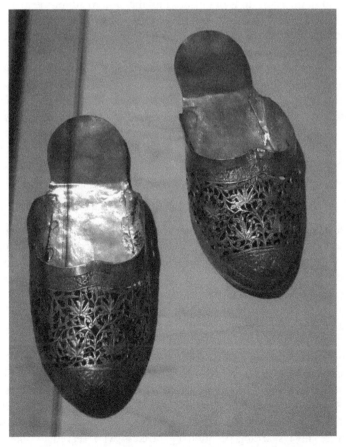

FIGURE 1.1 Indian bridal gift, silver filigree, North India, nineteenth century, exposition in the Bata Shoe Museum, Toronto, Ontario, Canada. Public domain via Wikimedia.

women. This meant that men had to refrain from marriage, or to marry relatively late. It also meant they paid a bride price to the family of the woman (Figure 1.1).

Between north and south India important differences in marriage customs existed. Females in the south received larger inheritances, which could include shares in the family's means of subsistence. This led to a pressure to delay marriage and to seek the partner among closely related kin in order to avoid the fragmentation of land. Thus, in contrast to the hypergamy found in the north, the south was characterized by prescribed kin endogamy, preferably among cross-cousins. This also meant that upon marriage a woman suffered less from submission to strangers, as she moved nearby and to people she knew well. Control over her property further enhanced a woman's agency, which translated into more divorce, remarriage, and transmission of property to a woman's own kin.[43]

During the nineteenth and twentieth centuries, a number of counteracting processes occurred. The English colonial government tried to improve the position of women by outlawing sati and female infanticide, by stimulating female education, and by raising the minimum age of marriage. The highest castes were receptive to British ideals of marriage by choice.[44] But, ironically, the middle and lower castes moved away from (relatively) free choice. Mass media spread Hindu ideals, and the expanding economy allowed social groups to fulfill aspirations of upward mobility and to adopt the marriage ideals of upper-caste groups (*Sanskritization*), to the detriment of women. Increasing incomes also allowed middle-caste families to retrieve their women from the labor market, as manual labor was considered polluting. Thus, wealth was translated into the seclusion of even more women.[45] Female labor was increasingly restricted to the most undervalued, menial work of poor women.

The Hindu marriage ceremony takes several days, and is full of symbolic actions aimed at instilling trust in the couples' bonding and mutual future. For instance, in the *Shilarohana* ritual "the bride puts her right foot onto a stone, implored by the groom to stamp as hard and as firmly as she can to symbolize that they will be strong and firm together to face ... the difficulties of the future."[46]

THE ISLAMIC WEST ASIAN AND NORTH AFRICAN FAMILY

In Islamic societies, the position of women was relatively strong in comparison to what we have described for India and China. Women could inherit (landed) property, albeit only half of what their brothers received. But the bride price received from the in-laws compensated for this. Ideally, women were married within the kin group, preferably to a cousin from father's side. But even if marriage was not endogamous, she remained part of her kin group after marriage, and she retained her family name.[47] Women were entitled to a dowry that was paid in instalments during her lifetime. This signals the continuing support and concern of her kin for her well-being. However, women could expect this support only if they did not press their claims on their shares. To ensure their kin's support, most women granted their brothers the usufruct of their shares. The continued protection of her father and brothers also meant that stains on her reputation reflected back on her family of orientation. Thus, her father and brothers remained the guardians of her (sexual) honor, which could lead to severe repressions in case of transgression. Marriages were always arranged, often by brokers who served as intermediaries in negotiations between families. Women married soon after reaching puberty and lived in secluded quarters (harems), and outdoors they had to wear a veil.

FIGURE 1.2 *Camel Conveying a Bride to Her Husband*, illustration from George Francis Lyon (1821) *A Narrative of Travels in North Africa in the years 1818, 1819, and 1820, accompanied by Geographical Notices of Soudan and of the Course of the Niger*. Public domain via Wikimedia Commons.

Very often, the husbands were older than their wives. Marrying a young wife enhanced male social status.[48] Men also had to delay marriage because they had to amass both the bride price for the parents and a dower (*mahr*) for his bride. One part of the mahr was directly paid to the wife whereas the rest was kept until widowhood or divorce. A woman's subjugation to her husband was underpinned by his one-sided financial input to the marriage, his older age, and his ample opportunities to repudiate her.[49] However, women had some economic independence, as there was no creation of a common conjugal fund. This allowed women to control their own property, which was also backed up by the courts.[50] But although they might have owned and controlled property, market activities were discouraged, in particular in wealthier strata: "distance from the market place was a sign of high status and an expression of the power and autonomy of the household to which a woman belonged."[51]

The space for courtship in Islamic countries was very limited, but court cases show that young people found ways to meet and sometimes even to enforce a choice marriage. The Koran itself is not always clear on specific norms and rules, and the interpretation of the Koran and the "tradition" (*Hadith*) or legacy of Mohamed's teachings differs from one legal school to the next. Thus, in Tunisia, for instance, women could benefit from the lenient interpretations of its local legal school. An example is a court case in Kairouan in 1876. Aïsha, virgin daughter of the late Sâlah' Methnânî, claimed that her brother had forced her to marry the old man Moh'ammad bin Fraj al-Methnânî. She did not accept this and demanded the cancellation of her marriage contract. The judge indeed ordered the dissolution of this marriage and a few months later she married the young man Muh'ammad bin Sâlah', by her own choice.[52] The assertion that Aïsha was still a virgin was of crucial importance, as premarital sexuality was a criminal offense in *shari'a* law. It is considered a crime against God (*hadd*) punishable by lashes if both are not married. In practice, it is difficult to prove and often milder punishments were given by the magistrates.

The court cases of Cairo, Egypt, give interesting insights into (the possibilities) for transgressing the injunctions against premarital contacts. In 1877, the magistrates dealt with the case of Hasna and Sa'd. The girl Hasna had been kept indoors but "Sa'd kept trying to attract her attention from the street, looking up at her window and entertaining her until late hours of the night, until he managed to convince her to leave the house." Apparently, their relation went on for several years. Then, one day "she visited his house to get some dough from his mother. She found him alone, and he deflowered her with her consent and promised to marry her." Hasna ran off with him, but they were caught by her brother who brought her to the police. They were sentenced to six-months imprisonment. Interestingly, her brother then applied for a reduction of the sentence on the ground of her being so young and gullible. The court consented and reduced her sentence to three months.[53]

In the final quarter of the nineteenth century, educated elites in the large Ottoman cities came under the spell of European, especially French, culture. In Istanbul, French romantic novels were eagerly read, and people began to discuss the merits and dangers of free partner choice. Very gradually, elite society opened up the opportunities for future spouses to get acquainted before marriage:

> Despite the veil and chaperoning, it became somewhat easier for young men and women of the literate classes to meet in public places, in parks, picnic spots, theatres, at weddings and celebrations. A furtive glance, a flirtatious turn under the veil, a handkerchief dropped, a flower in one's lapel, a secret love letter passed from hand to hand, these were some of the public symbols of a still forbidden, though increasingly tolerated, romance.[54]

THE CHRISTIAN FAMILY

Our discussion of the Christian family relates mainly to Europe, although many characteristics can also be found in the European "offshoots" or the (white) populations of North America, Australia, New Zealand, and South Africa.

Until now, we have discussed courtship in societies with strong patriarchal family systems. In such systems, the authority of the (male) household head was backed up by secular and religious authorities. But (Western) Europe had a "weak" patriarchy, in which the parents' hold on their children was limited. Ultimately, they could only obstruct an intended marriage by disinheriting the child.[55] The church was the main factor in undermining patriarchy by asserting that marriage was a sacrament, administered by the partners to themselves in their solemn marriage vow. Marriage was regulated in the sixteenth-century Counterreformation, when it was stipulated that these vows were to be properly spoken in front of a priest and witnesses, and to be duly recorded (Council of Trent, 1545–63), but the principle did not change. The Protestant Reformation did make parental consent to the marriage obligatory, but parents could never force a child to marry against their will.[56]

Since at least medieval times, couples in many parts of Western and central Europe (but also in several Eastern European regions),[57] headed their own households at marriage. They had to secure a means of living for themselves, which necessitated a period of working and saving and/or waiting for the parents to retire. These rules for household formation presupposed at least the compatibility of partners, as they were responsible for running their own household. Work in other households, as a farm hand or domestic servant, was a common experience for youths in Western Europe. In service, which could last until their late twenties, they could acquire the skills and save the money needed for their future households. And, of course, there were many opportunities to meet a potential spouse. Thus, the period of courting was protracted. In colonial America, there were plenty of opportunities to form a new household and age at marriage was accordingly low, especially for women. But during the nineteenth century, American marriage patterns converged toward the European model.[58]

The Christian family system offered plenty of "courtship space." But, as indicated in the introduction, social class determined to a large extent just how large this space was. In general, the more power and wealth involved, the fewer were the options for youths to choose their own partner, let alone to indulge in risky premarital sexual activities. In elite circles, nubile youths could meet the opposite sex, but their meetings were strictly supervised by a chaperon.[59] In other social groups as well, parents made sure to make the pool of eligible partners small. For instance, during the quiet winter months in the rural province of Zeeland, The Netherlands, the sons and daughters of farmers would go "walking": they stayed in the homes of befriended farmers with an eye on meeting a partner.[60] In many European regions, village fairs and dances (e.g., the British Maypole dance[61]) provided opportunity to meet freely, albeit under peer scrutiny. In several Dutch villages lovers could be "rented" for the duration of the fair. For instance, in Lochem (eastern Netherlands) girls would stand in a line and the boys would walk past, returning to make a mark with chalk on the back of the girl that had taken their fancy.[62]

Although choice was "free" in principle, marriage partners were almost always sought and found in the same social class as the parents. Nineteenth-century industrialization— which entailed increased geographical mobility, huge changes in occupational structure, and the rise of meritocratic ideals—did little to change this. At least, class boundaries did not become more "permeable."[63] Other forms of endogamy, for example, by ethnicity or religion also existed and could even become stronger. In late nineteenth-century Netherlands, competition for political control between religious denominations increased, and church leaders emphasized the need to choose a partner from one's own group. Moreover, the educational system (up to university level) was organized according to denomination, and the same was true for other activities such as sport. Thus, the chances to meet youths from other ideological groups diminished. During the heyday of this "Pillarization" (1935–55) the intensity of religiously mixed marriages was the lowest in Dutch history.[64]

In Eastern Europe, marriage choices of children were much more restricted. A good insight into courtship in Russia is provided by the ethnographies of no less than 1,218 rural communities collected around 1900 by Prince V. N. Tenishev.[65] Russian households were extended, meaning that sons remained at home and brought in their brides. The fathers, in name of the landlords, decided when and whom a son was to marry. Although the serfs were emancipated in 1861, peasant households remained part of the village collective and sons remained subordinated to their fathers. Commonly, marriages were arranged. A matchmaker "would visit the marriageable maiden's home and initiate the negotiations by declaring: 'Don't you have a calf for sale? I have a young bull'."[66] Factors involved included the capability for work of the girl, the relation between the families, and the bride price. After a visit by the girls' family, the arrangement proceeded to the bethrothal: "Kin on both sides gathered to drink and to pray for God's blessing. The senior males of the household concluded the financial arrangements and sealed the contract by clapping their hands together (rukobit'e). The date of the wedding was set. After that, if either party changed its mind it dishonored the other, and risked legal action itself. The wedding usually occurred within weeks after the contract was sealed."[67]

Going against the wishes of the parents was difficult for boys, as they were likely to be disinherited.[68] But after emancipation, with the fathers no longer backed up by the landlords, and with the gradual spread of wage labor, sons became more assertive and started to refuse an arranged marriage.[69] Girls had a bit more "leeway" in case they wanted to marry someone against the liking of their parents (mostly when the boys' family was considered of lower standing). She could simply elope, that is move to her lover's house and marry secretly, and informing her parents afterwards. In some regions of Russia, marriage by elopement was quite common.[70]

How did European societies solve the inherent tension between the (sexual) risks involved in courtship and the need to ensure the economic viability of new households? One of the most intriguing practices in which courtship was channeled and risks were mitigated was "night courting." Night courting implied nightly visits of lovers to their

FIGURE 1.3 Alexei Ivanovich Korzukhin (1835–94), *Eve-of-the-Wedding Party*, 1889. Heritage Image Partnership Ltd. Alamy Stock Photo. Image ID: DE2GWA.

girls. These visits could take collective or individual forms.[71] Collective forms could begin at a "spinning bee," where village girls spend the evening spinning together. Later in the evening, boys would join them for games, singing, and courting. Individuals pairs could pair off to find privacy. In more individual forms, boys were allowed access to their girl's bedroom, when the parents had already gone to bed. The stays of the lovers could last all night and could thus involve sleeping together. However, the love-making was supposed to be noncoital. To ensure this, the boys were to remain fully dressed, to stay on top of the girls' blankets, or even to be sewn in a sack (a bundle, hence the word "bundling"). This custom was to be found in many areas of the European countryside, especially in the northern parts, as well as in New England.[72]

Middle-class professionals working in the countryside and travelers were often puzzled and shocked when they heard of night courting and other activities, such as the elaborate tongue-kissing (*maraîchinage*) and mutual masturbation practiced by youths in the Vendée (western France).[73] Often, this behavior was seen as proof of the moral depravity to which the countryside had fallen prey to.[74] One of the most insightful contemporary observers of rural courtship behavior was the Norwegian Eilert Sundt (1817–75).[75] He visited several rural areas to discover the reasons for high rates of illegitimate births. One of his interviews shows how "collective" and "individual" forms of courtship could be intricately interwoven. A couple told him they had engaged in night courting for nine years before their marriage. The visits took place in a barn, where the girl slept with another servant girl, whereas in another bed two servant boys slept. This kind of sleeping arrangement for young laborers were not uncommon in rural Norway nor elsewhere.[76] The boy would visit his girlfriend when the others were asleep, in order to keep their relation a secret. But,

> as I said, there were several people in the animal barn, the door must have been opened and shut on Saturday nights and another boy might strike up a conversation with her. But if such a suitor made signs to lie down with her, then she had to stand up and sit on a bench with him or on the edge of a stall and direct the conversation to trivialities. In the meantime, her real boyfriend might stand outside in rain and bad weather and wait until there was silence inside, and if the visitor stayed a long time, and if a slight hint did not help, she could tell him straight, as for instance, "No, now it must be enough for tonight; I tell you, I do not want to put up anymore with your visit—you must go now."[77]

The couple kept this up for several years. When Sundt asked why they were so bent on keeping their affair secret, "the woman remarked that little good came of talking about these things because when servant folk wanted to meet each other, there were so many who wanted to interfere: the boy's parents would feel that the girl is not good enough, and the girl's parents could also find something to criticize in the boy."

According to Sundt, night courting was—in principle—a perfectly honorable practice, especially for farmer's sons and daughters living at home. But young workers sleeping collectively in barns on other farms, without supervision, and also without the means to set up a household in case the girl got pregnant, made it into a dangerous habit leading to illegitimate births. Proletarianization and increased mobility had disrupted the traditional rules and checks surrounding night courting. Not surprisingly, collective and more or less ritualized forms of night courting held out longest in relatively remote parts of the European countryside, in socially homogeneous villages.[78] Night courting seems to have been an exciting, preliminary stage in the courting of many rural youths. However, when the relation became serious, which might take several years, the prospected partner would still have to be presented to the parents, whose permission remained very important.[79]

Remarkably, night courting was also reported for sizeable parts of Russia.[80] Partner choice was clearly not always controlled by the parents. As elsewhere, boys would visit the evening gatherings of the girls, and later individual couples would pair off. The descriptions remind us that such freedom does not equate with gender equality. Boys were choosing their partner, girls could—at best—refuse: "Sometimes, girlfriends of a reluctant maiden, fearful that dissatisfied youths might not return, would press her to acquiesce: 'Sleep with the bad ones; better ones will come along', while the boys would shame and tease a reluctant maiden until she submitted."[81] Once a boy had made his choice, the others kept their distance. However, when a girl was experimenting in a similar way by having several affairs, she could lose her reputation and could even be beaten by her lover.

Possibly, the rules of night courting were somewhat more gender equal in Western Europe but here as well a clear "double standard" in courtship existed. Girls suspected of "loose" behavior were abandoned quickly, whereas, on the other hand, if a girl did not give in to male overtures at all, she might be considered too prudish.[82] Male dominance of courtship could include a great deal of violence.[83] And, of course, girls alone paid the price when they became pregnant and their lover refused (or was not allowed by his parents) to marry them.

In the choice of a partner, belonging to the right social group and possessing the experiences and resources to run a household were crucial criteria. But a new ideal was spreading, which emerged in the middle class and that reflected the withdrawal of women from the labor market. The ideal was that marriage was a union between "soul mates," true companions who shouldered the burden of running a household together in different but equivalent responsibilities. The norm emerged that courting should entail "falling in love" and that without this compelling emotion a marriage was not founded properly. This ideal can be traced in love letters that over time became more dramatic in their expression of passion (Figure 1.4). For instance, in 1871 Albert Janin wrote to his girlfriend: "I kissed your letter over and over again, regardless of the smallpox epidemic at New York, and gave myself up to a carnival of bliss before breaking the envelope." A few months later, he wrote her: "I cannot have a separate existence from you. I breathe by you; I live by you."[84] Sending printed Valentine cards to (potential) lovers became very popular, especially in America in mid-nineteenth century.[85] Romantic love entailed more private courtship, and also greater care in avoiding premarital sexuality.[86] In fact, the norm of women's chastity was strengthened and man had a valid reason to refuse marrying a girl who had allowed him sex during courtship.[87] There was no mercy for "fallen" women.

The romantic ideal was spread through plays and novels, and affected, as we have seen, the elites of places like Istanbul. But did they also affect the lower classes? From late nineteenth century onward, lower-class women tended to marry earlier and more often. But this does not imply they were captured by romantic notions of marriage. Probably, the reduced work opportunities for unmarried women simply left marriage as one of the few remaining options.[88] Working-class couples simply could not allow themselves to gamble on "love." "Love could not fill empty stomachs," writes Borscheid,[89] who claims that in Germany material criteria remained paramount in partner choice. But then, for a long time German couples had been used to legal restrictions on marriage (*Politischer Ehekonsens*). Until the 1860s, in Germany, Switzerland, and Austria applicants for marriage had to demonstrate sufficient means of sustaining a household before permission

FIGURE 1.4 August Toulmouche (1829–90), *The Love Letter*, 1883. Public domain via Wikimedia Commons.

was given.[90] Still, it remains to be seen how important financial calculations were during courtship. Some scholars have doubted whether courting couples were really capable of elaborate rational planning for the future. In Britain, for instance, many couples turned soon after marriage to their kin for financial support.[91]

At the end of our period, around 1920, the middle-class patterns of courtship were already shifting. The "calling" of a boy at his girls' house—on her initiative—to be scrutinized by her parents began to be replaced by the "date." Taking a girl out on a date to the movies or a restaurant, meant paying for her, and this implied that the initiative shifted to the boys. Going for a ride removed the couple even further from parental control. An anxious observer noted that a car was "a house of prostitution on wheels."[92]

Christian marriage rituals were standardized according to the rules laid out by the Council of Trent (see above). Thus, after public notice, banns were put up on three consecutive Sundays to announce the intended marriage, and people could come forward in case of serious objections. The public notice itself was considered the start of marriage festivities and a party was held the evening before. In the Netherlands, guests were treated to a liquor called "bridal tears" at this event. Then the couple would invite kin, neighbors, and friends for several receptions, and after the wedding ceremony itself the couple would visit kin who could not attend. During the nineteenth century and starting in the middle classes, the string of parties surrounding a wedding were reduced to the wedding ceremony itself, which became more formal and public.[93] An exception is the typical American phenomenon of the "bridal shower," a party in which the bride would be "showered" with gifts for her *trousseau*. These parties began in the late nineteenth century among the upper classes.[94] But by and large, the same tendency to simplify and "privatize" marriage was noted in America. For instance, since the late nineteenth century, American couples going on honeymoon would no longer take kin along.[95]

THE SUB-SAHARAN AFRICAN FAMILY

Due to the absence of corporately organized religions and enduring states, lineages and clans were the most important political, social, and religious entities in African societies.[96] Lineages are groups of about 100 to 200 people who share a common ancestor. A clan is a group of lineages claiming common descent from a (mythical) ancestor.[97] Lineages can be formed in different ways; in Africa patrilineal, matrilineal, and bilateral descent systems exist. Patrilineality is predominant in the northern part of sub-Saharan Africa, matrilinearity is found in parts of West Africa and large sections of equatorial Africa, whereas bilateral descent is mainly found in southern Africa.[98]

In all African descent systems, marriage was not an individual matter but an exchange between lineages. In patrilineal societies the bride wealth was very important, and negotiations could start early in a woman's life. The bride wealth went into a circulating fund that was used to procure wives from another lineage.[99] However, we should not equate this to "buying" a person. Basically, the transaction was restricted to a woman's offspring; it was her capacity to add children to her husband's lineage that counted, not the legitimacy of that offspring. The essential role of fertility becomes clear (e.g., among the Nuer) when, on divorce, the bride wealth had to be returned. The maximum sum was returned in case of an infertile marriage but practically nothing was repaid if the woman had borne numerous children.[100]

Although virginity in girls was mostly valued,[101] African youths were given ample opportunity for experimentation. For instance, late nineteenth-century reports on Zulus (South Africa) describe courtship customs involving coital techniques (*hlobonga*) meant to keep the hymen intact (otherwise the girls would fetch a lower bride wealth) and to avoid pregnancy.[102] A girl could engage in such sexual play with more than one lover but only one per month, in order to account for a pregnancy, in case it should occur.[103] Still, women were supposed to act chaste, to be modest and shy.[104] Another example are the Kenyan Kikuyu. Until the early twentieth century, Kikuyu youths engaged in highly ritualized collective night courting (*ngweko*). Girls would visit boys who shared a hut. The boys would undress completely, but the girls made sure to fasten their leather aprons in such a way that they functioned as a chastity belt. In this way, love-making was highly supervised by the peer group: boys who broke the rules were excluded from night courting.[105] The peer groups that were strongly connected to initiation rites (e.g., circumcision) suffered from attacks from the missions as well as the increase in migrant labor. This also implied that traditional—and rather effective—socialization and supervision of sexuality of youths in various African societies weakened.[106]

In many African societies, partners were often simply selected by the courting youths themselves. Once they made a choice, the negotiations between the parents would start. The bride wealth had to be paid by the father of the groom, and could amount to a sizeable part of his assets ("a third of his cows, half of his goats, and two months' salary"[107]). A girl's reproductive potential determined the price: younger as well as plump (healthy) women commanded higher prices, but lower prices were paid for older women and women who had given birth before marriage. However, in many African societies, youths and their parents were subject to the decisions of the clan elders, who organized economic activities as well as the marriage alliances. As the elders controlled the bride wealth funds, they often delayed the marriages of subordinate clan members, who had to work for them. In the colonial period, taxation, wage labor on plantations, and increased trade activities caused a strong monetization of all transactions. There was a strong inflation of bride wealth.[108] Inflated bride wealth also meant that women were increasingly seen as commodities from which maximum profit had to be reaped to repay the investment.[109]

FIGURE 1.5 *Zulu Maiden Attempting to Stab Bridegroom, An Act Symbolizing her Last Act of Freedom, Africa, c.* 1890. Universal History Archive/Universal Images Group Editorial via Getty Images.

African marriage rituals show that marriage is not seen as a singular event but as a protracted process.[110] Thus, they involve various stages, which, for instance, among the Kenyan Kipsigis begins when the young man's father "presents" a cow to the girl's father. This is just a signal to start the negotiations, which involves several more visits, including with the mother, in order to reach an agreement on the "presentation cattle." Then the young man himself, accompanied by a friend, goes to his father-in-law to be anointed. Then the girl, conducted by her father, mother, and siblings visits the house of the boy's. During a ceremony lasting several hours, they are tied (*ratet*) together by a bracelet of grass. The next ceremony is "viewing the cattle," which, however, may have to be postponed for several years depending on father's economic fortune. This ratifies the contract and is necessary before the final ceremony (*katunisyet*) can be held. This is such a large feast that it often has to be postponed until enough is saved. By then, the couple can have several children.[111] Similarly, the marriage rituals of Nigerian Yoruba revolve around the subsequent instalments in which the bride wealth is transferred.[112]

THE SOUTHEAST ASIAN FAMILY

In Southeast Asia, a "mild" form of patriarchy existed. Foreign observers frequently commented on the relatively equal position of women. An example is Albert Fytche, chief commissioner of Burma who commented in 1878: "[A Burmese] woman is ... not the mere slave of passion, but has equal rights and is the recognized and duly honoured helpmate of man, and in fact bears a more prominent share in the transactions of the more ordinary affairs of life than in the case perhaps with any other people, either eastern or western."[113] In large parts of the region, marriage norms were affected by precolonial Malay culture in which monogamy was the rule and in which women were allowed rights to property, including the bride wealth that was paid for her.[114] Ages at marriage (in Birma, Thailand, the Philippines) were relatively high for women. In some regions, such as Ceylon (Sri Lanka), marriage was bilocal, that is, the wife could either join her husband's family or the other way around. In other regions, for example Thailand, a "hiving-off" rule existed. In such a system, women married and brought in a husband, only to leave when the second daughter married and brought in her husband, and so on.[115] Buddhism, being not overly concerned with enforcing strict moral codes, contributed to relatively relaxed sexual norms in the region. Of course, for a long time Confucianism, Islam, and Christianity were influencing the region, but they were adapted to and modified by traditional (Malay) culture. Most European colonial authorities did not interfere with traditional family customs. However, they did have to deal with interethnic unions. For instance, in 1848 marriages between Christians and non-Christians were allowed in the Dutch East Indies, making it possible for the numerous cohabitations of European men and indigenous women to be legalized.[116] However, European women marrying indigenous men lost their "European" status as they had to take their husband's status (similar rulings existed in other Southeast Asian colonies and Siam).[117]

Family norms in Southeast Asia allowed adolescents some space for courtship: partner choice was not free but at least women had the right to veto their parent's choice (Birma and Thailand).[118] Divorce was very common in the region (including Java), with Malaysia even having the highest divorce rates in the world in the nineteenth and early twentieth centuries. Among the Buddhist Sinhalese of Ceylon (Sri Lanka), marriage was remarkably informal and "free." Women could try out a partner and cohabit before a relation was formalized (by granting use rights to land). Of course, this could lead to problems. In

1818, the Kandy court heard the case of "Appurala vs his wife" in which a couple having cohabitated for seven years fought each other on the question whether they were actually married or not.[119] The Sinhalese state recognized a legal marriage not on the basis of formal procedures but on whether the family heads had consented, whether the couple married within their caste and not within the forbidden degrees of kinship, and whether they had cohabited.[120] To be sure, partner choice remained part of a family strategy and parents frowned upon romantic marriage: "Marriage by choice has no claim upon kin for dowry, no claim for help in harvest and no claim for cooperation in marrying some ultimate daughter of the union."[121]

Not surprisingly, marriage rituals among the Sinhalese were very basic and often did not entail much more than the groom bringing a cloth to the bride's house. When she dressed herself in this cloth, he would conduct her to her new home.[122] Much more elaborate rituals were found among the higher ranks. First, an astrologer had to appoint the most auspicious day for the wedding. On the appointed day, the groom would bring a large number of presents (spices and food), to be carried by a group of lower-caste men. At the gate of the bride's home, he would pay a fee to her cross-cousin (often the son of the eldest brother of her mother), who according to Sinhalese norms had a vested right to marry his cousin. In this way, families counteracted property fragmentation caused by equal inheritance extending to daughters. Then, the visiting party handed over the presents and the night was spent eating and talking. At dawn, the couple were placed in a lucky direction, as ascertained by the astrologer, their little fingers were tied together, and they shared two balls of rice, symbolizing their mutual obligation to provide for food. Finally, a procession brought the couple to their home, where the feast would start. Pieris notes that the binding of hands—which symbolized indissolubility of the union—could be omitted as people were often not preparing for a permanent union.[123] A nineteenth-century observer claimed that the first fortnight was a trial period for the couple, after which their marriage could be easily annulled.

THE LATIN AMERICAN CREOLE FAMILY

In Latin America, colonization and slavery created a much stronger intermingling of cultures affecting marriage and family formation rules more than elsewhere. Colonial rules aimed to force the native Indian population to comply with Christian norms and regulations regarding family and sexuality. This meant breaking down the hold of the (patri)lineages on family marriages; village headmen no longer could arrange their subject's marriages and certainly not among kin. Apart from marriage by choice, marriage to nonrelatives, and nuclear households, the colonizers introduced testaments and private property. In addition, the Indians were taught that bodily pleasure was sinful.[124] However, the clerical ambition of restructuring family was often thwarted, as the clergy were too limited in number, in too much conflict among themselves, or too corrupt. Also, the indigenous population, decimated and subjugated as it was, managed to operate strategically within the new rules, creating new family forms in the process. Polygamous men would seek divorce, for example by confronting the clergy with the forbidden degrees of kinship, in order to retain their most favorite wife. But they would also form secretive relations, for instance with concubines disguised as slaves. Concubinage became an important alternative to polygamy.[125]

The mass importation of African slaves restructured colonial society once again. It became even more difficult to adhere to the Christian ideals of marriage, as the obsession with color distinctions made formalization of many relations impossible. However, the already existing "broad gamut of illegitimate relationships"[126] offered many opportunities for flexible adjustment.[127] For instance, according to the 1855 census of Salvador, Bahia (Brazil), more than half of all couples lived in a consensual union.[128] "Purity of blood" (*limpieza de sangre*) defined the status of the ruling white caste. White women were jealously protected and restricted in their courtship. Scarcity of available white women encouraged male sexual aggression toward black, Indian, or mestiza women. According to Therborn: "Male sexual predation became almost institutionalized among the white rulers. Within their racial boundaries, this proved role-models for the classes and races of the ruled males."[129] However, nonwhite women could also put sexual relations with white men to their advantage: becoming the mistress of a white man appears to have been a major route for upward social mobility of mestizo, mulatto, and black women.[130]

Of course, parental concern for family status often colluded with choices of youths who were relatively free to meet. In nineteenth-century Cuba, for instance, elopements occurred often when parents objected to a suitor's lower class. Couples eloped to start a consensual union and hoped to save money to marry eventually. When properly conducted, the marriage ceremony and festive celebration could be costly. Others eloped to gain immediate parental consent for marriage; they would return after a few days and pressured the parents to consent as now the girl had lost her virginity. To some extent, elopements were an "institutionalized" solution to the parental defense of status and relatively free choice.[131]

Couples could also defy their parents by going to court to seek permission to marry. A case from Buenos Aires, Argentina, nicely illustrates how discourses of class and race could clash. In 1832, Maria Rodriguez, a poor woman, argued before the judges that they should overrule her widowed mother's objection to marry a *pardo* (mixed descent) man named Andres Lorea: "It is true that the purity of my blood is well known. But if my lineage is well known, so is the fact that I am destitute and lack the means to survive." Furthermore: "My future groom, though pardo, is of proven character. And, as an employed wagon driver, he is in the position to provide for all of my wants and needs in a decent and comfortable manner." Even more succinct, Maria argued: "the purity of my blood cannot put food on my table." Eventually, the judge ruled in her favor, which fits a pattern of decreasing concerns for racially mixed marriages in nineteenth-century Argentina.[132]

CONCLUSION

We have seen how the risks caused by adolescent love and courtship have been mitigated or even annihilated in different family systems across the globe, as for example in child marriage in India. Societies often reduced risks by closely circumscribing the group of eligible spouses. An example is the proscribed cross-cousin marriage among the Sinhalese (Ceylon) and the ritual payment of fees to the cousin in case the bride married someone else. Another risk reduction was the physical seclusion of young women (India, Muslim world) to avoid unwanted connections. We have also seen how, even in such circumstances, young people could still enter premarital relations that sometimes resulted in elopements and court cases. In China, girls were married into another lineage in another village, which also put an effective limit to courtship. A final example are the American Creole societies that rigidly tried to keep the white blood "pure" by restricting mixed marriages. To be sure, young people in love could sometimes overcome barriers put in their way by eloping, by going to court, or by cohabiting. But these escape routes came at a cost, if not in the way of punishments, then at least of losing status and esteem. By and large, in large parts of the nineteenth-century world, there was little room for courtship understood as free partner choice based on emotional and physical contact.

Other societies offered more "courtship space," as in Southeast Asia. In middle- and upper-class Europe and its offshoots young people had chances to meet, although chaperons would make sure nothing untoward happened. Among the common people of Europe and North America much more freedom was allowed. Rituals such as night courting offered young people the opportunity to meet and to experiment with sexuality in a rather safe way. It was "safe" because love-making stopped short of full intercourse and especially because young men were controlled by their peer group, either by ostracizing them if they went too far or making sure they would marry the girl in case she had become pregnant. We have found such night courting in Europe but also in Japan, large parts of Africa, and—not discussed in this chapter—Polynesia.[133] Peer-controlled courting rituals notwithstanding, parents would still have a large say in partner choice. Moreover, the double standard of sexual morality meant that girls were less free to take the initiative but bore disproportionate risks.

Gradually, the European middle-class ideal of "romantic love" began to permeate courtship, not just in Europe but in non-European societies as well through European plays and novels, missionary activities, colonial laws, and local ruler's ambition to become "European." But the real victory of romantic love had to await the new century.

Courtship often had a ritualistic character, for instance in the rules surrounding night courting in different societies. But more formal rituals followed upon the decision to marry. In this chapter, we could not do justice to the enormous variation in marriage rituals across the world. However, they do have a number of elements in common. Many rituals deal with the transfer of a girl from one family group to another, as we have seen in the series of rituals involved in African interfamily negotiations and in bridal processions in which the girl is brought to her new family, as in China. Even in European rituals this element has been preserved in the form of the groom asking for the bride's hand and the father "giving away the bride" during the wedding ceremony. Wedding rituals often express the new unity of the couple, such as the Indian tying of hands or the foot-stamping ritual we have discussed above. Such rituals depend on the relative position of the conjugal unit—the more autonomy of the couple versus their extended kin, the more important it was to symbolize their unity.[134] Everywhere, fertility symbols were part and parcel of wedding rituals, such as the throwing of rice at the couple or making a wedding canopy from bamboo (India). In many societies, such as the Arabic, the consummation of the marriage was the most important part of the ritual, with evidence that the wife came to the marriage a virgin.[135] The evidence that the first child belongs to the rightful heir relates to the exchange of women between patrilineal clans. In this exchange system a strong sense of male honor interprets sexual intercourse as "violence" against men.[136]

The ways courtship is restricted or channeled toward formal marriage serve to mitigate the risks adolescent sexuality poses for families and society, and the rituals surrounding marriage often symbolize this harnessing of sexuality.

CHAPTER TWO

Religion

Between the Sacred and the Secular—Changes in Marital Life around the World

KARL KASER

The investigation of how and to what extent religions have had an impact on marriage and marital life is challenging because although considerable research has been conducted on the influence of individual religions on marriage, there are few comparative analyses comprising all or most of the world religions. My contribution will include Christianity, Confucianism, Hinduism, Islam, and Judaism, whereby with regard to Christianity I will distinguish between Catholicism, Orthodoxy, and Protestantism where appropriate. These world religions or religions with supraregional influence, which comprised the vast majority of the world's population around the First World War, seem to be the most relevant with regard to marital life. Buddhism is excluded here because of its focus on monastic communities and its disregard of worldly life.[1] I am aware that authors, especially those belonging to the "religions of the book," may not consider Confucianism and Hinduism proper religions.[2] However, others do by referring to religion as a system of meaningful practices in relation to personal and nonpersonal superhuman powers. In such a perspective, the question is not whether Hinduism and Confucianism are essentially religions but whether certain dimensions of these belief systems can be reasonably considered as religious.[3]

The scope of my chapter is not limited to the impact of religions on marital life, but extends its perspective to the emergence of their major rivals in connection with the regulation of marriage, namely, the state that aims to separate public and religious institutions and state administrations that spur the idea of secularization. This emerging confrontation created a complex interplay between static (sacred) and dynamic (secular) factors, characterized by advances and setbacks for the secular.

Since almost half a dozen denominations are included here, classification and groupings are crucial in order to maintain an overview. One important classification differentiates between interventionist (Abrahamic) religions and noninterventionist religions (Confucianism, Hinduism). However, religions and their impact on marital life could also be grouped in other ways. One consists in the distinction between primarily orthopractically and primarily orthodoxly oriented religions. Whereas orthopraxy prescribes concrete religious conduct in everyday marital life, orthodoxy stresses the observation of the spiritual component of religion. This means that orthopractically

TABLE 2.1 **Basic Orientations of World Religions and Family Ideology**

	Protestantism	W-Christian	E-Christian	Judaism	Islam	Hinduism	Confucianism
Intervention	*	*	*↓	*↓	*↓		
Nonintervention						*	*
Orthodox	*	*	*↓	[*]			
Orthopractice				*	*	*	*
Horizontal	*	*	*↓	*	*		
Vertical					[*]	*	*
	More gender equality, high age at marriage, neolocality, secularism, civil marriage				Patrilineality (ancestor worship), low age at marriage, arranged marriage, patrilocality		

Note: *↓ = the tendency of a religion to the category below; [*] = a minority tendency within a religion.

oriented religions have a more comprehensive impact on the nonreligious, secular spheres of marital life than orthodoxly oriented ones. Islam[4] and Confucianism[5] are considered the most pronounced orthopractical world religions. I would also add Hinduism, unreformed ultra-Orthodox Judaism (the Jewish law, the halakha, does not know a separation of secular and religious life), and ultra-orthodox denominations of Christianity to the list of orthopractically oriented religions. Another pair of categories that aids differentiation consists of those religions reinforcing horizontal family ties and those reinforcing vertical family ties. Horizontal orientation primarily focuses on the married couple and is more pronounced in the Abrahamitic than in the non-Abrahamitic religions. Among the important exceptions are marriages in Arab social contexts, which have a vertical orientation consisting of a preference for the father–son relationship and a patrilineal ideology linking the male ancestors with the contemporary living and the future born males. Hinduism and Confucianism emphasize patrilineality and ancestor worship; Shintoism (Japan) and Taoism (China) also support these kinds of values or at least do not suppress these features of family ideology. Verticality stresses the birth of sons and encourages the ideological devaluation of daughters and wives, as well as arranged marriage, while horizontality supports equality between the spouses and love marriages (Table 2.1).

My contribution consists of three sections, each with a particular structure. The first will look at spheres of marital life shaped by the above-mentioned religions before the age of increased state intervention. In the second section, temporal dynamics are emphasized, which were triggered by emerging secularization, the separation of the religious and worldly spheres, and civil marriage. Marital life was increasingly considered a societal field that should be regulated less by religious authorities and more by the secular state and its civil code. Since the intensification of colonial policies was one of the most important characteristics of the decades before the First World War, the third section will tackle the interaction of the marital practices of the Christian colonizers and the non-Christian populations of sub-Saharan Africa and India.

THE IMPACT OF THE WORLD RELIGIONS ON MARITAL LIFE—CONTINUITIES

This section starts with a few general remarks on the impact of the world religions on sex, marriage, and family life. The authors of a pertinent study[6] have identified sixteen fields of impact; only a few of the most relevant will be mentioned here. For each of the world religions, marriage constitutes a vital and valuable institution and practice that rests at the foundation of broader society; children constitute sacred gifts to a married couple and carry forth not only the family name, lineage, and property but also the community's religion, culture, and language. Each religious tradition eventually came to insist that marriage depends, on the one hand, on the mutual consent of the couple. On the other hand, each tradition emphasizes that persons are not free to marry just anyone they please. The divine and/or nature set the first limit on the freedom of the marital contract. With a few exceptions, parties cannot marry relatives by blood nor marriage nor people of the same sex. Custom and religion set the second limit: couples must be of comparable social and economic status and ideally of the same faith or caste. Figure 2.1 showing a grave from the nineteenth century documents that even

FIGURE 2.1 *"Grave with the Little Hands" in Roermond, the Netherlands. On the Catholic Side of the Cemetery Lady J.C.P.H. van Aefferden is Buried, Across the Wall, on the Protestant Cemetery her Husband, J.W.C. van Gorkum, Both hold each other hand.* Public domain via Wikimedia Commons.

the afterlives of those rare couples of mixed Protestant and Catholic marriage could become rather complicated.

The world religions, however, differ considerably in their respective views regarding the field of sexuality and procreation. Within marriage, religions vary with regard to the appreciation of erotic pleasure, with Islam and perhaps Hinduism being the most forthright in their affirmation.[7] Here, I think it might be useful to briefly discuss the religiously defined relations between the married couple, the aims of marriage, sexual morality, and the character of marriage. As already mentioned, a distinction can be made between interventionist and noninterventionist religious models.

Interventionist models—the Abrahamitic religions

Judaism, Christianity, and Islam emerged under specific social, cultural, political, and economic conditions and therefore the character of their intervention in previous customs differed. The family form endorsed by early Christianity was shaped by monogamy, the prohibition of concubinage, and the strengthening of husband–wife bonds through the condemnation of divorce.[8] Canonical marriage law, which had come into being by the end of the twelfth century, transformed marriage into an indissoluble sacrament based on mutual consent. The agreement of parents, even in the case of children, was not obligatory; clandestine marriages became fully valid.[9] This has often been referred to as one of the keystones of Western romantic marriages.

The Protestant reform movement was strongly opposed to canonical marriage law, celibacy, the acknowledgement of clandestine marriages, the ban on the dissolution of the bonds of wedlock even after adultery, and the monopoly of the church regarding marriage issues. For Protestants, marriage constituted a divine institution, a contract on the basis of mutual consent but not a sacrament.[10]

The Quran also introduced a number of reforms, especially with regard to women. For instance, it recognized a woman's right to contract her own marriage. The Quran sought to control and regulate the practice of polygamy, stipulating that instead of having innumerable wives, a man could marry up to four provided he could support and treat them equally.[11] Contrary to Christianity, in Islam marriage and the family are considered a major source of comfort and joy, including sexual pleasure, for both spouses.[12] This notion also includes less cultural and religious resistance to birth control. Compared to Catholic Christianity, Islam generally does not perceive family planning as a practice directed against the will of God. Allegedly, coitus interruptus was already practiced at the time of the prophet Muhammad; he did not forbid it.[13]

Islamic marriage laws prohibit a union between the same broad categories of kin as in Christianity.[14] However, Islamic law does not prohibit—nor does it recommend or impose—the marriage of first cousins. This pre-Islamic institution was, and still is, widespread among the Arab population of North Africa and in West Asia, as well as among the non-Arab population of Central Asia.[15] From the mid-nineteenth century, scientists warned of the deleterious outcomes of consanguinity; however, there were some scientists and doctors who argued that inbreeding offered major biological advantages.[16] This may be one of the reasons why today about 20 percent of the world's population lives in communities with a preference for consanguineous marriage.[17] Additional reasons for this kind of marriage include the beneficial opportunity to concentrate wealth within the family and to protect a daughter from being mistreated without consequences.[18]

The marriage laws of the Abrahamitic religions focus on the couple (and its children), emphasizing—contrary to Hinduism and Confucianism—horizontal and couple-centred marital ties. In Latin Europe under the influence of Christianity, ancestor worship was eradicated; spiritual kinship ranked higher than kinship by blood. This emphasis on the couple—supported by the free choice of the future spouse—went hand in hand with a relatively high age at marriage, as was widespread since the late Middle Ages.[19] In Orthodox Eastern Europe, however, ancestor worship in a Christianized version continued to exist and age at marriage remained low. Whereas in Latin Europe the share of people who remained single for life was high, in Eastern Europe marriage was nearly universal.[20]

This emphasis on the couple lost its basis in societies on the fringes of Catholicism—for instance in Latin America where the conjugal bond was characterized by significant instability, resulting in a high percentage of illegitimate births and unmarried mothers. To a certain degree, these unstable bonds were absorbed by the institution of *compadrazgo*, a form of ritual kinship that had not only important religious but also societal meaning.[21]

In Protestantism, there seems to be even more emphasis on the conjugal couple than in Catholicism. What Luther did was not only to urge his contemporaries to leave the monasteries and clerical celibacy, but to marry and establish their own homes. Moreover, his model of family life promoted more equality between wife and husband than was typical for his time.[22]

These couple-centered marital ties resulted, among other things, in strict sexual morality to be adhered to by both men and women. In this regard, Christianity took the harshest stance by confirming again and again that the sole purpose of marital sexuality was procreation and the only accepted mode of birth regulation was abstention.[23] Procreation as the primary purpose of marital sexuality is also emphasized by the Orthodox Church. However, sexual fulfillment also ranks high. In the Orthodox Church, sexual intercourse is described as *synousia*, meaning "a community of essence"—in a spiritual as well as a physical sense.[24]

The Catholic Church was not only radical in denying pleasure in marital sexual relations but also with regard to the indissolubility of the marriage bond: "What God hath joined together, let no man put asunder." Divorce was not permitted, only annulment. Among the theological points at the heart of disputes between theologians of the Catholic and Orthodox churches in relation to the sacraments, there was none of more practical significance than that of divorce. Orthodoxy provides some license for divorce in the case of adultery, which is considered as tantamount to death, namely a moral death that thus dissolves the bond.[25]

Judaism and Islam acknowledge the right of husbands and wives to divorce. However, a Jewish woman can be divorced without her consent; a man cannot.[26] The right of Muslim men to divorce is generally referred to as *talaq*, meaning "repudiation"—the release of a human being from any obligation. While the husband has the right to divorce, there are some restrictions: for example, there must be a plausible reason for divorce. Simply uttering "you are repudiated" three times in the presence of two other men is not always considered sufficient.[27]

In regard to monogamy and polygyny, Judaism and Islam differ from the Christian denominations. Whereas in Christianity monogamy in marital life constitutes an absolute dogma, Judaism has allowed, and some Islamic states still allow, polygynous constellations. Polygamy was not introduced by either Judaism or Islam; it had already been widely practiced. After long discussions, Judaism eventually outlawed polygyny in the eleventh century.[28] What remained, however, was an institution that looks like polygyny but has completely different roots: the levirate marriage—the marriage of a widow to her already married brother-in-law or another close male family member. Its primary purpose was to provide a son for the sonless widow in order to ensure the continuation of the line of her deceased husband.[29] Islam, moreover, limits the number of wives to four, which in itself represented a major step in restricting polygyny as the number of wives had previously been unlimited. The Quran permits polygamy only in specific circumstances, for instance if the husband is able to treat his wives equally.[30]

With respect to celibacy, Judaism and Islam also differed from Christianity—but even Christianity was divided on this issue. Judaism as well as Islam rejected celibacy.[31]

In early Christianity, anti-sex sentiment was shared by many.[32] As a consequence, the Catholic Church was able to enforce the prohibition of marriage and sexual intercourse during Lent and Advent. Research for the Netherlands in the nineteenth and first half of the twentieth centuries proves that the marriage ban was overwhelmingly respected.[33] Celibacy was an ideal for those who aimed for moral perfection. This resulted in the canonical requirement for priestly celibacy.[34] The Eastern Church was more moderate in allowing priests to marry. According to its canon law, ordained priests must maintain their marital status all their life—a condition that prohibits unmarried priests to ever marry and married priests to divorce. However, if a priest became a bishop his wife was obliged to retreat to a nunnery.[35] Luther categorically rejected priestly and monastic celibacy as leading to immoral sexual relationships and practices and condemned celibacy as contrary to divine law.[36]

These few examples document the interventionist character of the Abrahamitic religions, especially with regard to sexuality and procreation. Of these, Christianity reorganized marital life in the most radical way. If we take marriage as a measure for the extent of intervention, a range unfolds from the Catholic ideal of lifelong celibacy to marriage as a religious duty in Islam. In contrast to the Abrahamitic religions, which created new realities with regard to marriage and sexuality, Hinduism and Confucianism rather confirmed and stabilized existing societal relations in the period of their religious formation.

Noninterventionist models—Hinduism and Confucianism

The ideas that underlie the practices of Chinese patriarchal marital life can be related to Confucianism with some justification, even though many of them predated Confucius or were not elaborated until centuries after his death (479 BCE).[37] The canonical core of Confucian teachings on the family goes back to the Han dynasty (202 BCE— AD 220) when his texts were in wide circulation.[38] Similar is the case with Hinduism. Hindu patriarchal marital relations were enshrined in a 2,500-year-old tradition of law, with its paramount authority laid out in the Code of Manu produced in the centuries before the beginning of the Christian era. Although this law can hardly be compared to the marriage laws of the "religions of the book," important guidelines are included: marriage was and is considered a sacred act and the proper way for a person to respect their obligations to their ancestors. These duties can only be performed by men; a woman's sole form of virtuous life is devotion to and worship of her husband. Hindu marriage is indissoluble; a widow is therefore considered as socially dead.[39]

Both Hinduism and Confucianism reaffirm existing hierarchical societal regimes, vertical family relations, and ancestor worship. For significant parts of Hindu society, individual love and attraction are subordinate to the larger concerns of the family and patriline.[40] The purpose of marriage is to give birth to sons and to continue the line of the ancestors.[41] Marriage was primarily to ensure the continuity of the lineage and not the happiness of the conjugal couple.

Contrary to Hinduism, marriage in China was a secular arrangement and divorce was easy to obtain for the husband. Here, marriages were arranged between families and child betrothals were frequent, although the actual age at marriage was higher than in India—in the later teens for women. Concubinage was legitimate and common among the upper classes. The concubine lived in the household of the patriarch and her children were considered as equally legitimate as those of his wife. Institutionally, however, the concubine had a lower and weaker social position.[42] In Confucianism, the family is also understood as a chain stretching endlessly back to the ancestors and forever forward to the generations yet unborn.[43]

Sexuality in Confucianism and Hinduism is by far not as stigmatized as in Catholicism. Confucianism as well as Taoism teaches that sexual intercourse can be appreciated by all men and women.[44] Marital sexuality not only serves the purpose of desired male procreation but, just as in Taoism, health and longevity. The energy produced during intercourse between *yin* and *yang* is considered the ultimate force of creativity.[45] In Hinduism, conception is considered the result of a divine act because this is the moment when the soul enters the body along with the individual's past *karma*.[46]

To sum up, the impact of religion on marital life, despite all the interventions of the state to be investigated in the next section, was still considerable. However, by around 1900 it no longer remained unquestioned. This rough overview has not yet revealed that throughout the nineteenth century voices advocating secularization became louder and louder, and liberal political movements—not only in Europe—had started campaigns against the still evident influence of churches on partner choice, education, and marital life.

THE SACRED AND THE SECULAR—DYNAMIC FACTORS

Debates about who should be in charge of regulating marital life—religious institutions and/or the state—moved to the center of attention in the course of the nineteenth century, fueled by the American and French revolutions in the second half of the previous century. The decades before the First World War were characterized by a new and dynamic interplay between continuity and change, as well as between religious and secular forces. This will be exemplified by three observations: (1) an increasing dissatisfaction with the sacred forms of marital life, (2) the emergence of secularism, and (3) attempts to introduce civil marriage.

Increasing dissatisfaction with the sacred forms of marital life

In China, the first impact of Western education was felt in the cities during the later nineteenth century. Under missionary influence, boys were sent to study in the United States, France and England from the 1870s. At the same time, missionary schools were established in China itself.[47] Western influence should not be underestimated, but independently of this, Chinese reform forces started to encourage alternative forms of marital life already during the Taiping Rebellion (1850–64). In the "liberated" territories, the rebels prohibited polygyny and the deformation of girls' feet and forbade rape and the killing of newborn girls.[48]

Protests of women and youth—the two largest vulnerable groups—against the family values of Confucianism continued at the beginning of the twentieth century. Among the traditions they challenged in the first years of the century, the mutilation of girls' feet ranked most prominently.[49] The youth protests culminated in a demonstration in Beijing on May 4, 1919. This marked the beginning of a radical movement against the Confucian worldview, which was embodied in the hierarchical structures of the family. The army dissolved the peaceful demonstration by force but critique of suppression by the family, and demands for more freedom for youth, did not cease.[50]

Around the same time in the Islamic world, a kind of Islamic modernism was articulated. Egypt and India spearheaded the new thinking in the late nineteenth and early twentieth

FIGURE 2.2 George Rinhart, *A Wedding Party in Peking Bringing the Bride to her New Home*, 1900, undated photograph. Corbis Historical via Getty Images.

centuries. The Islamic belief system came under persistent criticism from diverse groups in relation to theological and social issues, including the status of women. European societies were perceived as residing at the pinnacle of world civilization, with the social status of women being the test of sophistication. The Islamic theologians who had accepted these ideas advanced a modernist interpretation of religion and a feminist reading of the Quran.[51]

Against this background, a discussion in the Islamic world about the future of the marital relationship began. The modernists demanded a reinterpretation or reformation of Islam in response to the new demands of modernity and change. Among the key areas of concern was women's status and thus educational and legal reforms regarding marriage, divorce, and inheritance.[52] Marriage was to be based on feelings of love, sympathy, and mutual affection, emphasizing partnership and reciprocal companionship. Men's power over women was to be limited and the physical abuse of wives discouraged. Polygamy was questioned, the age difference between spouses was criticized, and monogamy advocated as the best form of marriage.[53]

The emergence of secularism

These two examples should suffice to indicate the widespread tendencies directed against religious restrictions with regard to marital life. However, not only individuals and groups started to question the role of religious institutions, but states and their increasingly powerful administrations also became interested in neutralizing the impact of religious institutions on marital life. The introduction of civil marriage became a powerful instrument for realizing this aim. But its implementation required a complete, or at least extensive, separation of the state and religious institutions as a precondition—in other words, secularization. However, the emergence of a secular set of laws in the course of the nineteenth and early twentieth centuries did not necessarily imply that a secular state had completely replaced the influence of the churches, nor was the rise of secularism uninterrupted. Major European monarchies such as Catholic Austria-Hungary, the Orthodox Russian Empire, and the Muslim Ottoman Empire even successfully rejected the concept of secularization.

The separation of the spheres of the church and state in the United States and France was realized shortly after the respective bourgeois-democratic revolutions in the second half of the eighteenth century. Starting in these initial countries, the idea of secularization gained momentum and spread around the world. In Great Britain, the far-reaching secularization of the state was established between 1828 and 1835, though the Church of England remained the state church. At this point it should not go unmentioned that authors such as Callum Brown have brought forward the provocative thesis that secularization did not occur before the 1960s.[54] In most of the West European countries, the spheres of the state and church were already separated in the second half of the nineteenth century,[55] which did not necessarily mean that churches (especially the Catholic Church) had completely lost their influence on matters of marriage, for instance with regard to birth control. When fertility began to decline across Europe by the end of the nineteenth century, Catholics retained the highest fertility rates compared to the other major religious groups.[56]

In the Habsburg Empire, secularization was inaugurated by Emperor Joseph II in the second half of the eighteenth century. However, subsequent administrations did everything in their power to keep the significant influence of the Catholic Church on public education and marriage intact. Until the demise of the monarchy in 1918, it was not possible to establish obligatory civil marriage and divorce in Austria-Hungary.[57] Meanwhile in the Russian Empire, the Russian Orthodox Church successfully retained jurisdiction over marriage and divorce until the end of the *ancien regime*.[58] Six weeks after the October Revolution, in full civil war, the Soviets issued decrees aimed at the separation of the religious and public spheres.[59]

In countries such as Japan and China with their Confucian family tradition, things were more complicated. In Japan, the separation of the religious and the public spheres (guaranteed in the constitution of 1946) was irrelevant for the reformation of marital life since the obligatory veneration of the divine emperor was based on Shintoism and not on Confucianism.[60] More significant was the introduction of a civil code. Resistance against the imposition of Western civil codes in the Confucian world was considerable and the work of adapting them to local requirements in some areas took decades. In the case of Japan, laws passed in the decades after 1870 aimed at the separation of traditional Confucian doctrines from public law. The preparation of a civil code, a copy of the French original, began as early as 1870. But from year to year, more and more Japanese customary family law was included. Eventually, the civil code was passed in 1890 but was not adopted until 1898. Confucian family ethic remained pronounced, while at the same time the code represented a break with tradition insofar as customary law had known only obligations whereas the civil code formulated the completely new idea of the rights of family members. Since this notion was completely unknown, a term for "right" had to be created.[61] Critics of the law argued that now the couple was considered as the core of the family, contrary to the Japanese tradition of veneration of the patriline. Indeed, the law book hardly referred to ancestor worship. Nevertheless, the patriarchal concept of the family survived and the head of the household retained powers that other household members lacked.[62]

In China, Confucian customary family law sanctioned, for instance, the doctrine of the superiority of the father, husband, and senior over the son, wife, and junior in marital life. These regulations remained essentially unchanged until the end of the nineteenth century when a law reform movement began work on drafting a Japanese-inspired civil code,[63] completed just before the revolution of 1911 that turned China into a republic and in 1912 into a secular state. The code was made public only in 1916. After a number of further drafts, the new code was finally enacted fifteen years later, in 1931. Confucian ethical doctrines were almost completely expelled from the law. The authority of the father was reduced, the equality of the sexes introduced, and the husband's superiority over his wife no longer recognized.[64] However, it is unlikely that the protracted introduction

FIGURE 2.3 *Japan: A Young Japanese before her Wedding*, 1916. Ullstein Bild Dtl. via Getty Images.

of modern family codes led to immediate changes in the behavior of the Chinese and Japanese populations who had been shaped by Confucianism for many centuries.

In Islam, the separation of religious institutions and the state was hardly considered desirable. The Muslim vision of religion and the state was based upon the reading or interpretation of the Quran, as well as on the example of Muhammad and the early Muslim community. Spiritual belief and everyday behavior were considered mutually inclusive. Many Muslims were convinced that religion could not be separated from social and political life, since the first informs a person's every action.[65] It is therefore not surprising that the first serious attempts to separate the spheres of state and religion were undertaken only after our period of consideration, namely in the early Turkish Republic,[66] founded in 1923, and in Iran under the Pahlavi dynasty, established in the early 1920s.[67] However, this liberal period came to an end and gave way to new fundamentalisms. The foundation of the Society of the Muslim Brothers in Egypt (1928), which branched out into other Arab countries,[68] constituted a serious indicator of these developments.

In Latin America, however, the separation of the state and the religious sphere made considerable progress already in the second half of the nineteenth century. Under colonial rule in the Age of Enlightenment, the impact of the Catholic Church was reduced, the Jesuits were expelled, and the impact of the state on family and marriage increased at the cost of the church. In the postcolonial era, the church was confronted with public administrations that tried to reduce its historical, primarily economic, privileges.[69] In the Kingdom of Brazil, as a consequence of the republican coup of 1889, the church and state were separated. The constitution of 1891 omitted to mention God in its preamble. It gave all religions the right to open worship and forbade religious education in public schools.[70]

Civil marriage

Given this increase in the number of states worldwide that had started to separate the church from the state from approximately the mid-nineteenth century, the state moved to replace the church as a neutral authority governing marriage and family life by introducing obligatory civil marriage. Parties could still voluntarily subscribe to the internal marriage and family laws of their own religious communities, but the state's marriage and family laws were now supreme and in cases of conflict would preempt religious laws.

The French marriage law of 1792, which made marriage a secular act, constitutes a good starting point for further exploration. This revolutionary law required the civil registration of life-cycle events including the civil celebration of marriage in a town hall. Most of the ecclesiastical impediments to marriage were eliminated and marriage ceased to be regarded as an indissoluble bond. The law made divorce available to both men and women equally; liberty to live alone or to remarry was to be easily regained. A husband was permitted to remarry immediately, while a wife was required to remain unmarried for ten months.[71]

The revolutionary marriage law was extended also to the French Jews, who had been emancipated the year before. The French rabbinate had the task of resolving tensions and contradictions between civil marriage and the religious marriage law. French law stipulated that civil marriage preceded any subsequent (optional) religious ceremony. Reformed Judaism accepted the new legal forms of entering and dissolving the marital state, relegating rabbis to agents of the state, and the marriage contract to a formalistic exchange of vows. However, some traditional Jews married in a religious ceremony only. According to Jewish law, this kind of marriage was valid but not according to the law of

FIGURE 2.4 *Hebrew Wedding, c.*1900. Bettmann via Getty Images.

the state. Conservative and Orthodox Jews were now living under two jurisdictions—that of the state and that of Jewish law—and the two did not always match up. Divorce was the greater problem, since the state did not recognize the need for a religious divorce prior to remarriage, but without previous religious divorce Jewish law considered the second marriage adulterous and its children illegitimate.[72]

A further important incentive for civil marriage came from the Protestant state churches of Scandinavia, which in accordance with Lutheran theology had always recognized the legitimacy of secular family legislation in principle. They put up little or no resistance to civil marriage.[73] In Britain, family law reform is usually viewed as beginning with the English Matrimonial Causes Act of 1857. Six thousand clergy mobilized against it, but Parliament stood firm. The Act introduced two major reforms; firstly, all marriage and divorce jurisdiction was transferred from the church courts to the common law courts. In doing so, England followed the American example that had rejected ecclesiastical courts from the start. Secondly, the Act authorized private divorce on proof of cause, with a subsequent right to remarry for the innocent party. Innocent husbands and wives could now sue for absolute divorce on proof of the adultery of the other party.[74] In the second half of the nineteenth century, civil marriage proved increasingly popular in England and Wales and there is evidence of changing conceptions of the nature of marriage among the populace. By 1904, 22 percent of marriages were performed in county register offices.

The highest rates of civil marriage occurred in the more remote northern counties, in Wales, and in London.[75]

Shortly after the English Matrimonial Causes Act, the Italian *codice civile* of 1865 established a compromise between the positions of the Catholic Church and the state: marriage retained the secular character introduced by Napoleon, but divorce was precluded.[76] A decade later, the newly formed German Empire stipulated in an imperial act passed in 1875 that civil marriage would be the exclusive means of entering into marriage and also installed the basic right to divorce. This was repeated in the Civil Code of 1900.[77]

In Orthodox Eastern Europe, issues relating to the family and marriage remained under religious jurisdiction. The Tsarist family law left marriage matters to the religious authorities. The position of the national Orthodox churches remained unquestioned and their resistance against civil marriage could not be overcome.[78]

In the Islamic world, civil legislation and Islamic law (Sharia) appeared to be inseparable. Despite the reform movements mentioned above, there had been no modern reform of ancient Sharia law in any Muslim society by 1900. The first modern reforms of family law were promulgated by the Ottoman parliament in 1917[79] and became a model for some of its Muslim successor states. The law regulated marriage, family obligations, and divorce. Marriages had to be registered with civil authorities. Guardians were prohibited from marrying off girls younger than nine and boys younger than twelve years of age. The law left the traditional right for a man to marry up to four wives fully intact.[80] It was only with the establishment of the Republic of Turkey that a modern family law was introduced. President Mustafa Kemal ordered a law commission to import the Swiss Civil Code to Turkey, which took effect in 1926.[81] However, this did not automatically mean that all marriages were officially registered from then on. According to the Turkish Demographic and Health Survey of 1993, forbidden unions performed by religious ceremony only were commonly practiced all over the country; 7.5 percent of married women lived in such unions.[82] In Morocco, the French colonial administration was only charged with registering the marriages of Europeans and Jews. Registration was not made compulsory for Muslims before 1950.[83]

The introduction of obligatory civil marriage by the end of the nineteenth century in many Latin American countries increased the numerical disparity between informal and formal marriages. For the indigenous population opposed to the states organized by white and mestizo elites, this form of marriage was not attractive because it bore no relation to their religious or social customs. Resistance was expressed by the continuation of religious marriage practices without registration by the state. This resulted in high rates of illegitimacy. For instance, Guatemala introduced civil marriage as the only valid form of marriage in 1877. Whereas in the period 1865–70 the rate of illegitimacy had been only 17 percent, in 1920 it had already reached 48 percent.[84]

In countries such as Paraguay and Brazil, Catholic marriage as well as registered civil marriage was not very popular among the indigenous population. Thus, informal marriages were not the exception but rather the rule. For example, in Paraguay's capital Asunción in 1818 more than half of the newborn children were considered illegitimate.[85] In the 1850s and 1860s, 30 to 45 percent of the population of Salvador (the capital of the Brazilian province of Bahia) never formally married; approximately half of the city's households were found to be based on informal unions. A census conducted in the whole of Bahia in 1872 showed that only 25 percent of all women and 24 percent of all men were formally married.[86] Consequently, the percentage of illegitimate children was high.

FIGURE 2.5 *Indians in Brazil, Marriage Ceremony*, 1924. Bettmann via Getty Images.

The examples outlined above show that new legislation shaping the relationship between religious institutions and the state, and the introduction of civil marriage, was adapted in an increasing number of countries in various parts of the world from the mid-nineteenth century onwards. The secularist state increasingly replaced religious institutions as the prime authority regulating marriage and family life. Formally, the state's marriage and family laws substituted religious regulations. However, we should remain realistic as far as the implementation of the new legislation is concerned. The examples from Austria-Hungary as well as from the Russian and Ottoman empires show that even in some of the largest European countries the separation of the spheres of the state and religion could not be fully realized. In Orthodox countries such as Greece, civil marriage had to wait until far into the twentieth century. In many areas of Latin America, civil marriage was not attractive enough to become a serious alternative to traditional forms of marriage. The Muslim world remained practically untouched by civil marriage until the 1920s and most contemporary Muslim states still do not practice the separation of state and religious institutions. However, in subcontinents such as India and sub-Saharan Africa, the agenda was slightly different. They were not only exposed to European colonialism but also became targets of the ambitions of the Christian colonizers to eradicate non-Christian marital features.

THE COLONIZERS AND THE COLONIZED

In the course of the nineteenth and early twentieth centuries, most of sub-Saharan Africa was divided among European colonial powers, one of them being the British Empire that also administrated colonies in other parts of the world, such as the Indian subcontinent. The first missionaries to Africa arrived soon after European exploration in the fifteenth century. It was, however, not until the nineteenth century that missionaries entered into more profound and sustained contact with African peoples.[87] They brought with them new, and sometimes alien, religious-cultural models with regard to marital life. Colonial administrators and missionaries created a powerful axis that aimed at both exploiting the continent and Christianizing its populations.

The majority of the population adhered to so-called African 'indigenous religions'— belief in the existence of a supreme god, divinities, spiritual beings, ancestors and mysterious powers, good and evil, and the afterlife. Here, the supreme being is considered the source of all things: the creator, omnipresent and omnipotent. The final end and aspiration of every person is to attain the spiritual world of the ancestors, to be venerated by the descendants as an ancestor and eventually to be reincarnated. The forebears are regarded as belonging to the elders of the family with enhanced powers to bless, protect, or punish family members. They are invoked to share in gatherings, ceremonies and ritual communion. The ancestors are not only worshipped but are highly respected family members. They stand next to the divinities in the spiritual hierarchy and act as intermediaries between God and the members of their family.[88]

Ancestor worship constituted an integral part of the African indigenous religion and was strictly rejected by the Christian missionaries—whether Congregational, Methodist, Anglican, Lutheran, or Catholic—as non-Christian. In addition, the practices of successive stages of marriage, bride price and polygyny came into the focus of the mentioned axis. Three main areas of tension arose in the eyes of the missionaries: (1) the unromantic and duty-oriented style of African marriages; (2) the African custom of bride price, which missionaries viewed as the purchase of a bride; and (3) the impression of most missionaries that they were fighting a constant battle to uphold monogamy and eradicate polygyny.[89]

The strongest and most enduring point of tension between Christian missionaries and the indigenous population was the question of polygyny. Although the majority of marriages were monogamous—in Nigeria 70 percent of married men were monogamous in 1885—polygyny was seen as the most distinctive feature of the sub-Saharan marriage pattern. The desire to maintain polygyny was a limiting factor in African conversion to Christianity, especially in contrast to the success of Islam, which, in accepting polygyny, had been depicted as more harmonious with "traditional" culture. Some nineteenth-century missions in Congo and the Ivory Coast accepted polygyny, and in colonial Lagos 60 percent of men participating in Christian marriage ceremonies had multiple wives. In many missions, multiple wives were recognized if a man had married them before his conversion to Christianity. In other cases, only the first wife was recognized—all others were dubbed "concubines." In many congregations, if a polygynous man wished to attend church, he was forced to break up his family, separating himself from his so-called illegitimate wives and children. In general, the Catholic Church was rather strict regarding marriage; Protestant churches tended to be more tolerant and legalized customary marriages and the children born into them.[90]

The second area of conflict between the colonizers and the colonized concerned wedding practices. Christian marriage is based on consent and is celebrated in a single act: the wedding. In large parts of Africa, marriage constitutes a long process and is related to a plurality of rituals that represent the increasing interaction of two families with the aim of establishing trust and friendship. The primary aim of marriage is not the relationship between the couple but the ensured succession of the line of ancestors. After a long process of initiation, the formalities of marriage may be relatively short and social rather than religious. Betrothal is often arranged in childhood or early adolescence. Many actions form a true "rite of passage" in which the couple passes from childhood

FIGURE 2.6 *West-Africa, Togoland, German Protectorate, Local People Getting Married by a Christian Priest, Open-Air Wedding Ceremony, c.* 1900. Ullstein bild Dtl via Getty Images.

to the adult state, constituting a sexual union along with the assumption of a new name. Among some African peoples, marriage comes at the conclusion when the girl is taken to the bridegroom's house. The settlement of the rest of the bride price is considered to finalize the process.[91]

In the nineteenth century, this kind of customary marriage presupposed polygyny or did not exclude it. Christians who contracted a customary marriage were likely to face disciplinary measures in the form of temporary excommunication. The result was that nearly all married Christians were excluded from communion at one time or another in their lives, since a very small percentage had married in church in the first place, and even the percentage of those who later remedied the situation with a Christian wedding was relatively small.[92]

Belgium reacted differently to the challenge of polygyny. At the beginning of the twentieth century (1910), taxation on polygyny was introduced in Belgian Africa. Men with more than one wife were obliged to pay a supplementary tax for each wife beyond the first—from the second up to the thirtieth. The assumption underlying this kind of punitive, symbolic taxation was that it was too risky to simply attempt eradicating a deep-rooted customary practice; rather, polygamy should be discouraged.[93]

After some initial hesitation, Christian missions in Africa widely disapproved of customary or native marriage and promoted European-based ordinance or statutory marriage, for which they often pressed. Colonial administrations were supportive. The British, for example, began to issue a set of colonial marriage ordinances just before 1900. The first was the Gold Coast Marriage Ordinance of 1884. Its main purpose was to offer a British alternative to customary marriage: monogamous, difficult to dissolve, and with

British inheritance rights. In some cases, such as the Rhodesian Ordinance of 1901, the main thrust was to support women's rights within the customary system. There was silence on polygamy, but the ordinance did include a stipulation that no woman should be married against her will and it even installed a judicial redress procedure that she could resort to.[94]

The British colonial administration on the Indian subcontinent was also confronted with polygyny practiced by its Muslim population. However, the majority of the population was Hindu and pursued marital practices that the colonial government found necessary to eradicate. The most urgent issues relating to marriage in the first half of this century was the practice of suttee (sat̄ī—the self-immolation of widows), the killing of newborn females, and child marriage.

The funeral practice of suttee where a widow immolates herself on her husband's pyre was a model primarily for upper-caste Hindus. The Brahman code advocating suttee completely prohibited the widow from remarrying. This was a consequence of the asymmetrically sacramental character of Hindu marriage, indissoluble and unrepeatable by a woman, leaving the surviving widow the sole option of continuing her life as a social outcast. Virulent attacks on this code were made by social reformers of the nineteenth century. The government reacted and abolished suttee in 1829 without much success. Because of the rule of prepubescent marriage for girls and the frequently much higher age of their grooms, social death as a widow befell a large number of women while still in their youth. A reform campaign led to the Widow Remarriage Act XV of 1856 allowing Hindu widows to remarry, but the social price remained high. A few daring men who married a widow were excommunicated from their kin and caste. This debate, however, camouflaged the fact that the remarriage of widows was popular and practiced in various regions and among various castes. The colonial administration categorized this as a low-caste practice. However, the "untouchable" and peasant castes comprised the overwhelming majority of the population, especially of northern India. Even the non-priestly members of the Brahman caste practiced the remarriage of widows. Frequently, they were married to a husband's younger brother (Figure 2.7).[95]

The fight against the killing of newborn females was more complicated. First studies conducted by the colonial administration proved its wide distribution, but female infanticide was practiced above all in Northwest India. Depending on the region, there were 100 women to between 150 and 300 men. Many officials in the colonial administration shared the view that this practice was inextricably linked to Hinduism—if not enshrined in theological doctrine, then in practice. In fact, the killing of daughters had nothing at all to do with religious justification for this practice. Research shows that it was much more closely linked to changes in landholding legislation pushed through by the colonial government.[96] Nevertheless, in 1870 the Infanticide Act that prohibited the killing of newborn females was passed. However, this ban proved ineffective in erasing the practice. In 1910, the ratio of males to females in today's northern states of Punjab, Haryana, and Rajasthan was 100:120, 100:116, and 100:110 respectively.[97]

The last of this series of important laws with regard to marital life was the Age of Consent Act passed in 1891, which set twelve as the minimum age at marriage for females. The Hindu practice of child marriage allegedly goes back to ancient times. The principle seemed to be that the husband should be three times the age of his wife.[98] The law provoked hostile reactions on the part of the population that opposed every attempt by the state to regulate Hindu practices.[99] Indian nationalists opposed the "Westernization" of Indian women and the loss of their "Indian spiritual character" through this legislation.[100]

FIGURE 2.7 *Indian Wedding Chariot, c.* 1925. Bettmann via Getty Images.

It would be tempting to continue to detail the strained relations outlined here between the colonizers with their "civilizing mission" and the indigenous colonized actors, and their differing religious concepts with regard to marital life. However, the examples sufficiently show that the reform legislation achieved no conclusive results: neither clear winners nor losers. Contemporary India is confronted with problems that the colonizers were unable to resolve—if we consider the preference for male children and its consequences for the marriage market. Also, the "problem" of African traditional marriage practices with their successive steps towards a completed marriage remained unsolved. Today, this does not so much constitute a problem on the decolonized continent itself, but problems arise when agents migrate to other continents where marriage is concluded by a single wedding ceremony.

CONCLUSION

The main aim of my contribution has been to provide an idea of the impact of religions on marital life during a period when, after many centuries of having enjoyed a monopoly, first major rivals with regard to the regulation of marriage emerged. These were the state that promoted the separation of public and religious institutions and state administrations that spurred the idea of secularization. This emerging confrontation between the world religions and increasingly secular states created a complex interplay between static and dynamic factors as well as between the sacred and the secular. This interplay was characterized by setbacks for secular movements, which remained far from celebrating a worldwide victory until the end of the second decade of the twentieth century. It appears that in the period investigated here, the advance of secular legislation was most successful in the North Atlantic area—in Northwest Europe and North America—where societies were extensively shaped by Protestantism.

On the first pages, I introduced three pairs of categories that help to characterize the five world religions sufficiently for the purpose of this article: interventionism and noninterventionism, orthopraxis and orthodoxy, and religions reinforcing horizontal and religions reinforcing vertical family axes. Therefore, it is crucial to return to them here because they are useful for theorizing the complex interplay between the sacred and the secular. Many parts of the world adapted and introduced versions of the separation of state and church, as well as civil marriage, according to the Western blueprints that emerged in the Protestant states or, for instance, following from French revolutionary family law. As we have seen, these attempts were confronted with religiously augmented resistance of varying intensity. According to our theoretical considerations, countries shaped by religions that emphasized orthopraxy and reinforced vertical family ties (the patriline, ancestor worship) were challenged to the utmost since the adopted blueprint was formulated in a religious context based on a combination of orthodoxy with an emphasis on horizontal family ties (couple-oriented). Therefore, in societies based on Confucianism, Islam, and Hinduism, the potential for resistance was the greatest. But also for predominantly orthopractically oriented (conservative) Judaism of that time, the idea of the separation of a sacred and a secular sphere was hardly conceivable. The case of Christian Orthodoxy was very similar. Its natural resistance against the secular was additionally fueled by latent anti-Western attitudes rooted in the medieval schism of Latin and Greek Christianity. Even Catholicism showed considerable resistance against secular movements—not so much in the Latin American peripheries but rather in its European core regions.

At the same time as Protestant and Catholic churches were increasingly being put into their place by the secular state, they were able to play out their interventionist character in regions of the world where colonial administrations had come into power, such as in sub-Saharan Africa or India. Our examples, however, have demonstrated that almost endless compromises had to be reached with Hinduism and the traditions of the African indigenous religions. Sub-Saharan Africa, especially, did not become a primary battlefield between the sacred and the secular but between the sacred values of the natives and the sacred belief systems of the colonial rulers.

There is no doubt that the relationship between religion and marital life around the world changed dramatically in the course of the twentieth century. Except in the transatlantic area, the first two decades witnessed secular movements confronted by substantial resistance on the part of religious forces. The secular gathered decisive momentum only afterwards—without celebrating a final worldwide triumph.

CHAPTER THREE

State and Law

Four Models for Regulating Marriage

REBECCA PROBERT

All societies have a concept of marriage and all therefore need rules to determine what counts as a marriage within that particular society and what does not.[1] The creation and application of such rules requires a decision to be made as to the relative importance of the internal and external aspects of marriage: is it the intention of the parties to be married that matters most, or their compliance with certain stipulated rituals or formalities? And most fundamentally of all, who has the power to decide on what the rules are?

Such questions are key to the history of marriage in the nineteenth and early twentieth centuries. Across the globe, as empires rose and fell, the rules as to what was required for a valid marriage in any given place were subject to change. Revolutions and political crises led to the authority to decide what constituted a marriage being suddenly transferred from religious authorities to the state or vice versa. The creation of new nation-states required decisions to be made as to the relative importance of unity and the perhaps very different religious and cultural traditions of the territories being united. Similar dilemmas as to what should be recognized as a marriage were posed when imperial powers acquired more distant territories with even less familiar practices.[2] Even where a particular country did not experience political upheaval, the impacts of industrialization, migration, increasing religious diversity, or simply the awareness of changes elsewhere led to changes in the ways marriages were regulated.

These developments raised questions about the role of the state and the law, and about their relationship with religion and with the individual. The answers, however, differed between different legal cultures. Western legal cultures were seen as being characterized by a strong connection between the law and the state: it was the state, and the state alone, that created law, and law that underpinned the operation of the state. This was the idea of "positive law" as defined by the nineteenth-century English legal philosopher John Austin, which saw law as the commands of a sovereign. Law was understood as an autonomous system, a set of rules that operated according to their own internal logic. Religious influences were not absent, but religion was not an independent source of law. In other legal cultures, by contrast, the law was both less individualistic and less autonomous, with religion playing a more significant role as a source of law.[3]

In order to explore what role the state and the law played in the making of marriage this chapter will focus on the rules governing *how* couples could marry. After all, questions as to when a person is eligible to marry (in terms of their age and economic standing), who

FIGURE 3.1 Pierre-Marie Beyle (1837–1902), *The Wedding Procession*, 1879, oil on canvas, Christi's. Public Domain via Wikimedia Commons.

they can marry (in terms of gender and degrees of relatedness), and how many people they can marry (whether successively or simultaneously) tell us more about economic, social, and religious influences than about the role of the state and the law.

The chapter is accordingly structured around four different models of marriage regulation. The first model is that of mandatory civil marriage as a form created by the state alone, whether to signal the authority of the state and downplay that of the church, to separate the functions of the state from the church, or as a convenient way of ensuring neutrality between different religious traditions within the state. The second model is of marriages co-created by state and religion through legislation setting the terms on which religious marriages would be recognized as legally binding. Such developments reflected the cultural importance of religion while reducing the power of religious institutions to determine the validity or otherwise of a marriage. These first two options were more likely to be found within Western legal cultures. Yet the rise of state control was not universal, as the third model of marriages determined by religious rites and authority will show: within Islamic, Asian, and African legal cultures, entry into marriage continued to be governed by the religious affiliation of the couple. The fourth model is that of marriages created by the actions of the parties alone but recognized by the state: jurisdictions where marriages could be created without any ceremony at all were to be found within very different legal cultures, thus confounding any neat categorization or perceived hierarchy.

Within each section the aim is not to provide a comprehensive list of all of the jurisdictions that adopted a particular model but rather to illustrate different ways in which each of these models operated. The details of the precise processes that had to be followed in the making of a marriage will also be kept to a minimum, save where they are particularly illuminating about the aims of the lawmakers or the balance that was struck between different religious groups. The extent to which the laws were observed in practice also falls outside the scope of this chapter, save where popular opposition led to a speedy reversal of official policy or where particular cultural practices themselves shaped the law. But by paring down the discussion to the ways in which the balance between the state, the law, religion, and the individual was struck it will be possible to achieve a far greater global reach than would otherwise be possible in a single chapter.

STATE-CREATED MARRIAGE

In earlier centuries Protestant reformers such as Luther and Calvin had championed making marriage a civil matter, and Enlightenment philosophers had declared marriage to be a civil contract.[4] But the introduction of civil marriage did not necessarily reflect a culture of secularism, at least at a popular level. Instead, it could be used tactically, providing a neutral alternative in religiously diverse countries, a means of combating the power of the church within the state, or of reducing the influence of supranational religious organizations outside the state, or as a shorthand for signaling the modernity of the state and its alignment with the individualism and rationalism of Western legal culture. It was thus no coincidence that the advent of civil marriage tended to follow fundamental changes to the state itself, through revolution, renewal, or the reallocation of authority.

FIGURE 3.2 Albert Anker (1831–1910) *Civil Wedding*, 1887, oil on canvas, Kunsthaus Zürich. Public Domain via Wikimedia Commons.

Within this section, three different approaches to civil marriage will be considered: first, where it was part of a deliberate policy of secularization; second, where it was used to create unity; and third, where it was opposed and speedily reversed.

Secularization and loyalty to the state

In 1791 revolutionary France had declared that "the law considers marriage to be only a civil contract" and prescribed that civil marriage would be the only legally recognized form of marriage. This was accompanied a year later by civil registration of marriages, as well as of births and deaths.[5] Marriage, it was thought, was "a contract worthy of the keenest interest ... because it has individual happiness as its goal and also influences the power and splendour of Empires."[6] The requirement of a compulsory civil marriage was duly enshrined in the Civil Code of 1804, with the aim of using the ceremony to create an emotional link between the citizen and the state being reflected in the incorporation of a degree of ritual, comparable to that of a religious ceremony.[7] The marriage was required to take place at the town hall, in the presence of four (male) witnesses, where the officer responsible for celebrating the marriage would read to the parties the relevant parts of the civil code setting out their respective rights and duties within marriage.[8] This provided a means of not only informing the parties but also transmitting the state's ideology of marriage.[9]

The fact that marriage was now "available as a civil right for all rather than as a privilege for those of the same confession"[10] was seen as a marker of progress. Everyone was now equal before the law in terms of their ability to contract a legally recognized marriage, and the state stood as guarantor of the validity of the union. In return, it demanded compliance with a single set of rules and denied recognition to what minority religious communities had regarded as binding unions. This had particular implications for Jewish communities within France. Prior to the Revolution they had been largely autonomous, but civil marriage "became a publicly required contract in a way that religious marriage could not be."[11] The autonomy of religious groups was therefore constrained and their authority diminished.

Over the course of the nineteenth century a number of other jurisdictions adopted civil marriage as part of a more general process of secularization, including the Netherlands and the newly independent state of Belgium.[12] On the other side of the globe, as the Spanish Empire crumbled, its former colonies sought to shake off the influence of the Catholic Church by introducing civil marriage. Mexico made mandatory civil marriage a requirement in 1859, as part of a package of reforms intended to establish a secular state.[13] A political crisis sparked the introduction of civil marriage in Chile in 1884, despite the fact that Catholicism had been adopted as the official religion of the new republic in 1828.[14] And in Brazil, as in revolutionary France, civil marriage was introduced as one of the first acts of the new republic in 1889.[15]

Further dramatic change occurred during the early years of the twentieth century. Republican Portugal introduced civil marriage in 1910, following the revolution of that year. And right at the end of our period, civil marriage became the only form of legal marriage in those parts of Russia under Bolshevik control, just two months after they seized power in 1917.[16] The establishment of a regime that not only sought a separation between the state and religion but was avowedly atheist was very much an imposition on traditional culture, the Russian Empire having "almost completely missed" the reforms to marriage law that were happening elsewhere in Europe in the nineteenth century.[17]

Unification and uniformity

The unification of Italy in 1860 and Germany in 1871 provided the catalyst for the introduction of mandatory civil marriage in both states. In neither was this form of marriage entirely novel. The northern Italian states had fallen under the control of France in the early nineteenth century and had followed its lead in making civil marriage a legal requirement, although religious control over marriage had been largely restored upon the Restoration of the Bourbon monarchy in 1815. Large parts of Germany had similarly been under the control of the French Empire, and over the course of the nineteenth century a number of German states introduced civil marriage either as an option or, occasionally, as a mandatory requirement.

In both Italy and Germany, the introduction of a single form of marriage was intended to emphasize the unity of the newly created state. Both enacted new civil codes relatively quickly after unification, with the Italian Civil Code being enacted as early as 1865. In Germany mandatory civil marriage was introduced by imperial act in 1875, and confirmed by the newly drafted civil code in 1900, thereby also concluding a long-standing debate as to the appropriate form and function of the law in favor of uniformity as opposed to principles based on different cultural traditions.[18]

However, the religious traditions within the now unified states provided rather different reasons for opting for civil marriage in each case. In predominantly Catholic Italy, civil marriage symbolically emphasized the new state's "liberty from foreign influence and Church domination."[19] In Germany, by contrast, civil marriage was a practical solution, a way of ensuring consistency and neutrality in the face of the mixed Catholic and Protestant heritage of different states.

The justification of national unity could be used even where the state had not gone through any dramatic change in its constitution. In the religiously and linguistically diverse Kingdom of Hungary, the introduction of civil marriage in 1894 was depicted as a symbol of modernity, liberalism, and national unity.[20] This was vividly illustrated by the first civil marriage in the city of Komarom, at which the bride and groom demonstrated their patriotism by wearing Hungarian dress, while the officiant sported a tricolor sash and declared that "the unity of the political nation can only be achieved if the family itself is the basis of state existence, if marriage is placed under uniform state law."[21]

Opposition and reversals

Just as revolutions and political crises might lead to civil marriage being established as a symbol of a break with the past, so too opposition to such changes might lead to an equally symbolic restoration of religious marriage to demonstrate continuity and stability when power changed hands once again.

In Spain, for example, the 1868 Revolution led to the introduction of mandatory civil marriage in 1870.[22] Four years later, the new Republic was overthrown, and the possibility of marrying in a religious ceremony was restored.[23] In addition, any marriages that had been solemnized according to religious rites during the period of mandatory civil marriage were retrospectively validated.[24] By this means the state demonstrated its support for those who had adhered to their own religious traditions rather than complying with what had proved to be merely a temporary law. Even establishing civil marriage as an option later proved to be a challenge. In the subsequent Civil Code of 1889, Catholics were required to solemnize their marriage in a religious ceremony; civil marriage was only available for those who declared that they were not Catholics.[25] An attempt was made in 1906 to remove this requirement and make civil marriage available to all, at least as an option, but following opposition this measure was revoked two years later.[26]

In Cuba, too, as it was transferred from being a colony of Spain to a protectorate of the United States in 1898, civil marriage was briefly the only form of marriage recognized by the state, the new law being supported by nationalists as "eradicating the Spanish colonial legacy, and verifying national sovereignty."[27] In this case, however, opposition from the Catholic Church led to a swift reversal of policy and the acceptance of religious marriages as equally valid.

Overall, the introduction of civil marriage can be seen as being in opposition to existing cultural practices, but with the aim of shaping a new, modern, and secular system in which the state, rather than a religious authority, formed a third party to the marriage contract. Yet its introduction in a variety of different states, and its absence from other equally developed states, should make us pause before drawing any correlation between particular forms of legal culture and particular forms of marriage. There were still many other states within Western legal culture that did not even offer the option of civil marriage, instead requiring a form of religious ceremony to establish a legally binding marriage. Yet here too the increasing role of the state was to be seen in the way that the legitimacy of the religious ceremony was increasingly established and constrained by law, as the next section will show.

STATES DETERMINING THE STATUS OF RELIGIOUS MARRIAGES

Across the period there was an increasing tendency for states to legislate to set the terms on which religious marriages would be recognized as legally binding. While reflecting the cultural importance of the wedding as a religious rite, this tactic of legislating for religious marriage made it clear that it was the state that was the ultimate arbiter and guarantor of validity.[28] This was reflected in the definitions of marriage offered by one English judge, Sir William Scott, in the early nineteenth century. He suggested that within civil society marriage became "a civil contract regulated and prescribed by law and endowed with civil consequences" but added—probably mindful of developments across the Channel—that "in most civilized countries acting under a sense of the force of sacred obligations, it has had the sanctions of religion superadded: it then becomes a religious as well as a natural and civil contract; for it is a great mistake to suppose that because it is the one therefore it may not likewise be the other."[29] This acknowledged the importance of religion while subtly downplaying it as something additional to state-made law.

The downplaying of religious authority was reflected in the extension of formal recognition to a number of *different* religious routes, diminishing the importance of any single religious body within the state. Religion was increasingly classified as a private matter, as "classical liberal theory made sense of the diversity of individual religious beliefs by restricting them to the private while freeing the public to be ordered according to secular reason."[30] Such developments also provided a reason for the formal transfer of the jurisdiction to determine what constituted a valid legal marriage from the church and its courts to secular courts: if religion was to be a private matter, and different religions treated alike, it was problematic to leave the courts of any given religion to determine the civil status of a couple.

Within this model, three different approaches will be considered: first, legislating to allow for a number of different religious routes into marriage that had not previously existed; second, recognizing existing religious marriages and bringing them within a formal framework; and third, facilitating mixed marriages.

Legislation for multiple types of religious marriages

The marriage laws of the United Kingdom of Great Britain and Ireland—itself a new political creation—illustrate just how complex the relationship between the state, law, and religion could be. In 1800 there was one state and one Parliament but three different legal systems, multiple religious denominations, and overlapping but distinct approaches to the regulation of marriage.

Within England and Wales, the state had already begun to impinge on the church's control over marriage during the eighteenth century, but the changes that occurred over the course of the nineteenth century were far more radical. The Clandestine Marriages Act of 1753 had done little more than enshrine the requirements of the canon law in statute, albeit with new and harsher penalties for those who failed to comply with certain key requirements. The church courts had retained their power to adjudicate on the validity of marriages, and all except Quakers and Jews were expected to marry according to the rites of the established church, the Church of England.[31] Even in this period, then, state and religion were very much intertwined in the regulation of marriage.

Changes were motivated by the growth of nonconformity in the nineteenth century, although significantly it was only once adherence to the Anglican Church was no longer a prerequisite for participation in public life that Protestant Nonconformists and Catholics were able to marry according to their own rites. These religious developments coincided with a new interest on the part of the state in ensuring better recording of key demographic events and with a new administrative machinery that would be able to implement it. Reforms to the Poor Law had already divided the country into a number of civil districts that could be used as the basis for a new system. As the state took on more functions, it became all the more important to have such information about its inhabitants.

The resulting Marriage Act of 1836 provides a particularly interesting model of regulation combining increased state power with deference to the established church, recognition of religious diversity, and a desire to allow for a civil option that could be used by those of any religion or none. All those marrying other than according to non-Anglican rites, including Jews and Quakers, had to give notice to a state official, the superintendent registrar. There was even an attempt to introduce universal civil preliminaries, but this was strongly resisted by the Church of England and banns and licenses were retained as legal preliminaries to the Anglican service.

When it came to the celebration of the marriage, the degree of regulation differed between different types of marriages. Anglican marriages continued to take place in the parish church, and Jewish and Quaker marriages in their own places of worship. Outside these groups, the diversity of dissent was such that devolving the power to conduct marriages to religious groups was not really an option. The compromise was to license individual buildings that were used as places of worship: if twenty householders confirmed that they used a particular building as their regular place of worship, it could be registered as a place where marriages could be celebrated. In this respect the state could supervise exactly where marriages were being celebrated. Civil marriages, meanwhile, took place in the office of a superintendent registrar.

State control was further asserted by stipulating that *all* marriages should be centrally registered; responsibility for registration was devolved in the case of Anglican, Jewish,

FIGURE 3.3 Edmund Blair Leighton (1852–1922), *The Wedding Register*, 1920, oil on canvas. Public Domain via Wikimedia Commons.

and Quaker marriages, but all other marriages, whether civil or religious, had to be attended by a civil registrar. It was not until the close of the century that other religious groups won the right to register their own marriages.

In England and Wales the 1836 Act formed the basis for the evolution of new marriage rites. After all, Protestant Nonconformists—the Quakers excepted—had previously married in the Church of England rather than developing their own nuptial rites outside the legal system. English Catholics, too, had usually gone through an Anglican ceremony in addition to the Catholic rite, although by the 1830s concern had grown that the increasing number of Irish Catholic immigrants were marrying according to their own rites and were thus not married in the eyes of the law. In this respect the 1836 Act brought new legal and religious practices into existence.

Recognizing religious practices

Elsewhere, by contrast, the state began to recognize existing religious practices and bring them within the ambit of legislation. This was the case in Ireland, with its minority established church, majority Catholic population, and strong strand of Presbyterianism. The Marriages (Ireland) Act of 1844 was modeled on the 1836 Marriage Act in England and Wales but differed from the latter in giving Presbyterian marriages special recognition, alongside those conducted in the Established Church or according to Quaker or Jewish rites. Members of other religious denominations were permitted to marry according to their own rites in buildings registered for the purpose,[32] but Catholic marriages were specifically excluded from this provision and therefore remained governed by the canon law. It took another nineteen years for Catholic marriages to be brought within the legal framework of the state and even then there was little interference with the actual ceremony. Instead, couples were required to obtain a certificate in advance of the wedding and to register the completed certificate afterwards, although such registration was not essential to the validity of the marriage. In this way the state recognized and extended its authority over existing religious marriages with minimal change to the way in which such marriages were celebrated.

In Scotland, the position was still more complex. While the state recognized a broader range of religious marriages over the course of the nineteenth century, the changes related to what was recognized as a *regular* marriage, rather than what would be recognized as a *valid* marriage. At the start of the nineteenth century the only marriages recognized as regular were those celebrated before a minister of the Church of Scotland after banns had been called. At the same time, the law held that all that was needed for a valid marriage was the freely expressed consent of the two people involved and presumed that such consent had been given where the couple had sex following an earlier promise to marry, or where they lived together and were reputed to be husband and wife. Over the decades that followed, the incursions by the state onto this landscape of restricted options for regularity and almost infinite options for irregularity were relatively limited. Legislation passed in 1834 provided that clergy of any denomination could celebrate a regular marriage, but the requirement that banns be read in the parish church remained in order to provide a degree of uniformity. Civil registration was not introduced until 1855, almost two decades after its advent in England and Wales, and giving notice to the local registrar as an alternative to having banns called only became an option in 1878.[33] Nor was there any formal option of civil marriage, although the option of registering an irregular marriage has been seen as an effective alternative.

The variety of marriage laws within the United Kingdom, and the role played by missionaries of all denominations within the burgeoning British Empire, also meant that it was necessary for Parliament to legislate to ensure the legal recognition of marriages conducted in British possessions overseas according to different religious rites. As early as 1818, legislation established that marriages conducted in India by ordained ministers of the Church of Scotland should have the same force as those solemnized by clergymen of the Church of England.[34] By mid-century a broader approach proved necessary to ensure the validity of marriages conducted by Nonconformist ministers or by laymen acting under the authority of the governor general.[35] Modeled on the provisions of the 1836 Marriage Act, the 1851 Act for Marriages in India permitted couples to marry "according to such Form and Ceremony as they may see fit to adopt" as long as they had given notice to, and exchanged stipulated vows in the presence of, a Marriage Registrar.[36] This, however, was explicitly limited to marriages "where One or both of the Parties is or are a Person or Persons professing the Christian Religion,"[37] so as not to impinge on the privileges of other religious groups to determine what constituted a marriage. Just over twenty years later, further legislation was passed to allow marriage before a civil registrar for those declaring that they did not profess Christian, Hindu, Muslim, Buddhist, Parsi, Sikh, Jaina, or Jewish beliefs,[38] in order to provide an option for breakaway religious groups whose marriage rites did not conform to previous usages.[39]

Issues as to the recognition of marriages according to different religious rites also arose in the new Australian colonies, as the relationship between English law and the different religious traditions of the United Kingdom had to be worked out in the context of a society formed of former convicts and free settlers. The assumption that English law was applied so far as it could be was given statutory effect in legislation in 1828.[40] But an earlier local ordinance had specifically provided that existing marriages solemnized by ministers of the Church of Scotland or Roman Catholic priests would have the same force as those solemnized by clergymen of the Church of England, which would not have been the case in England and Wales at that time,[41] and there is ample evidence of marriages having been conducted according to Catholic or Presbyterian rites with the full knowledge and apparent approval of the colonial authorities.[42] When put to the test—in the context of a prosecution for bigamy—it was held that a Catholic marriage would be recognized as valid. In so deciding, Francis Forbes, the chief justice of New South Wales, made a direct link between the nature of the state and the laws that would be appropriate to that state, noting that Parliament could not have intended "to force the whole mass of English laws—the laws of an old and settled society ... to apply all ... at once to an infant community." The litigation led to more systematic regulation of the law of marriage, with legislation being passed to confirm the validity of existing marriages and set out what was required for future ones. Again, the role of the state here was limited to the recognition rather than the creation of marriage practices.

Legislation was also passed to allow for a range of routes to marriage within British North America. Local conditions heavily influenced the terms of an 1817 statute stating that marriages in Newfoundland would be void unless solemnized by a person in holy orders, unless they had been celebrated "under Circumstances of peculiar and extreme Difficulty in procuring a Person in Holy Orders to perform the Ceremony."[43] More precise provision was made by legislation in 1824 allowing licenses to be granted to religious teachers or preachers to conduct marriages where it was not practicable for the parties to be married in the Anglican Church, with those who exceeded their authority and celebrated marriages where no such difficulty existed being subject to fines.[44] Ontario, too, saw the emergence of a number of different routes into marriage. At the start of the nineteenth century it had recognized only marriages conducted according to the rites of the Church of England, but ministers from other Christian denominations acquired the right to solemnize marriages in 1847, and from 1857 all religious marriages were recognized.[45] Upon the confederation of Canada in 1867, its various provinces retained the power to regulate the solemnization of marriages, in order to allay the anxieties of Quebec's Catholic population.[46]

Legislating for mixed marriages

The fact that a state recognized different religious routes to marriage as legally valid did not necessarily ensure that these different routes were available to all. What if the parties to the marriage were of different religious faiths? Many religions had traditionally forbidden mixed marriages: should the state endorse that, override it, or sidestep it by providing a civil alternative? And what if it had simply overlooked the possibility of a particular combination?

Nineteenth-century Irish marriage law provides an excellent case study of both legislative gaps and changing attitudes to mixed marriages. In the eighteenth century Irish law had taken the step of recognizing marriages celebrated by Presbyterian ministers— as long as the marriage was celebrated between two Protestant dissenters.[47] It had not, however, specified the effect of a marriage celebrated by a Presbyterian minister where one of the parties was a member of the established church. In 1844 this omission led to the controversial acquittal of one George Millis in a high-profile bigamy trial: as a member of the established Church of Ireland, his first marriage, having been conducted by a Presbyterian minister in Ireland, was regarded as being no marriage at all.[48] The result caused considerable consternation, and legislation proved necessary to validate the marriages of those who had gone through similar ceremonies and to place the law of marriage on a more certain footing for the future.

The validity of marriages between Catholics and Protestants similarly depended on how it was celebrated. If it was conducted by an Anglican clergyman it was valid; if it was conducted by a Catholic priest it was void. Those who converted to Catholicism upon marriage might find themselves in a particularly difficult position, since the legislation also invalidated any marriage conducted by a Catholic priest between a Catholic and anyone who had been a Protestant within the year prior to the marriage. Wilkie Collins drew on this particularly harsh provision in his 1870 novel *Man and Wife*. In its opening pages we see a woman being spurned by the man she believes is her husband upon it being discovered that their marriage in Ireland was invalid, he having converted to Catholicism only shortly before their wedding.

The publication of the novel coincided with legislation finally addressing this particular issue, following a real-life case that had attracted much publicity and a storm of protest about the state of the law. Theresa Longworth, an Englishwoman, claimed that she had actually gone through *two* ceremonies of marriage with Major Yelverton—the first in Scotland, by a private exchange of consent; the second before a Catholic priest in Ireland. But the House of Lords decided that there was insufficient evidence of the first and that, as a Protestant, Major Yelverton could not have been validly married by a Catholic priest in Ireland. As one commentator noted, "in a nation of many intermingled creeds, it would surely be wiser to nullify marriages on account of the color of the hair of the parties than to do so upon the score of their religion."[49] The outcry generated by the case was one of the factors leading to the establishment of a Royal Commission to examine the laws of marriage in 1865. The disestablishment of the Church of Ireland in 1869 provided a further spur to action and the Matrimonial Causes and Marriage Law (Ireland) Amendment Act 1870 finally allowed mixed marriages of Protestants and Catholics to be celebrated according to the rites of either.

Elsewhere, civil marriage was introduced specifically to provide a means for those of different faiths to marry rather than as a neutral option open to all. In Sweden, religious plurality had existed since the late eighteenth century. Marriages had previously been required to be celebrated in the Lutheran Church, but first other Christian denominations and then Jewish communities were also authorized to marry couples.[50] When an option of civil marriage was introduced in 1863, it was only for those of different faiths who could not take advantage of any of the existing religious forms.[51]

Yet while in many states marriage was directly regulated through specific legislation, in others religious authorities retained jurisdiction over what made a marriage, as the next section will show.

REGULATION OF MARRIAGES BY RELIGIOUS AUTHORITIES

There was a variety of different ways in which marriages might be regulated by religious authorities. Within any given state, there might be one recognized religious authority or several. That religious authority might be either primarily domestic, associated with just one state, or transnational. The Catholic Church provides a good example of the latter, although its hold over the regulation of marriage in both Europe and South America was diminishing over the course of the period. As European powers expanded their overseas empires in Africa and Asia, the religious diversity of the colonized peoples meant that attempts to impose a single mode of marrying were unlikely to meet with success, and the personal laws of such peoples largely continued to govern how they married.

This section will consider first the links between religious authority and the identity of the state, then the way in which religious autonomy might both mute and support claims to territorial independence, and finally the intersection between law, religion, and custom.

Religion and the identity of the state

The widespread adoption of civil marriage, and the introduction of state laws governing religious marriages, might suggest that there was a smooth and inevitable shift of power from religious authorities to the state. In reality, the relationship was more complex. States might wish to draw strength and support from religious authorities, or make a connection between religious and national identity, as the examples of Austria and the Ottoman Empire illustrate.

Austria provides a good example not only of how power struggles between state and church might lead to jurisdiction being transferred back and forth but also of how a state might be pursuing its own agenda in ceding jurisdiction to religious authorities. Jurisdiction over marriage had been transferred to the state in the late eighteenth century, and the Civil Code of 1811 maintained this approach. Marriages continued to be conducted by priests, but it was the state that decided what constituted a marriage. After the Revolution of 1848, however, the Concordat of 1855 transferred jurisdiction back to the Catholic Church. As Ulrike Harmat has described, the close cooperation between state and church at this time meant that each began "to identify with the respective aims of the other," with the Crown and government beginning "to conceive of Austria as 'the Catholic great power.'" A little over a decade later, however, jurisdiction over marriage was transferred back to the state once more following a new constitution in 1867.[52]

Religion was also central to the identity of the Ottoman Empire, which operated under Islamic law, and religious norms were particularly important in regulating entry into marriage. Islam regarded marriage as a contract, rather than as a sacrament, and the presence of an imam was not required in order for it to be regarded as valid. Nor was any particular ceremony or ritual necessary. While the nineteenth century saw reform in a number of areas of law, with codes inspired by European models being introduced, these did not extend to the area of family law.[53] In that context, "the claims of the state as the originator of authoritative norms were attenuated by a proclaimed subordination to the norms of the *shari'a* as extrapolated, mostly, from the established and diverse jurisprudence (*fiqh*) of Muslim jurists."[54] By the start of the twentieth century, however, questions were raised about the need to reform the laws relating to marriage, and with the 1917 Ottoman Law of Family Rights "the state stepped up its regulation of the marital institution and self-consciously sought to bring the marriage practices of its citizens into sync with its vision of modernity."[55] In this case the role of religion was diminished not by internal or external power struggles but by a desire to project a different image of the state.

Religious plurality

While individuals within the Ottoman Empire had access to Islamic courts, this was not their only option. Given that "religious diversity was the norm rather than the exception"[56] across its territories, the "millet" system had long been in operation. This left the regulation of marriage and other elements of family life to be governed by the religious laws of the different religious communities, through agreements negotiated with their leaders.[57]

While this permitted the exercise of cultural autonomy by these different communities and so muted potential opposition to the state, it could also be used to make claims for territorial autonomy. When Greece gained its independence from the Ottoman Empire in 1832, a strong link was made between religious and national identity: the Greeks were portrayed as a separate people "unified under the 'garb of religious difference'" within the Ottoman Empire.[58]

Religion, law, and custom

The ways in which marriages were regulated across the developing British Empire demonstrate the complex relationship between law, religion, and custom. In India, for example, it had been established by the end of the eighteenth century that the regulation of marriage would be governed by the laws of the Qu'ran in the case of Muslims and, in the case of Hindus, by Sanskrit texts which the British colonial rulers called the Shaster.[59] In the decades that followed, however, the limited understanding of the way in which Muslim and Hindu law had operated led to what was effectively a new body of law emerging,[60] within a "a plural legal order that replicated the main features of European jurisdictional boundaries between canon law and state law".[61]

Religious plurality was if anything even greater in Africa. In those parts that came under British control, it had been the "multitude of indigenous tribal systems" that determined what constituted a marriage, with norms differing between tribes.[62] African customary law was initially "dismissed by the early missionaries and colonial officials as a barbarous and inferior system of law."[63] Such attitudes were illustrated in the 1887 case of *Re Bethell*,[64] in which the question to be decided by the English Court of Chancery was whether a marriage had taken place between an Englishman, Christopher Bethell, and a member of the Baralong tribe, named Teepoo. Christopher had traveled out to South Africa and taken up residence at Mafeking, among the Baralong tribe. He indicated that he wished to be part of the tribe and to marry according to their customs. Evidence was

FIGURE 3.4 Eugène Delacroix (1798–1863), *A Jewish Wedding in Morocco*, 1839, oil on canvas, Louvre Museum, 1000 I Museums.

given to the court that marriage according to Baralong custom required the bridegroom to slaughter a sheep, ox, or cow and give the head and hide to the bride's parents before the marriage was consummated, but that no further ceremony was required, and that custom had been followed in this case. Those arguing for the validity of the marriage rested their case on the well-established legal principle that the validity of a marriage was to be determined by the law of the place where it took place. On the other side, however, it was argued that "the *Baralong* tribe have not laws but only customs when they marry"—in other words, that the principle could not apply—and that unless there was a mutual exchange of consent "there cannot be that which English law recognizes as marriage."[65] The judge, Justice Stirling, made it clear where his sympathies lay by interrupting on more than one occasion to ask whether the relationship described "was a marriage at all"[66] and held that there was no marriage that the court could recognize, since the union described was "a marriage in the Baralong sense only."[67]

Despite such attitudes, with the adoption of the policy of "indirect rule," African customary law was held to have a place within the formal legal system.[68] But as in India, the process of recognition and incorporation was not value-neutral, whether in substance or in form, or in the way that it was transmitted, understood, or applied. Male elders who were identified as "chiefs" had a privileged position in describing customary law, and their version often enhanced their own authority.[69] Colonial administrators translated fluid practices into specific rules.[70] Practices that were regarded as "repugnant to justice and morality" were simply disregarded.[71] A further layer of complication was added by the enactment of legislation creating optional procedures for entering into a marriage that would exist alongside customary and religious law.

In New Zealand, meanwhile, ideas about law and marriage were entwined with a particular view of the emerging nation-state. Local ordinances were passed to regulate marriage relatively soon after it became a British colony but did not extend to the native Maori population, the assumption being that the latter would continue to marry according to their own laws. Yet before long, as Nan Seuffert has shown, there emerged a view of Maoris as primitive and uncivilized, without a system of law. The result was that the validity of Maori marriages fell to be determined by colonial laws: as one judge put it, "there is only one marriage law in New Zealand for all races ... and the so-called marriage according to Maori custom is no marriage in law."[72] When the English courts were called upon to consider the validity of a marriage between an Englishman and an Aboriginal woman in *Armitage v Armitage*, the discussion of the precolonial position was decidedly cursory, it simply being noted that the "alleged husband" had said "that he was married according to the customs and usages then in force in New Zealand" but "there is no evidence before the Court of what those customs or usages were."[73] Further justification for nonrecognition of Maori marriages by the state was found by linking Maori marriage laws with concubinage and polygamy, supposedly premodern concepts that could be unfavorably contrasted with "notions of civilization and progress associated with the modern nation-state."[74]

Somewhat ironically, the perception of certain lands as "barbarous" also led to the English courts developing a concept of marriage that harked back to the "law of nature" and that was in many respects akin to a form of personal or religious law, albeit one justified in more nationalistic terms. In *Ruding v Smith*, Sir William Scott invoked the idea that there was a law higher than the law of the land, an *ius gentium* or a custom common to all nations. This, he thought, provided the basis for the recognition of Anglican marriages between English men and women "settled in countries professing a religion essentially different."[75] In that particular case the marriage had been celebrated at the Cape of Good Hope by the chaplain of the English forces, but the idea that the British took their own law with them was nonetheless quickly extended beyond British troops fighting overseas to all cases where there were deemed to be "insuperable difficulties" in complying with the local law,[76] or where the British were establishing themselves in a country that was deemed to be "uninhabited" or "barbarous." The validity of marriages conducted in such places fell to be determined by English common law, at least until it was supplanted by local regulation. Yet in holding that all that was required was an exchange of consent in words of the present tense, nineteenth-century judges misinterpreted what the English common law had required for a valid marriage before legislation was passed in 1753. It was nonetheless a convenient mistake, since it neatly side-stepped the requirement that marriages be conducted by an Anglican clergyman and recognized the role played by missionaries and ministers of all denominations across the British Empire.[77]

So the recognition of religious marriages within a plural legal system was not confined to Asian, Islamic, and African legal cultures. But it operated very differently within the imperial context, as those versed in Western legal cultures tended to understand religious laws and customs through a particular lens. Religious laws were crystallized as formal law, while redefining the laws of indigenous peoples as "customs" enabled them to be displaced as a source of law altogether. The emphasis on personal laws also created barriers to intermarriage between those of different faiths.

By contrast, developments elsewhere involved the emergence of a new form of marriage created with no ceremony at all, as the final section will demonstrate.

LEGITIMACY WITHOUT STATE INTERVENTION

In *The History of Human Marriage*, published in 1891, Edward Westermarck loftily proclaimed that "among primitive men marriage was, of course, contracted without any ceremony whatever; and this is still the case with many uncivilised peoples."[78] The linkage of "civilization" and "ceremony," and the assumption of a clear line of progression was, however, complicated by the possibility of marrying in Scotland by a simple exchange of consent and by developments in the United States.

At the start of the nineteenth century the newly independent United States was beginning to forge a new and distinctive American family law.[79] Most states already provided for a choice of civil or religious marriage rites, but new developments were to make marriages even easier to enter into, with the concept of "common-law marriage" emerging in the New York case of *Fenton v Reed* in 1809. In allowing marriages to be entered into entirely informally, this new type of marriage both prioritized the choice of the couple over the laws of the state and widened the state's reach in terms of the imposition of obligations on husbands and wives.[80] Its radicalism was obscured by the fact that it was presented as being rooted in English law, but while English law would indeed have regarded the fact that a couple had cohabited and were reputed to be married as evidence from which it might be presumed that a ceremony of marriage had taken place, it would not at the time have regarded a simple exchange of consent as amounting to a valid marriage.[81]

Despite the novelty of the doctrine, a number of states subsequently adopted a concept of common law marriage[82] and in *Meister v Moore* the US Supreme Court held that there was a "common-law right" to form a marriage by a simple exchange of consent. Acknowledging that statutes in many states regulated "the mode of entering into the

FIGURE 3.5 John Lewis Krimmel (1786–1821), *The Country Wedding (US)*, 1820, painting.
Public Domain via Wikimedia Commons.

contract," it held that statutory provisions requiring a formal license and ceremony were
to be construed as merely directory unless the legislation made it explicit that a failure to
observe such formalities would result in the invalidity of the marriage.

Not all US states adopted the view that marriage laws were directory rather than
mandatory. Massachusetts, Tennessee, North Carolina, and Maine never recognized any
form of common law marriage. Even amongst those that did, there was a distinct lack
of uniformity in how the courts determined when precisely a common law marriage
might be held to have come into existence,[83] and indeed in the types of states to adopt
the concept.[84] Over the course of the nineteenth century, statutory requirements were
gradually relaxed only to be tightened again at its close. New provisions for the giving
of notice before marriage and its registration once it had taken place were introduced
by legislation.[85] From the last quarter of the nineteenth century, states began to abolish
common law marriage, and by 1920 it was only fully recognized in twenty-six states and
partially recognized in a further six.[86]

The growing importance attached to the role of the state in the making of marriage
was reflected in an 1892 decision of the Supreme Court of Washington, in which it was
asserted that "by adhering to the statutory provisions … parties are led to regard the
contract as a sacred one, as one not lightly to be entered into, and are forcibly impressed
with the idea that they are forming a relationship in which society has an interest, and to
which the state is a party."[87] In other words, the ties to the state were sacred.

CONCLUSION

In the early years of the nineteenth century, the German jurist Friedrich Carl von Savigny had argued that law could only be understood as part of culture: in his view, law was "first developed by custom and popular faith, next by jurisprudence—everywhere, therefore, by internal silently operating powers, not by the arbitrary will of a law-giver." The Age of Empires saw many challenges to this idea of law as evolving in line with culture. New states might deliberately use laws as an instrument of modernization, of nation-building, or of authority.[88] Where the deep religiosity of the people within a particular state clashed with the desire of the state to impose a single form of marriage, the result might be opposition and swift repeal, grudging acceptance, or the continuance of religious ceremonies with no formal recognition.

As this chapter has shown, while the pace and extent of change varied between different legal cultures, there was a very clear shift toward according a greater role to state laws. This process was only accelerated by the First World War. Henceforth the state was to play a far greater role in the regulation of everyday life, and it is no coincidence that two of the empires within which marriage law had changed very little over the previous century—the Russian and the Ottoman—both made changes to their marriage laws in 1917.

While the move to greater regulation by the state has brought greater certainty, this has been at the expense of making compliance with certain stipulated formalities the touchstone of what makes a marriage that will be recognized by the state. But even the most innocuous-seeming regulations as to notice and registration are not value-neutral. The often unintended effects of the laws of marriage upon individuals has long engendered a debate—one which continues down to the present day, with widespread cohabitation outside formal marriage and the modern practice of religious-only marriages—as to whether this focus on formalities offers sufficient protection to those members of society whose voices are least readily heard.

CHAPTER FOUR

The Ties That Bind

Family and Kinship in Europe and Asia

SATOMI KUROSU AND

K. DILHANI WIJESINGHE

This chapter focuses on marriages in Europe and Asia during the nineteenth century and early twentieth century. Marriage is the tie that binds a couple together, secures the stability and well-being of the household, guarantees specific rights to the offspring, and maintains kin networks. It thus makes the transmission of property and human and social capital possible.[1] Marriage is therefore considered either a means for social reproduction[2] or a strategy for alliance.[3] Marriage has been important in all cultures, but the emphasis and the methods of forming and securing ties in the nineteenth century were diverse and depended strongly on religious, cultural, socioeconomic, as well as demographic backgrounds.

To start the complex discussion of why and how ties are bound in various cultures, we address a set of questions: (1) Why are ties bound? (2) When to tie a bond? (3) With whom are ties bound? and (4) How are ties secured and strengthened? We first discuss how diverse cultures approach marriage differently. We ask why people marry, what symbolizes the transition from singlehood to being married in terms of wedding and postnuptial residence, and how marriage relates to reproduction. We then compare the age at first marriage together with the question of whether or not to marry, as indicated by the proportion who never married. These demographic means of selected (available) communities/countries are used to illustrate an overview of marriage patterns. The third question, selection of spouse, is vital, as marriage involved not just two individuals but two families and/or kinship groups. We pay special attention to the issue of whether to marry within the same social class, kin, or descent group (endogamy) or outside (exogamy), either as a rule or a strategy of alliance. The fourth question deals with the practices of dowry and bride price. We also discuss some characteristics of Asia to show how ties were strengthened or reconnected via motherhood and remarriage. Finally, since the temporal scope of this chapter includes a period of drastic change in a world of modernization, we end with the discussion of how these characteristics changed or persisted toward the twentieth century.

WHY ARE TIES BOUND? CULTURAL AND CONTEXTUAL MEANING OF MARRRIAGE

Why do people marry?

The majority of Asians and Europeans did marry in the nineteenth century although the timing and intensity might have been different. Why are ties bound? Far beyond individual sentimental relationship, the early modern period required and/or utilized the institution of marriage for at least four reasons. First, marriage was necessary for individual survival where the level of mortality was high and the level of social security or any alternative to family support had not yet developed. The Eurasia Project on Population and Family History (EAP)[4] indeed found that individual survival was much improved when people were married compared to being widowed in East Asia.[5] Marriage was a provision for old age. Second, marriage was a way to legitimize procreation, socialize children, safeguard the next generation, as well as continue the family line. Third, marriage could be used to supply labor for farming and for domestic work, although some societies such as Western Europe preferred to hire servants over the use of daughters/sons-in-law as a temporary solution.[6] Fourth, marriage was a way of forming alliances between and among households and kinship. For example, Pakistani Punjabi landlords used marriage strategically to seek maximal political advantage and minimal household disruption through marriage arrangements.[7] Marriage was a means to strengthen family ties and to protect the pedigrees of the family as well as distribute family resources.

While these meanings of marriage are shared by people of many cultures, there were variations in how they approached it, resulting in different characteristics of marriage between the early modern East and West. We discuss three aspects: wedding, the postnuptial household, and the relationship of marriage and reproduction.

Wedding

Any society recognizes marriage as a crucial point of transition for an individual as they shift from the family of origin to the family of procreation. In both West and East, the wedding ceremony and banquet probably best symbolize this transition and the ties that are bound between individuals as well as the two families and the concerned parties. As Ehmer illustrates with an example from eastern rural Finland, wedding ceremonies, with their splendid rituals and exchanges of gifts, are clear evidence of the forming of alliances between families or clans: at a wedding "two kinship groups met each other. The rites they performed together symbolized an agreement between the former kin group and the new kin tie created by marriage."[8] In southern Sweden, relatives, neighbors, and villagers attended the wedding feast and gave gifts that facilitated the setting up of the young couple's household. The wedding feast could be costly for the landed family in that "traditional material abounds with accounts of how parents, from the time their children were very young, saved for their future weddings."[9] Marriage was also an elaborate and ceremonious process in India[10] and other parts of Asia, where wedding celebration was costly and involved, particularly among upper-class families.

In Europe, marriage used to be a religious event and included mandatory validation by the church, with the consequence that the role of institutions, especially ecclesiastic ones, was decisive in maintaining the European marriage pattern.[11] After the French Revolution, civil marriage was introduced and validation by the state became more important,

FIGURE 4.1 *A Marriage Ceremony, A Couple Taking their Vows in a Church Ceremony, c.*
1897. Photograph by the Hulton Archive via Getty Images.

although many areas still continued to hold religious ceremonies for civil marriages.[12] By
contrast, marriage in Asia was a civil/family matter well into the late nineteenth century in
many areas. It was the community and kin that took a vital role in the process of marriage
or gave social legitimization via customary rituals and celebrations.

A report from European travelers and missionaries to Japan in the late nineteenth
century gives an interesting account of this difference. For them, a Japanese wedding
appeared too simple, consisting of a mere exchange of sake cups, and they disapproved of
the lack of religious and social legitimization of the marriage ceremony.[13] As this example
shows, unlike the *Samurai* (elite/administrative) class, the marriage of commoners (which
was the majority) did not require any formal application for marriage to the domain
authorities, unless it concerned a marriage with someone from outside of the domain. Even
for this, the requirement was due to migration and not marriage. Religious organizations
(temples, shrines) and the state did not have any role in legitimizing marriages until the
end of the nineteenth century.

Postnuptial arrangement

Postnuptial living arrangements illustrate the main difference between the forming of
ties in Europe and Asia. In Western and northern Europe, marriage meant the formation
of a new household where young couples formed a new unit (neolocal) independent of

FIGURE 4.2 *Bride and Groom at Wedding Ceremony, 1900s Japan.* Duits Collection/
Meijishowa.com.

their parents. Young people delayed marriage until they owned sufficient resources. Some
probably missed their chance either by waiting to accumulate sufficient resources or not
being able to find the right partner. In Asia, young married couples lived in the parental
household with either the husband's (virilocal) or wife's parents (uxorilocal). The couple
did not have to accumulate funds; instead their parents and kin members had strong
influence over the timing and arrangements for marriage.[14]

Even among European societies, where neolocal arrangements were the dominating
pattern, it was not uncommon to have virilocal and uxorilocal marriages in urban areas
of Europe. This was called the "launching pad" model, where a new couple temporarily
resided with the parents of one of the spouses.[15] Even in the stem family found in central
and Western Europe, this simply took the form of *Ausgedingefamilie* (retirement family),
under which headship was handed over to the heir at the time of his marriage and is
therefore considered akin to the simple, nuclear family.[16] Saito claims that this type of
stem family is different from that found in Japan, in terms of living arrangements and
parental involvement in marriage.[17]

In early modern Japan, where the stem family was considered ideal and the practice
prevailed, the eldest child (most commonly the eldest son, but sometimes the eldest
daughter) continued to live with their parents after marriage, bringing their bride or
groom into their parents' home.[18] The inheritance of family property was in principle
impartible and belonged to the child who continued to live with the parents after
marriage. Virilocal marriage was preferred, but sonless families often used uxorilocal
marriage. Uxorilocal marriage was also used in merchant families as a strategy to recruit
an able/talented son into the family business. In Southeast Asian societies, where the
family system was almost universally bilateral, newly married couples often joined the
wife's family.[19] Such bilateral/matrilocal arrangements often relate to female autonomy
and economic productivity.[20]

Virilocal marriage, in contrast, is often associated with strict normative control over
premarital sex and partner choice, and the decision-making power was in the hands of
the household head. Patriarchal and virilocal marriage were identified in northeastern
China, where the system of extended and joint family prevailed[21]: married couples lived

FIGURE 4.3 *Chinese Bride and Bridegroom, Canton, China, c.* 1900. Photograph by the Print Collector via Getty Images.

in a large household together with the husband's parents, unmarried sisters, married brothers, and even cousins. All patrilineal sons inherited equal shares of family property. Virilocal marriage was considered to be a socially superior way of marrying in China,[22] and uxorilocal marriage was considered a last resort for men because of poverty and therefore was not favored.[23]

In Sri Lanka, Gamage reports that, traditionally, *deega* (patrilocal) and *binna* (matrilocal) marriages were prevalent.[24] In the *binna* marriage, the husband lived in his wife's parental home and she had an equal stake in her parent's estate with her brothers. A *binna* husband had no privilege in his wife's house. Thus, just as in China,[25] wealthy men who were natives of the village did not intend to marry matrilocally; poor men, on the other hand, settled matrilocally though the proportion was not very high.[26]

Marriage and reproduction

Yet another important difference found in EAP is the relationship between marriage and reproduction. The interval between marriage and reproduction was much longer in Asia than in Europe. In the West, marriage was followed immediately (simultaneously, or even preceded) by reproduction, while in the East, it took much longer: i.e., marriage was only part of a process that led to reproduction.[27] This may reflect a quintessential difference in the nature of marriage in Asia and Europe. In general, marriages in nineteenth-century Europe started as loving companionships between individuals who had chosen their partner themselves and were already accustomed to each other following a shorter or longer period of engagement. In Asia the relationship often started as a companionship between children who often did not know each other. This was because "decisions about marriage and adoption were instruments of family policy, the outcome of deliberate assessments of family needs, means and aspirations."[28]

Thus, the difference in age at marriage was much larger between the East and the West compared to that of age at first birth.[29] Even though people married early in China and Japan, young couples did not start to procreate immediately; the average waiting time for the first recorded child in China and Japan was four to five years after marriage.[30] In northeastern Japan, couples often lived apart after marrying because of labor service (*hoko*), and frequent divorce also disrupted reproduction. What is more, frequently practiced infanticide contributed to the delay as well as to lower marital fertility.[31] Another East–West comparison study also found that the birth interval between wedding and first birth for women from Lugang (Taiwan) was about 6.5 months longer than for women from Nijmegen (the Netherlands).[32] It is important to note that they attribute the lower fecundity and marital fertility of Chinese women, not to impoverishment and malnutrition nor infanticide,[33] but to the nature of matchmaking and marriage.[34] They suggest that early marriage arranged by parents created a result opposite to parents' expectations. The young couples "were expected to begin reproductive intercourse without a period of cultural foreplay" and thus "could not live up to the fertility level of the couples in the West."[35]

There are three types of marriage system that illustrate the idea that Western marriage is an "event" while Asian marriage is a "process" and that further complicate the relationship between marriage and reproduction: commuting marriage, child marriage, and trial marriage. First, in the practice of commuting marriage, as revealed by ethnographic studies, the wife or husband visited each other for a certain period of time before moving into one of their natal households. This temporary commuting marriage was found in Japan, southern China, and Southeast Asia and is considered to relate to a more liberal attitude toward mating as well.[36]

Second, child marriage was common in many regions of Asia. In some parts of China, marriage of young daughters (*Tongyangxi* or *Shim-pua* marriage) is found. A young girl is adopted and brought into the boy's household at a very early age; the pair grow up together as brother and sister; and are then declared to be husband and wife when they reach maturity.[37] Just like uxorilocal marriage, this type of marriage varied by region. The prevalence of child marriages among Hindus in India is attributed to ancient Hindu scriptures that suggest a girl should be married before she attains puberty, and certainly right after her first menstruation.[38] The parties do not begin to cohabit immediately after the marriage ceremony. Conjugal relations are generally preceded by a second ceremony, called *gauna* or *vida*.[39] Between the time of her marriage and the *gauna* ceremony (which is roughly the period between puberty and the institutionalized recognition of her potential motherhood), the bride lives with her parents. When marriages are held later, when both parties are grown up, as is the case with educated families, the *gauna* ceremony is performed at the time of the main marriage ceremony. Raghuvanshi summarizes studies for India and found that the father was blamed and considered a sinner if he could not arrange his daughter's marriage before she was eleven in the Bihar and Patna districts.[40] Marriage could take place in several stages, and much earlier than puberty. Bengalis, for example, tended to pair off the marriageable couple very early and used to hold a marriage ceremony even when the couple were infants, but the consummation of marriage took place at the age of fourteen on the male side and ten or eleven on the female side.

Third, trial marriage reflects a flexible attitude toward marriage. Divorce was rare in many European countries and did not become a social issue until the end of the nineteenth century. It was often not allowed and was too costly for laboring classes to initiate.[41] In contrast, divorce was easy in several Asian countries including Japan, Java, Malaysia, Indonesia, and Taiwan.[42] Divorce often took place within the first few years after marriage. In northeastern Japan, divorce was immediately followed by remarriage and a significant number of men and women even repeated this process.[43] The short duration of marriage was considered a "trial marriage"[44] and provided an opportunity to test whether the bride/groom fitted in with the household and the village community. In Southeast Asia, young couples freely resorted to divorce when they found the partner of an arranged marriage was incompatible. Divorce could be initiated by women as well. This is very different from the European situation, where it was much more difficult for women and often impossible. Recent studies suggest that this was also the case in Japan.[45] Unlike the patriarchal or Confucian image of a wife being expelled from the household because she did not meet expectations, as in nineteenth-century Korea,[46] divorce was more of a mutual agreement and an egalitarian process among commoners, and the wife's family or village officials were instrumental in the process.

The three marriage characteristics discussed above suggest that in many areas of Asia, reproduction did not take place at once. Rather, reproduction often came long after the two parties began living together, testing, and/or getting used to each other. Hindus and Bengalis in India did not cohabit immediately after the marriage ceremony; young daughters in China also had to wait until they reached puberty. Divorce was also prevalent in early modern Japan and Southeast Asia, and therefore the disruption of marriage hindered immediate procreation. Thus marriage was strongly associated with reproduction in both Europe and Asia, the difference being that reproduction was immediate upon (or even earlier than) marriage in Europe, while marriage was only a path toward possible future reproduction in Asia.[47]

WHEN TO TIE A BOND?

The timing of marriage was obviously affected by these cultural differences. When do people marry? In addressing this question, we also need to pose a question about whether people marry or not. The age at first marriage and the proportion who never married have been the most widely researched parameters in the discussion of marriage patterns ever since Hajnal laid out "European Marriage Patterns."[48] Hajnal's claim that Europeans married later and a larger proportion remained unmarried than in the rest of the world, has been examined and reassessed for its fit to geographic location and interpretations.[49] Possible interpretations are: (1) that these figures "may well hide substantially different realities"[50]; (2) there are differences between regions and within countries[51]; and further, (3) apparent aggregate differences may conceal numerous similarities between Europe and Asia.[52] Bearing these in mind, our intention here is to present an overview of marriage patterns to reflect the cultural and contextual meaning of marriage discussed above. It should be noted that the selection of figures also reflects the availability of relevant sources and development of the study of historical demography in the region.

We compiled figures for ages at first marriage and proportions never married at age forty-five to forty-nine from EAP and selected European and Asian countries from other studies in Table 4.1. In order to see the geographic variation, Table 4.1 includes various levels of observation: national, regional, and at village/parish level. When the mean age at first marriage is not available, singulate mean age at marriage (SMAM) is used.

TABLE 4.1 Mean Ages at First Marriage and Proportion Never Married, Selected Populations in Europe and Asia

Areas and Populations	Mean Ages at First Marriage		Never Married % at 45–49	
	Men	Women	Men	Women
Sweden				
1801–1850 (SMAM)	27.5	25.9	–	–
1851–1900 (SMAM)	28.3	26.2	–	–
1861–1870	28.8	27.1	–	–
1871–1880	28.8	27.1	–	–
1881–1890	28.5	26.8	–	–
1891–1900	28.8	26.8	–	–
Southern Sweden (EAP)				
Scania 1815–1864	27.6	25.1	6.9	11.6
Scania 1865–1894	28.4	26.0	13.8	23.6
Eastern Belgium (EAP)				
Sart 1812–1899	30.3	27.1	16.1	11.7
Pay de Herve 1846–1900	31.1	29.1	21.6	21.3
Central Italy (EAP)				
Venice 1850–1869	27.7	24.7	25.7	19.3
Follina 1834–1888	28.4	24.9	10.0	13.3
Treppo Carnico 1834–1867	29.5	27.0	22.9	19.2
Casalguidi1 819–1859	27.6	24.8	14.5	10.0
Germany				
Fourteen villages 1800–1824	28.3	26.2	–	–
Fourteen villages 1825–1849	29.4	26.9	–	–
Fourteen villages 1850–1874	29.5	26.9	–	–
Fourteen villages 1875–1899	28.3	25.5	–	–
Netherlands				
Nijmegen 1830–1849	28.3	26.9	11.1	15.1
Nijmegen 1850–1869	28.8	27.6	–	–
Nijmegen 1870–1889	28.9	27.4	14.2	23.0

Areas and Populations	Mean Ages at First Marriage		Never Married % at 45–49	
	Men	Women	Men	Women
Japan				
1879 (Yamanashi, SMAM)	23.8	20.6	3.2	1.2
1910	26.9	23.0	–	–
1915	27.4	23.2	–	–
1920	27.4	23.2	2.3	1.9
Northeastern Japan (EAP)				
Niita and Shimomoriya 1800–1839	18.7	15.6	4.8	0.6
Niita and Shimomoriya 1840–1870	18.9	16.5	–	–
Northeastern China (EAP)				
Liaoning 1800–1849	22.0	19.9	13.5	0.7
Liaoning 1850–1899	21.2	20.2	–	–
Liaoning 1900–1909	20.2	19.1	–	–
Shuangcheng 1866–1899	21.6	20.0	10.4	3.1
Shuangcheng 1900–1912	22.0	22.9	–	–
Korea				
1800–1849	16.5	17.3	–	–
1850–1899	15.5	16.8	–	–
1900–1949	16.3	16.7	–	–
Taiwan				
1905 (SMAM)	–	18.1	–	–
Lugang 1886–1900	24.4	18.2	–	–
Lugang 1901–1915	23.0	18.8	4.2	0.0
India			(age 35–39)	
1891–1901	20.0	12.8	5.7	2.8
1901–1911	20.4	13.1	3.8	1.3
1911–1921	20.7	13.5	4.8	2.0
South India				
Travancore 1901	23.4	17.4	–	–
Travancore 1911	23.4	17.7	–	–
North India				
Rajastan 1891	20.2	13.0	–	–
Rajastan 1901	19.7	13.7	–	–

TABLE 4.1 (*Continued*)

Rajastan 1911	21.0	13.0	–	–
East India				
Bihar and Orissa 1891	19.0	11.2	–	–
Bihar and Orissa 1901	19.0	11.4	–	–
Bihar and Orissa 1911	17.0	11.6	–	–
Sri Lanka (SMAM)				
1901	24.6	18.3	–	–
1911	26.5	20.8	–	–
1921	27.0	21.4	–	–

Note: SMAM (Singulate Mean Age at Marriage) is used when mean age at first marriage is not available. EAP indicates that figures are taken from the work of the Eurasia Project (Lundh et al. 2014). Swedish figures are based on tables 9 and 13 in Lundh (2003). German figures are based on table 6.1 in Knodel (Knodel 1988). Japanese figures are based on table 2 in Saito (2005). Mean ages at first marriage are from the Vital Statistics; SMAM for 1879 is Saito's calculation from a pilot census of Yamanashi prefecture. Korean figures are based on table 2 in Park (2008). Figures for Taiwan and the Netherlands are based on tables 3.2, 3.3, and 3.4 in Engelen and Hsieh (2007). The proportions never married in Nijmegen and Lugang are based on Nijmegen censuses (1849, 1879) and Lugang household registers (1916). Indian figures are selected from tables 2 and 3 in Agarwala (1957). Sri Lankan data are based on table 3.11 in CICRED (Department of Census and Statistics) 1974.

Table 4.1 confirms the general pattern that Asian men and women married earlier than their European counterparts. In Asia, the mean age at first marriage was between 11 and 23 among females and between 18 and 27 among males, while in Europe it was between 25 and 29 for females and 28 and 31 for males. The most outstanding East–West divide was the proportion of never-married women. The proportion of unmarried women at the end of childbearing age was extremely small among Asians. Although statistics are not easily available, female marriage was early and universal in the rest of Asia, including Southeast Asia.[53] Celibacy rates among Asian men are also much lower than those of European men, with one notable exception in Chinese males, among whom the proportion unmarried at age forty-five to forty-nine is not much different from that of Europeans. This is considered a direct demographic consequence of a gendered mortality pattern, in which a disproportionate number of females died at very young ages: fortunate males could marry, while a large proportion of unfortunate men never married, spending their lives as bachelors.[54]

Asian women and men married early and also within a narrow age band.[55] For example, women in Europe did not marry until age twenty and only half of them got married by age thirty. In contrast, 80 percent of northeastern Japanese and 40 to 50 percent of Chinese women in the EAP study were already married at age fifteen to nineteen years. Almost all of them were married by age thirty. It was even more striking among Indian females that 79 percent were married by age sixteen, and 96 percent by age twenty.[56]

These Asian cases imply a strong adherence to the social and cultural norms regarding the appropriate age to get married.

WITH WHOM ARE TIES BOUND?

In pre-industrial societies, choosing a marriage partner was a crucial process, as it was a concern for individuals as well as households that shared consumption and production.[57] In Asia, marriage was often arranged. In China, not only did families arrange marriage in accordance with a set of refined customs and rites, but the state also codified some customs to regulate the process of union formation as well as divorce.[58] To arrange a marriage in India, family connections were properly ascertained, and seers, astrologers, and mullahs were consulted regarding the future of the couple.[59] There was even a professional matchmaker, or *ghatak*, who was responsible for maintaining elaborate family histories as well as negotiations for the upper caste in Bengali society, since a good marriage depended on the availability of detailed information on family histories and genealogies.[60]

What were the concerns of individuals and families in the choice of partners? Here, we pay special attention to the issue of marrying within the same social class (endogamy or homogamy), or not (exogamy or heterogamy). Endogamy or exogamy might be culturally, religiously, or legally prescribed, or they could be strategically used for alliance. The criteria for endogamy/exogamy could be socioeconomic status, kinship, caste, religious group, ascribed status, or even locality (village, community). These criteria overlap and sometimes conflict with each other. We also have to bear in mind that differences between ideal and reality always existed.

Social class

Marrying within the same social group, socioeconomic homogamy, was preferred and persisted as a way of maintaining the family status and prestige in nineteenth-century Western Europe.[61] A study of five cities in nineteenth-century Belgium, even suggests that "social closure strategies were efficient in that they apparently prevented upward marital mobility for lower-class grooms."[62] In rural Japan, marrying within the same social status and pedigrees was also preferred, as was marrying within the same village. In agricultural societies, endogamous marriages were the best fit for integrating the functions of two households to cooperate with each other in cases of rituals, festivals, and the exchange of agricultural tools and horses on a daily basis.[63]

Patrilineal joint families in China and India both favored women marrying up (hypergamy) and men marrying down (hypogamy). In China, many virilocal marriages were hypergamous and virtually all uxorilocal marriages were assumed to have been hypogamous.[64] This led to the delaying of female marriage among higher status women in Liaoning and Shuangcheng.[65] The practice of female infanticide intensified female hypergamy and male hypogamy or celibacy. In India, hypergamy (anuloma or "with the hair") has historically been a core principle of dharmic Hinduism.[66] In contrast, hypogamy (pratiloma or "against the hair") simply degraded the woman and her family, while doing nothing to raise the status of the man.

Yet another important basis for class endogamy comes from the caste system. In colonial India, Nepal, Pakistan, and Sri Lanka, local kings as well as British rulers administratively helped to establish and maintain the caste system, and marriages were socially stratified

FIGURE 4.4 *Bride and Bridegroom of One of the Lower Divisions of the Sudra Caste, India.*
Illustration from Joyce Thomas Athol and Thomas Northcote Whitridge (1908), *Women of all Nations; A Record of Their Characteristics, Habits, Manners, Customs and Influence.* London: Cassell. Public domain via Wikimedia Commons.

based on this system. In particular in India, the caste system was well elaborated and connected to the marriage and gender hierarchies. By marrying within the same caste, class difference was further consolidated and social connections were passed on within family and caste community.[67]

Consanguineal marriage

Consanguineal marriages—marriage between cousins or relatives—have long been banned by the church in Europe.[68] However, they were practiced in various parts of Europe by the nineteenth century.[69] In fact, according to Ehmer, the goal of social endogamy in marriage strategies became more compelling in the nineteenth century than it had been in previous centuries.[70] Ehmer surveyed the studies of that century and found kin-based marriage strategies to prevent dispersion of property and to maintain the integrity of familial patrimony in various locations in Europe, including rural and urban areas of Germany, Italy, France, Spain, Belgium, and Sweden.[71] Consanguineal marriages were considered reliable for business alliance or to prevent the dispersion of property, maintain the integrity of the family patrimony, and combat the social and economic problems of the modernization process.

Cousin marriages were favored in South Asia, including Pakistan, Sri Lanka, and Southern India.[72] For example, people in Pakistan practiced sibling-exchange marriages (*watta satta*). In *watta satta*, a pair of siblings from one household marries a pair of siblings from another household. These are usually (but not necessarily) first cousin marriages, and the children of such marriages are related to each other as double first cousins, through both their fathers and their mothers. Cousin marriages were therefore useful to strengthen ties between kin who held land in common.[73] Moreover, cousin marriages were easier to arrange, helped to keep property and other assets within the family, expressed the solidarity and honor of kin, and in turn supported the region's gender norms, which required male control of women in a kinship.

Marrying outside the descent group was a concern in China and Korea. People avoided marriage with the same surname and almost no one married patrilineal kin.[74] Men of Punjabi landlord families also married women who were not patrilineal kin.[75] Unlike these examples, Japanese peasants preferred marriage within *dozokudan*, a group of households based on a common ancestor and with a hierarchical order based on their economic relationship, regardless of patrilineal (or matrilineal) kinship.[76]

Monogamy, polygamy, and polyandry

Yet another criterion for binding ties is not the question of whom but the question of how many spouses. Monogamy and polygamy practices are based on how many partners are bound together via marriage betrothal. In Europe, monogamy was prescribed by the church, and no other form of marriage was accepted with respect to the number of wives.[77] The general Southeast Asian norm was monogamy moderated by relatively easy divorce, and polygamy was found only among royal courts.[78] In China, marriage was monogamous, though relatively few polygamous marriages were practiced among the elite during the nineteenth century, a man could have several spouses other than his wife, with the title of secondary wife or concubine.[79] Within the family, a secondary wife or concubine had a lesser status than a first wife. If the first wife failed to have a son, the sons of the secondary wife or concubine could inherit the father's title. Chosŏn society in Korea was a polygamous society, especially among commoner or slave classes. However, a man was allowed to formally marry one women. Only the death of a previous wife or a divorce allowed a concubine to become the legal spouse.[80]

Among the Kandyan Sinhalese of Ceylon, poor farmers as well as wealthy elite gentlemen have practiced polyandry, as "both social classes recognized polyandry to be moral as it teaches man to be unselfish and solidarious."[81] The wife was shared exclusively by brothers since it was considered immoral for her to be married to those outside of the family.[82] Only biological brothers or close fraternal kin who could not afford individual wives supported and built up marriage unions together with their brothers or cousin brothers. Environmental limitations or economic constraints have been suggested as the paramount factors of polyandry.[83] Family relations associated with polygamous marriage are also complex: polygyny increases conflict both between father and son and between brothers.[84] In contrast, polyandry practices, as found in Ceylon, reduce the potential hostility between sibling brothers.[85]

HOW ARE TIES SECURED AND STRENGTHENED?

Dowry and bride price

Dowry and/or bride price, or other forms of gift/money exchanges between families at the time of marriage, were important in securing marriage and family relationship in both early modern Europe and Asia. A dowry was a transfer of money or gifts from the bride's family to the groom's family, or from the bride's family directly to the marrying daughter. For wealthy families, a dowry could be property, and the transfer would help to maintain the social status of the daughter.[86] Bride price is typically seen as the payment given by the husband or his family to the bride's parents for the rights to her labor or reproductive capacity.[87]

Since women in Europe had the right to inherit property, the dowry was a premortem transfer of resources that would remain with the married couple but be the formal property of the wife.[88] In Sweden, the principle of equal inheritance rights for men and women was introduced into legislation in 1845.[89] However, the eldest son was often favored in practice, so sons and daughters who were not chosen to take over the family farm were compensated with outlying land for cultivation or movable property, sometimes given in advance as a dowry. The most usual gifts included cows, furniture, bedding, linen, and money.

In Tuscany, Italy, providing a dowry was almost an obligation for the bride's family independent of social status, including day laborers as it helped them to set up a new independent household. More pricy items marked the dowry of brides of higher social status (land, jewelry, money, etc.) compared to those of lower social status (some sheets, bed linen, etc.).[90] In the event of the husband's death, the dowry was returned to the widow. This gave an incentive for the deceased husband's family to discourage the remarriage of the widow. If parents could not provide a dowry, sometimes the woman had to save for the dowry herself or could get support from charitable organizations.[91]

In both China and Japan, wedding celebrations and gift exchanges were more common in the upper social classes. Bride price was a necessity to secure marriage, while dowry was optional. The content and amount of dowry varied in Japan. The amount of dowry was decided based on the betrothal and the socioeconomic status of the bride's household.[92] In general, the recruiting household paid betrothal money to the native household of the bride. The brides also brought in dowry in the form of money and/or landholding, together with their personal belongings (clothes and furniture).[93] The land and property of a bride were transferred to the native household of her husband. Thus, upon divorce, she could not claim the dowry back, but her personal belongings remained hers. In China, bride price was more important toward the bottom of the social ladder, and dowry was essential among the social elite.[94] Parents were more likely to marry their daughters into families capable of providing a higher price. This brought about the different positions of men and women in the marriage market: marriage for women was highly hypergamous, while for men it was hypogamous as discussed in the earlier section (see "Social class" above).

India has a long history of dowry practices. Dowry was a prerequisite for a marriage, and the amount and value of the dowry might depend on various social characteristics such as social status, caste, etc. The father had to collect her dowry from her birth, as almost all girls married at a very young age. Having more than one daughter was therefore considered a heavy burden for a family, and many resorted to the practice of female infanticide in order to relieve this burden.[95]

Children and motherhood

In many Asian societies, ties bound via various types of marriages discussed in the previous section probably required further assurance. Often, motherhood enabled a woman to gain a status not otherwise attainable. In South Asia, status graduation through motherhood was so marked that barrenness was a dreaded condition[96]: if a woman did not produce children, her husband had the prerogative to divorce her or marry another; sterility spelled social and emotional doom for the woman as "she is considered an ill omen both for the household and the larger society." In East Asia, having a child, or better, a son, assured her status in the household. It was socially and economically imperative for the Chinese family to have at least one surviving son and, if possible, also a combination of sons and daughters.[97] In Japan, the marriage reached its most stable position when a couple had a boy and a girl, as the ideal for couples was to reproduce a mixed set of offspring.[98]

Remarriage

In both Europe and Asia, remarriages were quite frequent because of high mortality at the time.[99] Remarriage practices, however, varied by region, depending on social and legal context. Remarriage was prohibited for Hindu women in India until the Act of 1856, while it was easily accessible for Southeast Asian women. Chosŏn society in Korea also imposed a ban on female remarriage.[100] According to EAP, remarriage was least common in China and more common in Japan, while European countries fell in-between the two distributions.[101] Despite the differences in frequency, similar patterns were found: remarriage was more common among men than women and among younger rather than older individuals, and occurred within a very short time after the marital dissolution. It should be noted, however, that the length of time between becoming a widow and remarriage grew longer in the latter part of the nineteenth century due to the introduction of the romantic marriage ideal.[102] Furthermore, just like first marriage, the individual likelihood of remarriage was affected by socioeconomic status and presence of kin.[103] Notably, the presence of an adult son reduced the chance of remarriage of widows in East Asia, as their patrilineal succession was fulfilled. Adult daughters reduced the chance of remarriage among widowers in Western Europe, as an adult daughter could help out with domestic duties and could replace a wife.[104] Above all, remarriage was extremely likely when widowers/widows had minor children, suggesting that marriage ties, whether from first marriage or remarriage, were important for raising children in early modern societies.

SUMMARY AND OUTLOOK: MODERNIZATION AND REDEFINING "TIES"

In this chapter, we have reviewed the complex and diverse questions of why, when, with whom, and how ties were bound and secured in early modern Europe and Asia. While marriage was pivotal for individual and family lives as well as social organization in both regions, it was early and universal in Asia and late and not universal in Europe. Although the intention of this chapter was not to contrast East and West, the long-standing divide allowed us to consider the meaning of marriage. We suggested three characteristics that might distinguish the Asian marriage from the European one: marriage was still considered a civil/family matter; parental involvement in arranging marriage and co-residence; and a longer process from marriage to reproduction. However, in finding partners, there were variations within East and West as well as similarities between the two. Examples of marrying within the same group (endogamy) and outside of the group (exogamy) were found. Each society had different criteria and priorities for finding a good partner based on the relevant sociocultural or legal rules, including social class, kin relation, locality, etc. Dowries and bride price were important for securing ties in many societies. We further discussed the high importance of motherhood (i.e., having children and sons) for securing marriage in India and China. Remarriage was also a way of reshaping households and individual lives in many societies of Europe and Asia.

How did these characteristics change or survive toward the end of the nineteenth and early twentieth century? Again, large regional and socioeconomic variations exist in the way that marriage responded to a period of drastic change in the world of industrialization, modernization, urbanization, and secularization. It has been strongly theorized that industrialization and urbanization changed marriage and family life as well as household composition. The reality, however, is that complex and empirical studies place more emphasis on continuity than change.[105] Nevertheless, our final task here is to understand some of the characteristics concerning the continuity and/or change of marriage culture observed in various parts of Europe and Asia.

There was a general improvement in living standards in Western Europe and East Asia.[106] People lived longer and were more able to plan their family formation and reproduction. Given this, the drop in the proportion of remarriages in the nineteenth century can be explained to a large extent by a corresponding decrease in adult mortality.[107] EAP found a decline in remarriage in Scanian parishes and northeastern villages in Japan and China. A complementary explanation for the decrease in remarriages in Europe would be the development of new forms of social security and pension systems during the nineteenth century, while at the same time a change in preferences took place as Victorian morals and the ideal of romantic weddings were becoming more widespread,[108] leading to a shift from instrumental to romantic marriages.[109]

In Europe, Ehmer maintains that "at the end of the nineteenth century—despite all the modification and shifts—the traditional character of marriage seems to have remained intact" and that "marriage was still a stable and durable institution, which, as a rule, did not end until the death of one of the spouses."[110] Nevertheless, the relationship between a couple became more sentimental, partnership became more defined by gender roles, and, in various ways, privatization of marriage developed. For example, in Flemish communities during the course of the second part of the nineteenth century, there was an increasing trend toward choosing family members (brothers and brothers-in-law) as witnesses to the marriage ceremony, which was interpreted as an increasing familiarization of relations.[111] The model of male breadwinner and female homemaker that emerged in the developed world in the first half of the nineteenth century became widespread after the 1850s.[112] However, this was not the case for families in lower socioeconomic groups, as the income of the wife remained essential despite the increases in men's wages.[113] Matthijs asserts that "marrying young and creating an identity around expressive family and motherhood tasks was, for many women, a reaction to and a remedy for their public exclusion and economic subordination."[114] Divorce began to become a social problem in nineteenth-century populations in Western Europe as they witnessed demographic transitions, democratization, and urban industrial processes.[115] Yet, while there was some innovation before the First World War, some claim that there was definitely no real breakthrough until women in the West gained more equality.[116]

Such changes are not so apparent in most of Asia. In China, late imperial marital patterns remained salient well into the twentieth century.[117] In India and other parts of South Asia, caste endogamy and the dowry system seem to have persisted and even intensified.[118] However, a closer look at the institution of marriage might lead to the discovery of changes in the practice of arranged marriages and land inheritance, as, for example, among Pakistani Punjabi landlords,[119] and in the city of Calcutta, where traditional matchmaker *ghataks* were replaced by matrimonial advertisements and marriage bureaus.[120] Some changes might have been initiated legally, for example, by the

Age of Consent Act of 1891 in India, which set the age for the consummation of marriage at twelve.

Major change started to become apparent in the latter part of the nineteenth century in northeastern Japan and in colonial Southeast Asia. The rise of female age at marriage is observed in most regions of Japan, most likely due to improved female status in the late nineteenth century.[121] Concurrent with these changes, arranged marriages became popular. Such temporary changes in the values and customs of marriage were further influenced by governmental efforts to abolish various customs that were considered barbaric by Western morals prevalent at the time. This included institutionalized premarital sex and trial marriage, which resulted in high divorce rates. This was also the point in time when "puberty" started to be emphasized. Interestingly, similar changes occurred due to Western modernization in colonial Southeast Asia.[122] In both Southeast Asia and Japan, the imposition of the Western model, including gendered roles of male breadwinner and domestic female, emphasis on virginity, etc., made society more patriarchal. The "invented" tradition of strong and patriarchal marriage became the basis of marriage and family behaviors in the new century.

Regardless of change or continuity in its meaning and timing, the institution of marriage remained an important and integral part of individual life courses and family cycles in any culture until the early twentieth century.

ACKNOWLEDGEMENT

We would like to thank Christer Lundh, Osamu Saito, and the anonymous reviewers for their constructive comments on the draft.

CHAPTER FIVE

The Family Economy

Families, Work, and Marriage in the Western and Non-Western World

ANGÉLIQUE JANSSENS

INTRODUCTION

The Age of Empires (1800–1920) is the period witnessing the breakthrough of industrialization, large-scale urbanization, and modern economic growth. Full-fledged industrial economies appeared in some parts of the world, most notably in the northwestern part of Europe and the United States, whilst other parts of the world began to lag behind in terms of economic development. Economists have coined the term "The Great Divergence" to discuss the emergence of this enormous divide at the global level that to a large extent still exists today.[1] This should, however, not be taken to mean that the world outside Europe and the United States remained untouched by these global economic developments. Far from it: its consequences were felt across the globe. Worldwide markets became integrated and in many cases destroyed traditional manufacturing based on family economies in Latin America, the Middle East and Asia. These global market forces had an enormous impact on people's everyday lives and sometimes but not always on the individual's chances at contracting a marriage and the timing of this important life-course event. For families and households around the world many new challenges presented themselves both at the individual and the family level.

In this chapter we will first of all consider the nature and the extent of social and economic change in different parts of the world in the nineteenth century in order to sketch the diversity in these developments between continents and between countries. This will also show that there can be no universal picture of the way these changes impacted upon the household economies of the big mass of the working population. In the section on family economies we will nevertheless try to present the broad picture of how and where economic development changed the way families organized work and income. In subsequent sections we will discuss the ways in which these changes impacted upon the roles of men and women in the domestic economy and more specifically on the normative relationships between men and women, and between husbands and wives. We will also take a closer look at the children in household economies. Throughout these sections we will discuss the implications for marriage opportunities and for the ages at which young people were able to break away from their parental household to engage upon married live.

THE RISE OF INDUSTRIAL SOCIETIES

The traditional historical narrative on the nineteenth century has a strong focus on the radical changes introduced by the Industrial Revolution. Indeed, there is no denying that this process of change ultimately and fundamentally changed the world we inhabit. However, we cannot say, not even for Europe or the Western world at large, that all nineteenth-century nations turned into typically industrial capitalist societies. With this concept I refer to societies in which the industrial sector dominates the economic structure and where most of the labor power is engaged in industrial production based on capitalist principles. Some countries in the West did transform into industrial capitalist economies, but most did not. We can therefore not speak of a clear juxtaposition between an industrialized Western world, as a whole, versus a non-modernized non-Western world by the end of the nineteenth century. In Europe unquestionably two industrial giants can be discerned on the eve of the First World War. If we measure industrial performance in terms of total industrial output, these two giants are England and Germany. However, this measure favors larger populations, and in addition it does not tell us anything about living standards. For our purposes it is better to look at industrial performance in terms of per capita output. If we take that perspective, the image changes in crucial ways. As Figure 5.1 shows, Belgium is more industrialized than Germany throughout the entire nineteenth century, and by 1900, due to the rapid economic development of Germany in the previous two decades, the two countries end up at very similar levels of industrial development. France follows these European leaders at some distance, and countries such as Russia and Spain can be found right at the end of the list of European industrial economies.[2]

Outside Europe, the United States began its comet-like rise in the 1860s as the leading economic power in the world, surpassing the industrial pioneer—the United Kingdom— at great speed by the 1910s. However, what Figure 5.1 also shows is the remarkable similarity in industrial levels between the different parts of the world at the start of the period, around 1750. At that time industrial output levels of countries such as Japan, China, and India were not substantially different from those in the West, leaving the United Kingdom aside for a moment. In fact, the economic situation in the East was remarkably close to what we find for European countries such as Spain, Russia, or even Germany. Within Europe a clear dividing existed between the northwest and countries in the southern and the eastern part. Hence, to think about the world at the threshold of the nineteenth century as a world consisting of on the one hand a solid Western block of economic change and innovation, against a non-Western block on the other characterized by economic backwardness and retardation is clearly quite wrong. The pre-industrial world was remarkably similar between the different continents, at least in terms of industrial capacity. In the course of the century, however, an enormous abyss opened up that accelerated in the second half of the nineteenth century between the industrial countries in the West and all other parts of the world. Even so, large non-Western countries such as India and China were still industrial powers in their own right, due to their large population size. Still, as their industrial sector depended on traditional

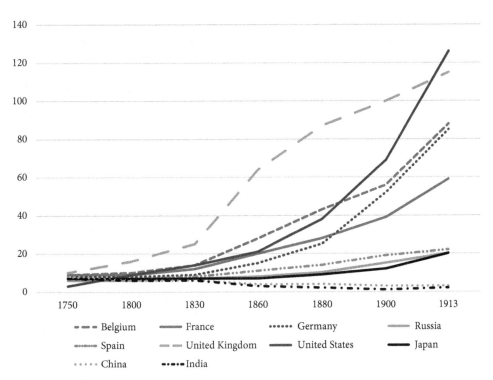

FIGURE 5.1 Level of industrialization per capita in triennial annual averages, except for 1913 (Index Numbers – United Kingdom = 100 in 1900). Graph by Angélique Janssens. *Data* Source: Paul Bairoch, "International Industrialization Levels from 1750 to 1980," *Journal of European Economic History* 11 (1982): 269–333.

technologies these were far less productive than those of some countries in the West. The huge diverging global developments in economic structure and productive technologies have had an enormous impact on people's everyday lives and the ways in which people were able to shape their personal and family life; issues that will be discussed further on in this chapter.

Clearly, England is the pioneer in industrialization. England's industrial development, beginning as early as the mid-eighteenth century, was based on cotton, at first using water powered machines but soon switching to steam power.[3] In 1797 there were already 900 cotton factories, and by 1830 one in six workers was employed in this single industry.[4] The staggering rise of cotton production in England was also felt elsewhere. It led to an enormous boom in cotton exports to all continents of the world. Moreover, the English cotton industry depended entirely upon imports, cotton was not a locally produced raw product. The huge rise in the demand of raw cotton meant that imports into the United Kingdom from around the world necessarily had to increase as well. In the course of the nineteenth century all industrializing economies on the European and American continent generated an a never-ending hunger and thirst for a wide variety of industrial inputs, such as minerals, new types of metal, and other raw materials such as rubber. Many countries around the world were thus drawn into the resulting global streams of trade. Whether this resulted in sustained local economic growth depended much upon the characteristics of these countries' export sectors. If they were dominated by large foreign companies working low wage laborers in a narrow range of products, economic growth was usually unable to transform these countries' economies in any structural way. In these cases European economic influence and penetration was restricted to a temporary overexploitation of that country's natural resources after which it was often left behind in a poorer state than it was before, especially if traditional economies had become disrupted in the process.

On the Latin American continent only Argentina was able to benefit from the new global economic connections; that country became a successful exporter of a broad range of products. Argentina also became the most industrialized country on the Latin American continent, closely followed by Chile and Mexico. Latin American industrial developments were mostly dominated by the food sector as well as by the textile industry. In these industries women's and children's labor were traditionally highly represented. However, the countries of Latin America were not really able to connect to the industrial dynamic going on in North America and Europe; poverty remained high, internal demand kept lagging behind and Latin American industries were not capable of breaking into foreign export markets.[5]

The Asian continent again does not present a uniform picture. Until 1895 the Chinese prohibited the establishment of foreign enterprises, which seriously restricted industrial expansion. For the greater part of the century China remained as it had been before, an economy primarily based on agriculture and a pre-mechanical but highly sophisticated craft production. In each of these sectors family based enterprises were the norm. Pockets of industrialization were emerging though, from the 1860s and 1870s onwards, when the powerful Chinese state began to develop a number of industrial projects, related to shipbuilding, arms production, mining, and textiles. However, full-scale industrialization was not the norm. On the Indian subcontinent industrialization also took place, starting in the second half of the nineteenth century.[6] Indian commercial entrepreneurs developed an industrial textile sector—jute in Calcutta and cotton in Bombay—which even managed to conquer Chinese and Japanese markets. These exports were the main factors in India's ninefold increase in the world market for cotton thread, from 4 percent in 1877 to 36 percent in 1892. The Indian cotton sector was definitely a sector with a considerable size and vitality, but the industrial textile sector played a minor role in the Indian economy as a whole. One of these successful cotton entrepreneurs was Jamsetji Tata (1839–1904), whose sons later founded the famous Indian Tata Steel company (in 1907). Thus, in India regional pockets of highly dynamic urban areas were created, which attracted a distinct group of waged proletarians and factory laborers who had migrated from the countryside. However, throughout the entire nineteenth century the backbone of the Indian economy continued to be based upon small-scale peasant agriculture, solely relying upon family-based labor.[7]

Japan represents one of the most remarkable state-driven industrialization projects of the nineteenth century. The Japanese economy, while being highly developed, as well as urban and commercial, with an integrated national market already by the mid-nineteenth century, was primarily based on small-scale artisanal and proto-industrial production for a range of nonagricultural products of high quality, amongst them silk.[8] Families obviously played a pivotal role in these industries. Agricultural production was also at a high level in Japan and steadily producing high yields and capable of sustaining industrial investments through land taxation. After the fall of the Tokugawa shogunate—which had kept Japan secluded from the West—in 1867 the new Meiji regime took up its mission to industrialize and modernize Japan as part of a broader policy of national renewal. The Japanese elite had come to realize that industrial development was the key to the country's success in its competition with Western powers. This not only involved industries serving military purposes (shipyards, steel, etc.) but also textiles. In Osaka and Kobe steam-driven cotton factory production arose, which existed side by side with local proto-industrial family based cotton production, earning Osaka the nickname of "Manchester of the Orient".[9]

By 1910 only 10 percent of the population in the United Kingdom was still employed in agriculture.[10] However, countries in which industry was the leading sector of employment were scarce in the nineteenth century; outside the United Kingdom this was restricted to Germany, Belgium, and Switzerland. In all other countries agriculture remained the dominant sector of employment throughout the nineteenth century keeping families the key players in economic production. Moreover, the expansion of the world economy and the increase in world population greatly stimulated agrarian production. Consequently, by the end of the nineteenth century worldwide most people were engaged in agriculture. Some countries, such as the Netherlands, were neither primarily agrarian nor industrial; this country had an important service and trade sector, employing large

FIGURE 5.2 *Large Silk Mill in Japan, c.* 1910. University of Victoria Libraries. Public domain via Wikimedia Commons.

numbers of people. This should not be taken to imply the total absence of any type of change in agriculture. Agricultural production necessarily had to increase in order to feed the steeply rising populations and the larger numbers of people living in cities; these pressures prompted the adoption of new techniques, new crops, as well as technological change. Not surprisingly, agricultural productivity improved first in those countries that were also the first to industrialize. Nevertheless, also here, families remained the basic economic unit organizing production processes.[11]

Finally, the rise of large-scale industrial production in the nineteenth century does not imply that artisanal production by craftsmen in independent workshops had disappeared. Even in Europe craftsmen retained their central position in towns but also in the countryside. They continued to work in much the same way as they had done before; some artisanal sectors even gained in importance. As cities grew in size, the need for artisanal production increased as well. Many of the goods purchased by inhabitants of towns and cities were still produced in workshops run by craftsmen and their family members, such as good-quality clothing or shoes, jewelry, kitchen tools, and various types of ironware, or were bought from small business and tradespeople, for instance groceries such as bread, milk, and meat. In all of these businesses families remained at the center of the production process. We will now turn to a discussion of how these economic continuities and discontinuities affected family economies for the big mass of ordinary people in different parts of the world.

FIGURE 5.3 *Chinese Family including Female Members, a Rare Scene as Strict Confucian Families did not Allow Women to be in the Company of Guests or Out of Their Homes, China,* 1874–75. Photograph by Boiarskii, Adolf-Nikolay Erazmovich. Public domain via Wikimedia Commons.

FROM FAMILY ECONOMIES TO FAMILY WAGE ECONOMIES

In the section above we have identified families as key players in economic production, despite the huge economic changes sweeping around in various parts of the world. Before the nineteenth century families and households had often functioned as *family economies* with a dual role as units of production and consumption, for instance on farms and in artisanal shops. This does not imply that waged work did not exist before industrialization. On the contrary, some households were entirely dependent upon waged work. Inheriting the family farm was often the prerogative of the eldest child, forcing all siblings out of the household to seek an income elsewhere as farm laborers on neighboring farms or as domestic servants in urban labor markets. Moreover, a substantial proportion of economic activity took place in small artisanal workshops based on hired labor even before the nineteenth century, also in the United Kingdom.[12] Outside Europe, non-inheriting children in farming families were also often forced to move out of the parental household if they wanted to marry. For instance, in China so-called joint families, consisting of parents, their children and spouses, and their offspring, were extremely rare.[13] Chinese young men and women who were not able to acquire a viable economic niche for themselves, whether in agriculture or in artisanal production, were forced to remain unmarried and either continue co-residence in the parental and/or fraternal household as coworkers or move to other households as hired laborers and servants. In addition, even producer households such as farming families, were often partly proletarian before the nineteenth century. They could only continue their independent farming if some of the co-residing adolescent or young adult children were able to contribute to the family fund through waged work. The patrilineal stem family was also the dominant family and household model in Tokugawa, Japan; here the eldest son was allowed to marry and bring his wife to live in his parents' home.[14] Non-inheriting children were forced to seek a marriage and livelihood elsewhere, for instance in the household of an inheriting son or daughter. In the case of an inheriting daughter, these households could decide to adopt the son-in-law as their own, so that the stem family line could be maintained, which was an important cultural value in the Japanese family system. Still, in both Asia and Europe access to economic resources, in other words access to the means to earn a living, was strongly linked to marriage, especially for non-inheriting men.[15]

The economic historian Jan de Vries has argued that before the Industrial Revolution European families began to intensify the labor force participation of their members to satisfy the household's growing demand for all sorts of consumer goods.[16] De Vries coined the term "Industrious Revolution" for this change in the orientation of households away from subsistence and toward marketed goods. Nevertheless, the spread of industrial production greatly stepped up the spread of proletarian labor relations and led to the more or less complete disentanglement of productive relations and domestic ones for large numbers of families, especially in the cities. Before the nineteenth century proletarian families might combine waged work with some form of small-scale agricultural work, growing vegetables in their garden plots and keeping a pig or goat in the backyard.[17] As the century wore on, these small-scale agricultural domestic production units were increasingly difficult to maintain.

As the scale of production increased, employment opportunities opened up for young adolescents. For them factory work provided an independent avenue towards marriage and the setting up of their own homes. At a young age factory workers could earn a handsome wage, there was little that prevented them from taking their pay and leaving the parental family economy. Thus, with the rise of industrial capitalism the numbers of families lacking any means of production, neither land nor tools, grew explosively. Increasingly, the dominant family type was one in which any type of production process was lacking: the family economy came to consist of wage workers only. And as long as economic tides were favorable and productivity could grow, there was no structural limitation to the number of new family wage economies that might be established. Such a development would break up traditional Malthusian controls on marriage, which had limited access to marriage for a certain proportion of the population entirely and had postponed entry into marriage for others.

Family wage economies were generally characterized by large differences in economic well-being depending upon the stage of the family life cycle. As Benjamin Seebohm Rowntree, an English social reformer and industrialist, discovered at the end of the nineteenth century, working-class families experience several periods of relative affluence, interrupted by periods of poverty and outright misery.[18] These poverty squeezes were determined by imbalances between the number of mouths that needed to be fed against the number of family members in waged work. Right after marriage husband and wife continued in paid employment, but after the arrival of several young children the first poverty squeeze presented itself as the wife was forced to give up paid work and concentrate on childcare and domestic work. The presence of many young children weighed heavily on the family budget, which now had to draw on the often insufficient income of the male head of the household only. As subsequently children began to enter the labor market, the total family income began to increase again relative to the number of its members. Most families would reach their highest level of financial well-being when all children were engaged in paid work as young adults. However, ultimately poverty loomed large, this time deeper than ever before, as children would marry and leave the household, often coinciding with parental earning capacity severely being depressed due to frailty and old age. Hence, parents were often desperate to retain children in their household as long as they possibly could.

If the expansion of wage labor in Western European countries promoted children's early economic independence from parents, did that lead them to abandon their elderly parents to suit their own economic interests? The historical record shows that this did not happen to any large extent. Even though the proportion of married people did increase somewhat in some European countries, pre-industrial marriage patterns were by and large maintained. This led some authors to describe the history of nineteenth-century marriage in Europe as "the story of the dog that did not bark."[19] A radical break in marital patterns, as economic theory had predicted, did not really occur during the nineteenth century. Similarly, differences in marriage traditions between Western and Eastern European countries, as was first described by John Hajnal, remained as they had been before.[20] In Eastern European countries marriage was more frequent than in Western European countries, and marriage ages were lower. Earlier generations of historians often described European marriage practices as a simple dual system with large differences between an undifferentiated "west" and an equally undifferentiated "east." More recently it has been shown that differences are more gradual, the further one travels to the east, the lower the age at marriage and the higher the marriage frequencies that can be found for early nineteenth-century communities.[21]

If Western European youngsters did not massively enter into early marriages when economic opportunities in wage labor opened up in the nineteenth century, this shows that the European marriage pattern did not just function as a demographic system but also as a system of values.[22] For one thing, these values centered around the couple's necessity to set up a household of their own, and to have at least a minimum of property (housing, domestic goods, and some tools) as well as an economic niche that would prevent the new family from falling into complete destitution. Young couples in most social classes were highly motivated not to step into "improvident" marriages—as contemporaries labeled these early proletarian marriages—because a timely marriage was central to working-class notions of respectability. In addition, young adults continued to adhere to family values that prevented them to rush into extremely untimely marriages. Only very few marriages in western European urban areas were contracted before the bride turned twenty or so years of age. Most young men and women were prepared to remain loyal to the parental family economy, not only by co-residing with elderly parents but also by pooling their wages with parents and siblings.[23]

Some authors, however, have stressed that factory towns were different. The English historian John Gillis spoke of nineteenth-century English manufacturing towns as "marrying places."[24] In such an economic context, and under favorable economic tides, the relatively high factory wages would entice both male and female children to leave the parental household at an early age, to embark upon their own family life. Gillis also believed these early marriages resulted from a break with the requirement that newlyweds ought to set up an independent household. Evidence on marriage patterns in textile cities in various places in Europe does indicate that marriage ages for female factory workers were significantly lower than for women in more traditional female occupations, for instance women working as domestic servants.[25] The relatively high female earning potential is generally believed to have played a role in lowering ages at marriage, not just for the female factory workers themselves but also for their male partners, especially if the latter were also employed in factory work.[26] The joint earning power of these factory couples was generally high at an early age and was not likely to increase further with advancing age; hence, postponement of marriage made little sense. Still, examples where nineteenth-century industrialization went hand in hand with relatively late ages at marriage are not difficult to find; for instance in the French arrondissement of Lille, an industrial textile region, men and women married rather late. The great majority of men married not earlier than age twenty-nine and for women this was around twenty-seven years.[27] At the same time fertility in these marriages was high, so with decreasing mortality trends population pressures mounted. Families responded in traditional ways by keeping a tight control over access to marriage. Thus, Malthusian controls and normative attitudes toward the proper age to marry also remained in operation in contexts of industrialization. A similar conclusion has been drawn for the highly industrialized region of eastern Belgium where marriage ages were quite similar to those found in Lille.[28]

In general we might say that marriage ages of nineteenth-century couples did not experience dramatic changes nor did household disruption take place.[29] In some countries marriage ages were not much lower in the later parts of the period compared to those at the start of the century, whereas in other locations the age at marriage rose between 1800 and 1900. Recently it was shown that in the Netherlands female marriage ages increased somewhat after the mid-nineteenth century. Dutch women were on average almost twenty-six years old at the time of their first marriage; for men the average age at first marriage was around twenty-eight.[30] A similar development has been noted for the United States where female ages at first marriage peaked toward the end of the nineteenth century.[31] This indicates that despite a fundamental restructuring of the economic basis of the family, the traditional *moral* economy of the family stayed largely intact. Sons and daughters remained loyal to parents and siblings, and in the face of the vast changes surrounding them, people largely held on to traditional ways of coping with the social and economic pressures arising from these changes. In such a context family support remained of crucial importance.

WOMEN'S WORK

Historians have amply documented the essential role women played in the nineteenth-century economy.[32] Ideally, for our account on the impact of economic change on family economies and on marriage practices we would like to distinguish between women workers who were married and those who were not. However, historical sources such as national labor statistics never reveal the marital status of the workers they are reporting on and neither do factory archives. Population statistics, such as censuses, population registers, and vital registers, also seldom record the occupations held by married women. Even for unmarried women a certain amount of under registration is unavoidable. Hence, most studies of the development of women's work cannot explicitly single out married women. In this section therefore I will describe the development of women's work in more general terms, and in the subsequent section I will focus more closely on married women's work and male breadwinning in as far as we have historical material available. If we want to understand married women's work it is important to sketch the more general development of women's work, because as we shall see later on the extent to which married women were engaged in paid work depended to a large extent on the demand for women's work from the side of employers.

Historical studies have made clear that women and children were often the first to be drawn into factory work. Indeed, many of the new technologies invented for the English textile industry were designed with a female and child labor force in mind.[33] Thus, the Lancashire cotton mills employed many women and children, as carders and piecers, but also as spinners or weavers.[34] This did not represent a breach with the English pre-industrial period in which women's and children's work in both agriculture and domestic industry was of long standing.[35] Elsewhere, women were hired only if male labor supply was insufficient. This latter factor was for instance decisive in the Dutch case. When the cotton textile mills in the east of the Netherlands were going through a rapid phase of expansion, from the 1860s onwards, large numbers of women, including married women, were hired. They were, however, the first to get thrown out again when demand for textiles slackened by the 1930s.[36] Women's industrial wages were less than those of males; however, compared to other occupations open to women, such as domestic service, the Lancashire factories paid women much higher wages. Elsewhere in Europe the situation was no different. These lower female wages sometimes prompted factory owners to substitute male workers for female labor. This was the case in Scotland for instance, where women even made up the majority of the textile workforce.[37] Similarly, in the woolen mills in Verviers, Belgium, factory owners employed large numbers of female workers.[38] In Japan, the vastly expanding cotton and silk-spinning industry employed primarily women, mostly from poor farming families who could scarcely survive without their daughters' waged work. Most of these female cotton and silk workers were very young, under the age of twenty, and were working long hours under appalling conditions and were housed in wretched circumstances in supervised dormitories. These textile mills were perfect breeding grounds for tuberculosis, as has also been found for nineteenth-century Europe.[39]

Outside Europe the increasing industrialization and resulting boom in European textile production often served to marginalize traditional female work, most notably in Asia. The flood of cheap European textiles, first from England, but later on also from other European countries such as the Netherlands, onto Asian markets had a detrimental effect on the importance of local weaving and spinning activities, traditionally carried out by women.[40] Nevertheless, new opportunities offered themselves as well. For instance, in Indonesia women successfully switched to the production of *batiks* or entered other often well-earning occupational activities in agriculture or trade.[41] So that by the end of the nineteenth century women's role in economic activities on Java overall had not seriously declined; measured as the proportions involved in gainful activities, women were as often employed as men.[42] This does not imply that women and men occupied equal positions, neither in the household nor on the labor market. Important differences remained between the economic roles of men and women. As was the case throughout Southeast Asia, women were more often family workers, which kept the women themselves and their earnings under tight control of fathers and husbands. Hence, the development of women workers' independent spending power and autonomy remained seriously curbed. Also, in most other Asian countries this would imply that women were primarily employed in agriculture but Java seems to have been an exception as female family workers were to a large extent employed in nonagricultural occupations, that is in trading and manufacturing. This reflects the relative importance of these economic sectors in the Javanese economy. Also in Thailand and the Philippines the proportions of women active in the labor force were considerable at the start of the twentieth century.

FIGURE 5.4 *Women at work on a plantation in Java, c.* 1920. Photograph by Ohannes Kurkdjian. Public Domain via Wikimedia Commons.

However, commercial and industrial developments in other Asian countries could and did come with clear negative effects on the economic and social position of women. It has been suggested that this was related to stronger patriarchal controls in those countries, most notably in India and China. For instance in India the development of the local textile industry served to progressively differentiate between male and female tasks, which reinforced traditional notions of female dependence and seclusion. Here the factory system from its beginning in the nineteenth century preferred and employed chiefly men. The two major textile sectors, cotton in Bombay and jute in Calcutta, had about one woman to four men in their workforce at the most, and over time the number of women was only reduced further. Thus, men were increasingly drawn into the industrial labor force whilst women and children remained behind and increased their nonpaid labor, making women's work less visible and undervalued. The dominance of men in the industrial workforce was first facilitated by an ample supply of male labor, and later on by the gendered pattern of labor migration, drawing single men from ever larger distances into the centers of the Indian textile producing regions. These migration options were not open to single women; only women suffering from social stigma's such as widowhood, desertion, bareness or accusations of unchastity could afford to migrate to urban areas.[43] The diverging examples of India and Indonesia outlined above serve to remind us that the effects of Western economic and political expansion were not following a single and uniform pattern.

Hence, in India women's work continued to take place within rural domestic units of production, although they might also be hired out to other farming families. In this way, married women might supply about 20 percent of the household's income, which might easily mean the difference between family poverty and starvation. Whatever the precise amount of women's contribution to the household, women's earnings would always be looked upon as "supplementary" income. In India married women might undertake a large range of additional economic activities, however, they would only do so when male incomes were depressed. In most regions women's work outside the home in general was casual, poorly paid, and intermittent. Women would collect and sell firewood, grass and fodder, and cow dung cakes. They would make baskets, dairy products, or process grain for the market (cleaning, husking, pounding, and grinding rice). Many sectors were closed to them, as women were unable to work in independent economic roles. The traditional ideology of female domestic seclusion stipulated that women were kept away from the outside world, so they could only work as a member of a household team.[44]

Our focus on the effects of economic and social modernization should not lead us to overlook the fact that the largest proportions of working women in the nineteenth century were not employed in industrial work. Even in mid-nineteenth century England most women worked as (non-farm) domestic servants or as needle workers; and these sectors were almost exclusively female. The cotton industry came only third and agriculture fourth as sectors in which women worked.[45] This was no different on the European continent or in the United States. In the Netherlands, domestic service was the dominant single occupation for young women around 1900.[46] Female factory work was limited to the few geographical pockets of industrial development, for instance in the textile area in the east of the country or in the pottery town of Maastricht. Moreover, in most countries factory work was limited to single women, for married women the full-time commitment required by factory work complicated their participation in industrial work.[47] In the final decades of the nineteenth century technological change in European agriculture also diminished the importance of traditional female tasks in rural areas, for instance in the sphere of milking and butter making. The introduction of creameries moved these operations into factories that were solely run by men.[48] Similarly, the replacement of domestic production in such industries as garment production—which had been dominated by women—by factory production as well as the growth of heavy industries all contributed to declining levels of female labor force participation.

On balance this implies that women's opportunities for waged work diminished in the course of the nineteenth century. It was only with the rise of the service sector in the twentieth century that work opportunities for women expanded again in a meaningful way, for instance in offices, shops, schools, and the medical sector. This development testifies to the important role played by the demand for women workers that not only created a diversity over time but also between locations and sociocultural contexts, as we have seen above. Generally, the precise intensity of women's involvement in paid labor was the result of a complex mix of factors, among them—apart from the demand for female labor—male wages, levels of education, the number and ages of children in the household, as well as cultural norms about proper roles for men and women.[49] It is precisely in the latter area that we can witness important shifts occurring in the second half of the nineteenth century; this is the issue to which we will turn now.

THE MALE BREADWINNER FAMILY: IDEAL AND PRACTICE

Women had always worked, both before as well as after marriage, in most of the centuries that preceded the one that we are looking at here. It is easy to think that the rise of industrial capitalism would *necessarily* imply the emergence of the male breadwinner family. After all, women's labor could hardly be united with the demands of factory work, which was not only located outside the household but also required a steady workday of ten or more hours at a stretch. Women could no longer combine household duties and childcare with productive labor as they had done earlier when working on farms and in the putting out industry. However, as we have seen above in the everyday practice of working-class family life, women's productive work and paid labor hardly disappeared from the scene everywhere. What did change though was the way in which female paid work was perceived and labeled. In the second half of the nineteenth century in large parts of the Western world the idea arose that fathers should be breadwinners and mothers caregivers who should limit themselves to domestic duties. This also implied that men should be paid a "family wage" sufficient on its own to maintain wife and children. This ideal of the male breadwinner was primarily aimed at excluding married women from paid work. Whether children were employed and were working for wages outside the household was generally considered less harmful for the ideal of male breadwinning. Indeed, children remained central to the family economy until well into the twentieth century and were widely regarded as valuable family workers. There was also a clear economic rationale involved here. Children's incomes were more often than not much higher than what wives could bring in. Moreover, mothers could then specialize in domestic duties that would support adolescent and young adult child workers.

Where did the ideal of the male breadwinner family stem from and why did it arise? The British historian Wally Seccombe identified its age-old predecessor as being the "family provider," a notion that can be found in patriarchal ideologies in many different cultures.[50] The idea of the family provider was connected to the notion of women and children as the weaker family members, in need of protection and economic security. Fulfilling the role of family provider would legitimize the husband's domestic authority over his wife and children and secure his position as head of the household. In the nineteenth century this notion of the male family provider was seized upon to articulate the claim of men, and above all of trade unions, to stake out their claims for higher male wages, a family wage, and at the same time the exclusion of married women from the paid labor force. Seccombe and many other historians have connected the rise of the male breadwinner ideal to the perceived threat of the increasing competition for work and wages from the many women and children who entered the industrial labor market.[51] Moreover, instead of working under the male head of household's supervision within the safe confines of the family economy, women's work, and women's remuneration, became individualized and women would be working alongside unrelated men. All this afforded women a public presence outside the household and a certain degree of independence, posing a serious conflict with traditional gender norms. For skilled workers trade unions the claim for a family wage and the exclusion of married women from the workforce offered an attractive strategy to secure their members job security and wage levels. The fight for higher male wages based on the male breadwinner ideal closely fitted middle-class notions about women's proper place in the home and the devastating effect upon the country's morality emanating from women's factory work. Structural economic change encroached upon traditional work roles and patterns for all family members, and thus providing impetus for the weakening of patriarchal power of men over women, and of fathers over their children.

Whether working-class families were putting the male breadwinning ideal into everyday practice was quite another matter. This was dependent upon many factors. If the husband's income was insufficient for a family to survive on, or if his income was irregular, wives would often work for wages. In the Western world this economic motive was the prime factor for working-class women to continue in paid employment after marriage. Families could often hardly afford to keep the wife at home and out of paid employment. In the United States even as late as around the turn of the twentieth century married women typically worked in the early stages of the family life cycle.[52] Husbands' incomes were rarely enough to cover all expenses when children were young and unable to contribute to the family economy. Families therefore needed an additional worker, and this was necessarily the wife. As multiple studies have shown the presence of a child under age two prompted the labor force participation of the mother.[53]

Wives' contribution to the family economy through paid work was also dependent upon local labor market opportunities. Here women could and sometimes did face restrictions, such as has recently been argued by Humphries and Weisdorf.[54] These authors argue that as the nineteenth century wore on and the factory system became more developed married women's labor opportunities came to be entirely restricted to casual work. Women's family obligations precluded employment in factory work as they were not able to meet the demands of commitment and regularity required by industrial work. However, female wages in casual work began to lag seriously behind both male wages as well as female wages for longer term work contracts, which would apply to jobs in farm work for instance, in the first half of the nineteenth century, making it much more difficult for married women in England to contribute in substantial ways to the family economy. This encouraged an early development, in England in the nineteenth century, of the male breadwinner family at a time when men's wages were insufficient to feed an entire family.[55]

Still, other studies show that nineteenth-century industrialization was not incompatible with married women working in factories. In sectors such as textiles, where women's

FIGURE 5.5 *Child labor in informal home enterprises, United States, c.* 1910. International Ladies Garment Workers Union Photographs (1885–1985). Photograph by Lewis Hine. Public domain via Wikimedia Commons.

participation had a long tradition, it was quite common for married women to stay on at the mill and retreat as the older children began to bring in income of their own. In these families the male breadwinner ideal was necessarily much less important. Van den Eeckhout has described the existence of this practice in Belgian textile families as late as the start of the twentieth century.[56] In the majority of urban textile families the mothers were actually in paid employment. Her study demonstrates that the male breadwinner ideal was more common amongst artisanal families who were not only able to put this luxury into practice but also were likely to be more susceptible to what was basically a middle-class family ideal. Male breadwinning offered them an important feature to increase the social distance separating them from the lower social strata. Another example comes from the Seville tobacco industry, where female workers remained in high demand until the mid-twentieth century so that both unmarried as well as married women participated in large numbers.[57] Due to the low level of capital investment, which existed until the mid-twentieth century, the tobacco industry allowed its workers high degrees of flexibility in working hours and work routines. Hence for a long time married women were able to combine industrial work with household duties. In France where the labor market needs worked against the exclusion of women from industrial work, working-class families combined a rhetoric of the family wage with labor strategies designed to enhance and diversify the wage earning capacities of all its members, including those of wives.[58] These examples demonstrate that married women's gainful employment depended upon many largely local and regional labor market factors and was certainly not solely determined by a rising ideology of the male breadwinner.

Outside Europe and the United States variation in breadwinning patterns was perhaps even greater. In Latin America and the Caribbean for instance the ideology of female domesticity was strong and the division between the male public sphere and the female private sphere much more pronounced than in European cultures. However, even there male breadwinning was far from universal. In nineteenth-century Mexico women constituted one-third of the workforce, and amongst the Afro-American and Afro-Caribbean populations female economic dependence upon men was unknown.[59] Also in Asia (south and east) male breadwinner household arrangements were largely absent. In nineteenth-century India a clear separation between household tasks and production was not made. Productive functions of households continued to exist for a long time after the beginning of industrialization in India, as we have seen above. Especially in poor households, women combined a large variety of tasks, often simultaneously: consumption, wage earning, domestic production, and reproduction. Whatever productive activity women would undertake, increasingly these economic activities were regarded as secondary, as extensions of their housework, and quite distinct from the cash remittances of the men. The more this cash nexus of male labor increased in importance, the more female labor was subsumed within domesticity, and the more it came to be devalued. This formed a basis for the gradual emergence of notions of male breadwinning, but in India that took place only in the course of the twentieth century. When demands for a family wage eventually arose after approximately the 1920s, this was partly the result of the instigation of British labor reformers. However, the Western notion of a male provider did fit easily with traditional Indian family ideology on property and labor arrangements that subordinated women and children to men in general and fathers in particular. The introduction of these Western ideals, however, did not change the continued importance of female work to the family economies in farming.[60]

CHILDREN IN THE FAMILY ECONOMY

One of the important issues in the debate on the social effects of the Industrial Revolution on the family economy is the question concerning the impacts on the working conditions and the livelihoods of children. In his renowned classic titled *The Making of the English Working Class* the English historian E. P. Thompson spoke extensively about the fate of little children toiling in English factories as one of the worst abuses of the factory system. In this book Thompson eloquently and passionately confirmed what he called the traditional view that "the exploitation of little children on this scale and with this intensity, was one of the most shameful events in our history."[61] This book revived the old perspective that viewed child labor primarily through the lens of morality. In later approaches to the history of childhood and child labor in the industrial era scholars began to ask very different questions. We will discuss these briefly in the following paragraphs but only in as far as they are relevant in providing insights into the changing economy of families.

Thompson provides ample details about the terrible conditions under which children were employed in England's "satanic mills." Not only were they working long hours, twelve hours or even more a day for six days a week, but Thompson also shows how these child workers were ruthlessly exploited and oppressed. He presents the story of a young boy who was found standing asleep with his arms full of wool. It appeared the boy had been working for seventeen hours that day. The next day the boy was dead. Children were especially prone to heavy exploitation if they had no relatives present in the factory who were working side by side with them, for instance for orphans and illegitimate children. In the early factories families often tried to transfer the family economy system to the factory work floor so that fathers or mothers were hired as work teams together with their children. Factory owners saw the advantage: parents could discipline their children and introduce them to the industrial rhythm of the factory system.

Thus, for Thompson the effects of industrialization on children was not just about the issue whether or not child labor increased but above all his work addressed the qualitative changes of child labor, that is, whether or not the conditions under which children were working had worsened. Piece rates increased children's work intensity and their individual factory labor removed them from the protection of kin members. Also, the factory system drew children of very tender ages into the workforce, from age four onwards, and negatively affected their health.[62] Other authors were more prone to stress the continuity between the employment of children in rural households and their industrial work. These historians argued that families were trying to optimize their family economies.[63] Increasing the pool of workers and the level of monetary contributions benefited the living standards of all members of the family including the children themselves. Children's factory work here appears as a rational economic choice, and indeed many studies suggest that if families had high numbers of offspring, children were more likely to be working.

Much of the difference in judgment on the numbers of children involvement in the English factory system depends on the period that is being discussed.[64] Recently, a new

FIGURE 5.6 *A little spinner in the Mollohan Mills, Newberry, South Carolina, United States,* 1908. Photograph by Lewis W. Hine. Public domain via Wikimedia Commons.

consensus has emerged suggesting that the worst excesses of the industrial system in England were beginning to disappear by the middle of the nineteenth century, such as the employment of extremely young children below the age of ten. Moreover, in the later decades of the nineteenth century real wages began to rise, albeit slowly, so that parents could afford to forego the paid employment of the youngest of their children.[65]

Also elsewhere in European countries and in North America the nineteenth century saw a rise in the level of child labor but as the century wore on labor markets began to crowd out children. This process has been termed the "adulting" of the labor market and of family economies.[66] The age at which individuals entered the labor market for a first time had risen. Moreover, children in the Western world were more and more relegated to the marginal economic sectors and were no longer found in the major new industries of that period, such as electrical companies or chemical industries. A separate children's labor market had come about by the end of the nineteenth century in which children were employed for such jobs as messenger boys or newspaper distributors. The decline in the proportions of children in the labor market, say below the age of fifteen, has clear relationships with the increase in male wages as was already mentioned.[67] Similarly, in late nineteenth-century American urban working-class families, the likelihood that children were sent to school rather than to work was significantly higher if father's earnings were relatively high.[68]

However, other factors also contributed to the decline of child labor. State action is one set of such additional factors: states were introducing labor laws prohibiting the labor of very young children in factories, and they were issuing schooling laws. Many of these labor laws were ineffective, however, because they were hardly enforced, although some did make a decisive difference. Elsewhere, in the United Kingdom for instance, child labor was already declining well before the adoption of the so-called factory laws.[69] Furthermore, technological change and employment strategies by employers played a role in reducing the importance of child labor in the course of the century. Employers began to switch toward intensive employment strategies with a focus on high-quality labor and lower hours worked rather than extensive strategies focused on long hours, high labor turnover and cheap labor of low quality. This also implied switching from child labor to adult labor. Finally, cultural norms regarding very young children began to change toward the end of the century. Increasingly children began to be viewed as dependent individuals in need of care and protection within the home.[70]

Did nineteenth-century industrialization outside Europe and North America intensify children's work roles in family economies? Japan presents an interesting case. After the opening up to international commerce in the 1850s, Japan experienced a strong wave of factory industrialization, especially in textiles. These early textile mills employed a large proportion of the total female workforce: in 1899 as much as 80 percent. But many young female workers were also found at work in rug making, rope braiding, and matchmaking.[71] Nevertheless, the Japanese evidence suggests that overall children were not sent out into factory work before adolescence. Japanese family economies seemed more often to have opted to supplement the family income through adult, that is, married women's work instead of by the paid employment of very young children. This constitutes a strong difference with European and American families who often preferred to substitute women's work for children's work, if they possibly could. Rich historical evidence taken from family budgets shows that in working-class households in Belgium and Spain around the period 1890 and 1900 very young children worked to compensate for the withdrawal of the mother from the paid labor market.[72]

It is very easy to see why the expanding work opportunities in the nineteenth century, particularly in factory work, were quite worrying for contemporaries, especially for mothers and fathers. On the one hand, it must have been attractive for fathers that children and adolescents could be sent out to do waged work. This was very useful for families with many mouths to feed, and it was also useful if the family counted more workers than its production base could employ. Under these circumstances waged work by its youngest members could bring in extremely useful monetary additions to the family purse. On the other hand, if children were increasingly able to make use of individual labor opportunities, this might move them outside the sphere of patriarchal power. Fathers would no longer be able to keep an eye on their offspring and to control their whereabouts. More worrying, however, was the fact that in the course of time employers were increasingly paying wages directly to the children and adolescents themselves rather than to fathers as representatives of the family economy. It was felt that this would severely undermine paternal authority. Also, if children were not dependent on fathers for work and wages, it would encourage independent behavior in all sorts of ways, ways that were mostly conceived of as encouraging immorality. For instance, children might decide to keep some of the money to themselves and spend it on what parents considered frivolities or immoralities, such as drinking and dancing, or fancy dresses and outfits. Or it might be an incentive to leave the parental household earlier than parents would see fit and get them into difficulties on account of improvident marriages. These would be marriages with an unsuitable partner and without sufficient money to establish a "proper household."

Losing the wages earned by children and adolescents must also have been a nightmare for working-class parents for other reasons: family economies were simply too dependent on child and adolescent labor throughout the entire nineteenth century. Of course, the proportion of the family budget brought in by co-residing unmarried children of various ages varied along the family's life cycle. It especially began to peak when the father was in his thirties. At that stage of the family cycle the father's earning power began to decrease, mothers would be bringing in very little money on account of age and household duties, whilst adolescent children were beginning to reach the height of their adult earning capacity. On the London labor market, as late as the early decades of the twentieth century, male household heads' incomes peaked at age thirty-five after which decline set in.[73] A study in the United States showed that by the time the father was in his fifties, very likely about one-third of the family budget was brought in by the couple's children.[74] In Europe that proportion could be even higher. In Spain, for instance, proportions as high as 40 or 50 percent of the family budget earned by children have been found, and for heads in their sixties this proportion might even rise to as high as two-thirds of the total family budget.[75] This brings into very sharp focus the enormous importance of children to nineteenth-century family economies, giving parents every reason to try to prevent their children from marrying early. This conclusion applies not only to European families. Similar labor strategies have been described for rural Japanese families in which sons and daughters were sent out into service or into other types of temporary waged work, whilst trying to fit the timing of the children's marriage to meet the material demands of the family economy.[76]

Throughout the nineteenth century children remained crucial to working-class and farming parents' survival, despite the increases in the ages at which children began to work in the final decades of this period. Children's contributions to the family purse and their allegiance to the parental economy remained strong so that wealth continued to flow

FIGURE 5.7 *Japanese Ainu family in front of their dwelling in the Department of Anthropology exhibit at the 1904 World's Fair.* Photography by Jessie Tarbox Beals, Missouri History Museum. Public Domain via Wikimedia Commons.

from children to parents. It is only in the twentieth century that these intergenerational flows of wealth were reversed, when wealth began to flow from parents to children as a result of rising costs of education and further increases—until age sixteen—of mandatory schooling. These increases in educational levels would fundamentally change family life in two important ways. Not only did education raise the total net costs of children but also education—and above all education of girls—changed family values and the desires and aspirations of parents toward their children. Parents began to want to provide a better future for their children. This would fundamentally end the historical period in which children were regarded as child workers. Moreover, it prompted families to limit the number of children they would have: parents began to opt for fewer children in which they would invest more. This fundamental shift in family values played an important role in the decline of marital fertility and the size of families.[77]

CONCLUSIONS

In the Age of Empires global economic change transformed the world inhabited by nineteenth-century families. The Industrial Revolution divided the world into continents characterized by economic progress and technological change, primarily located in northwest Europe and later on also the United States, and continents that were drawn into ever-growing global streams of commerce as markets of industrial inputs and selling markets for cheap industrial European products. Fueled by the revolutions in the production of cotton the United Kingdom became the world's leading industrial power early on in the nineteenth century. These first English factories were drawing in considerable numbers of children and women workers without whom the Industrial Revolution could perhaps not have borne fruit. In later stages of the English industrial development, and in particular when steel and electrical companies began to be the driving force of the industrial sector, adult men began to replace women and children as the dominant industrial workforce. Outside Europe and North America local markets changed work roles and productive relations, sometimes destroying traditional local handicraft industries, on other occasions creating new opportunities. These could, however, not prevent a further drifting apart of the continents, both in terms of economic development and technological change as well as in terms of the living standards of the large mass of working-class families.

In this process the economic make-up of families and households changed fundamentally. The Industrial Revolution transformed work relations, work rhythms, and labor discipline. It individualized the economic roles of parents, husbands and wives, and of children. Families became dependent on the anonymous powers of a global market that were capable of mercilessly destroying families' earning powers and traditional ways of working and living. However, families were and remained pivotal in people's lives and in their livelihoods. Families could help to "weather the storm" of economic change and survive the pressures families experienced at various stages along the family cycle.[78] For urban families who had become entirely dependent upon waged work, whether in the industrial or the artisanal sector of the economy, the first few years after the couple's marriage when both husband and wife could work earnings might be relatively plentiful. With larger numbers of very young children in the household it became more difficult for the wife to work full hours putting great strains on the family budget. Family affluence was built up when children began to bring in wages making up for the serious reduction in earning abilities of the male head of the household after age thirty-five. The waged work of the wife, who was paid significantly less than that of her sons, was substituted for work activities by the couple's offspring.

Labor force participation by children and adolescents was not seen as damaging the male's role of family provider; it rather testified to his ability to maintain discipline in the family. In the second half of the century paid work outside the family sphere by the wife increasingly became another matter. Men defended their prime position in the labor market against the competition by the cheap labor power of women and young children by demanding a family wage and sometimes even by striving for a (partial) exclusion of women from certain jobs and sectors in the economy. In practice, however, families carefully maintained a diversified labor market strategy, and when the situation demanded or when local labor opportunities were favorable married women did work for wages, whether outside the household or within, in different types of domestic production for the market. Families were acutely aware of economic hardship that might present itself, for instance at the death of the main provider. Outside Europe families could seldom afford to completely forego the productive activities of women. Especially within rural family economies the work process simply implied that certain productive tasks needed to be carried out by women. However, the expansion of waged market work in newly arising industries in Asian countries did introduce sharp differences between men's remunerated work and women's unpaid work within the family that was not beneficial for the position of women in families and marriage.

Even though the further expansion of waged work and the greater individualization of work roles for children and adolescents implied a greater independence of children vis-à-vis parents, we cannot say that this brought high degrees of instability to wage-working families. Indeed, in some factory towns the access to marriage had increased and the age at first marriage had declined somewhat. Still, there is no evidence of children fleeing their parental homes and leaving behind elderly parents in poverty and destitution. In this sense industrialization did not seriously erode ties between generations. There is enough evidence to support the idea that children continued their strong allegiance to parents.

CHAPTER SIX

Love, Sex, and Sexuality

Balancing Economic Considerations, Sociocultural Expectations, and Personal Desires

PAUL PUSCHMANN

Writing histories of love, sex, and sexuality is complicated, because information on emotions, erotic phantasies, sexual preferences, and bedroom practices is not easy to catch in the historical source material, as most people did not freely share such private information.[1] Moreover, some of the historical records have to be interpreted with caution, as they might tell us more about ideology or politics—for example, marriage advice literature, love letters, novels, and even medical books—than about true feelings and actual practices.[2] The reverse is also true: what people did cannot be equated with their personal and sexual preferences as their agency was limited and the main decisions in the private lives of individuals—for example, whom they chose as a partner, with whom they had sexual intercourse, whether they married or not, whether they remained faithful to their partner, whether they got divorced, etc.—were strongly influenced by the people and institutions around them.

Before we start our account on love, sex, and sexuality in the Age of Empires, it is important to briefly discuss and define the key concepts. Expressions of love are found in a very wide range of historical and contemporary societies. An anthropological survey by William Jankowiak and Edward Fischer found direct evidence of "romantic love" for as many as 147 different cultures.[3] This suggests that love is a universal concept and is part and parcel of human nature. Helen Fisher demonstrated indeed that love has a biological basis and she distinguishes three motivation systems in the brain, which are related to lust, romantic love, and attachment, the three basic components of love.[4] Lust is the feeling that makes one want to have sex with a person; romantic love—when one is madly in love, often accompanied by the feeling of having butterflies in the stomach—makes sure that mating efforts are targeted toward one person; and attachment is what keeps a couple together in the long term, enabling them to rear offspring together. Feelings of lust, romantic love, and attachment guide the social behavior of individuals, consciously and unconsciously, but the behavior is moderated and mediated by ideology, economic incentives, culture, and religion on the macro-level.

With sex we refer in this chapter to all forms of sexual behavior including, for instance, masturbation, non-penetrative sex, vaginal intercourse, oral and anal sex.

Sex is essential for human reproduction but it is also a source of physical pleasure and psychological satisfaction. Sexuality is closely related to the bodily process of sex, but the concept itself encompasses a much larger set of norms, values, believes, feelings, and behaviors related to sex. More specifically, sexuality refers to the ways in which people experience and express themselves sexually.[5] Sexuality is thus also about how individuals present themselves as sexual beings to the outside world. This goes beyond sexual experiences and is also expressed in the way we dress, stand, sit, walk, dance, etc. Sexuality is a cultural and historical construct, which varies across time and space.[6] Sexuality is tightly connected to one's gender identity (e.g., male, female, transsexual) and one's sexual orientation (e.g., heterosexual, homosexual, bisexual, asexual).[7]

Since this chapter is part of a cultural history of marriage, the emphasis of the text lies on heterosexual experiences. Given the expertise of the author, and the availability of scholarly literature, the focus is on the Western world, but key features and developments regarding love, sex, and sexuality are also discussed for various Asian, African, and Latin American countries in order to reveal similarities and differences across cultures

The chapter is organized into five sections and a conclusion. The first section deals with the question: how much room was there for love and romantics in the choice of a marriage partner? It has been argued that Western countries witnessed during this epoch a shift from instrumental to romantic marriage. Based on the available scholarly literature, it will be evaluated to what degree this new ideal was put into practice and how partner choice took place elsewhere in the world. In the second section—from love tragedies to happy endings—the rising ideal of romantic marriages will be linked to shifting trends in fiction on love and in particular the introduction of the story plot with a happy ending. Marital love and intimacy are at the heart of the third section. The fourth section deals with the weakening link between sex and reproduction, as a result of the introduction of birth control in Western countries. The last section aims to shed light on whether sex and sexuality were increasingly being repressed or whether a trend toward liberation set in.

LOVE AND THE CHOICE OF A MARRIAGE PARTNER

Although people have always fallen in love, throughout most of history, love had little or nothing to do with the choice of a partner for life.[8] Marrying a partner out of love was felt to be dangerous and unwanted, since a marriage would end if mutual love disappeared, and this would not only bring two individuals into trouble but also their offspring, parents, and wider kin network, as marriage was in the first instance an economic bond between two individuals and their families. A marriage led to the extension of the family's labor force and the pooling of resources. It involved major transfers of money, land, means of production, jewelry and other valuables by ways of dowries and bridal gifts, and it could also involve the transfer of a farm or a workshop. For a woman marriage was the best possible investment in her economic future, while for a man it could mean a major financial injection, especially in societies in which the bride received a dowry at her wedding.[9] Given the economic nature of the relationship, and the fact that it involved the well-being of two families, marriage partner choice in premodern societies was instrumental and guided by economic and political motives.[10]

Marriage required trust as it went hand in hand with investments. A marriage with the right partner secured the continuation of the family line through (male) offspring, created harmony, and could lead to an increase in social status as well as economic and political power of the families involved. By contrast, a marriage with an unsuitable partner would cause family disputes, disgrace, loss of income and wealth as well as loss of power. In addition, marriage usually involved some kind of arrangement between the generations regarding care with respect to illness and old age of the parents in return for capital investments and inheritance.[11] It is for this reason that most marriages in premodern societies were not the result of free partner choice but were arranged by parents, the larger family, or with the help of a match maker, which for instance was very common in India.[12]

Since most nineteenth-century societies were patriarchal, men had on average considerably more agency than women regarding the choice of their future spouse. In fact, women were often forced into marriage. In a very diverse range of African, Asian, and Latin American, but also in some Western countries such as Ireland and Australia, bride kidnapping was practiced in the nineteenth century.[13] In such cases individual men or groups of men—the latter often in times of war—abducted women, raped, impregnated, and forced them into marriage. However, bride elopement existed also. In such cases the agency of the women involved was larger, as the targeted women actively cooperated with their kidnappers or even planned the whole enterprise from the beginning in order to compel parental approval of the marriage (Figure 6.1). Such forms of consensual abductions were the exceptions to the rule, since parental authority and control were usually absolute. Nevertheless, even in nineteenth-century patriarchal Egypt, which was characterized by very strong parental authority, court records reveal that certain women managed to marry the men they fell in love with, even though parents and brothers opposed it. In this respect, an ultimate way of enforcing a marriage was by becoming pregnant, with all potential risks involved, ranging from punishment by law —including imprisonment—to rejection or even murder by the family (honor killing).[14]

In nineteenth-century Northwestern Europe and North America, arranged marriages were rather uncommon—except for the aristocracy—and partner choice was in principle free, as already from the Middle Ages on, the church had severely limited the power of parents in this respect.[15] However, church involvement in marriage affairs also meant that the number of potential marriage candidates was highly limited, given the strict rules regarding kinship. Moreover, individuals were expected to marry someone from the same racial, ethnic, socioeconomic, cultural, and religious background, and preference was usually given to partners from within the same community. Consequently there was what Jan Kok and Kees Mandemakers called "free choice from a limited supply."[16] Before a marriage was contracted lovers had the chance to get to know each other during courtship. This allowed them to test whether they were a good match and whether they could get along together. These conditions must have been perceived as a privilege by those who met each other for the first time during the wedding, as was, for instance, very common in many Asian and North African societies.[17] The other opposite in terms of familiarity with the partner was formed by Chinese minor marriages, as parents adopted a girl early on, raised her with their son, and finally declared them husband and wife.[18]

Although many Enlightenment thinkers strongly warned against marriages based on love, in Northwestern Europe and North America mutual feelings and companionship became in the course of the eighteenth and nineteenth century more valued, and love

FIGURE 6.1 Edmund Blair Leighton (1852–1922), *The Elopement*, 1893, oil on panel. Public domain via Wikimedia Commons.

became increasingly a condition for marriage.[19] This shift from instrumental to romantic marriage partner choice, which was also reflected in marriage manuals of the time, was fostered, amongst others, by industrialization. Proletarianization meant that there was no farm or workshop, nor particular professional skills to transfer from one generation to the other. This prospect caused a further deterioration of the power of the parents.[20] Children of laborers could simply ignore the wishes of the parents regarding their partner choice and marriage timing as they would face no financial consequences.[21] Next, industrialization made sure that early on in their life young men and women could earn a wage and sustain themselves independently. Thanks to the introduction of welfare provisions—for instance the installation of pension systems and the construction of retirement homes—the elderly became less dependent on their children. These developments fostered individualization, and as a result parental involvement became even smaller than it had been during premodern times.

Thanks to the rise of modern welfare states, which in the long run created a higher standard of living and a safety-net for individuals and families, the lower classes had to worry less about bare essentials in life. Consequently, other values in a partner—apart from their ability to strengthen the socioeconomic position and reproductive capacity of the family—were being increasingly treasured—such as personality, sociability, appearance, taste, and especially educational background. The latter would become even more important in the course of the twentieth century, and not only because it became a genuine predictor of future earning power and a new social class marker[22] but also because it allowed two individuals to communicate on the same level. The latter was indeed a key feature of romantic marriage: it was a union of two equal individuals. Instrumental marriages, by contrast, were mostly unequal; the husband usually overpowered his wife as he was older and more experienced, but the reverse existed also, for instance, when a farmer's widow got remarried to one of her younger farmhands. In various European countries the advent of romantic marriage is reflected in the nineteenth century by a trend toward age-homogamy, which shows that the ideal of romantic love started to take root: marriage was increasingly a union between two equal partners.[23]

However, the romantic marriage ideal became far from fully internalized among Western populations during the Age of Empires. This is also reflected by the fact that the boundaries in the marriage market by social class, migration status, religion, race, and ethnicity remained relatively rigid.[24] If people had chosen to marry purely out of love, marriage heterogamy would have increased significantly. Nevertheless thanks to the advent of new modes of transportation—steamships, trains, and trams—migration was facilitated and the area from which a partner was sought gradually increased, as is shown by the growing average distance between the birthplaces of spouses.[25]

That boundaries in the marriage market persisted shows also that more instrumental incentives kept influencing marriage decisions to a considerable degree and especially the economic background of the partner. This becomes immediately clear when one reads through nineteenth- and early twentieth-century marriage advertisements, as single men and women had clear expectations about the income and wealth of their future partner for life. A sample of ninety marriage advertisements published in Dutch newspapers from the period 1800–1950 revealed that some three-quarters of the singles explicated the economic background of the partner they were looking for.[26] The financial position was indeed the most important explicated criteria singles were looking for in their future partner, followed by age (54 percent), character (50 percent), and religion (42 percent). The appearance of the partner was explicated in 25 percent of all marriage advertisements. These results suggest that contemporaries were not totally blind to such factors as personality and physical looks. Marriage partner choice had become more than pure rational choice. However, it was only during the latter half of the twentieth century that in Europe and North America factors such as educational attainment, physical attraction, personality, lifestyle, and hobby's became really decisive, a trend that is again reflected in Dutch marriage advertisements of the latter half of the twentieth century.[27]

Although outside North America and Europe arranged marriages stayed the norm in most societies during the whole of the nineteenth and early twentieth century, important change was underway in Latin America. More and more opposition arose against arranged marriages and a trend toward free partner choice is observable. This cultural shift was supported by changes in law in Argentina, Mexico, and Cuba, which granted young people more opportunities to overrule parental opposition to a marriage.[28] In Brazil, arranged marriages became less common from the 1850s on, and courtship and

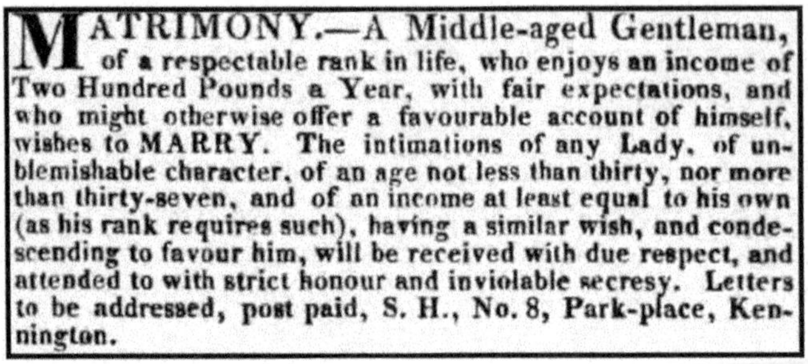

> **M**ATRIMONY.—A Middle-aged Gentleman, of a respectable rank in life, who enjoys an income of Two Hundred Pounds a Year, with fair expectations, and who might otherwise offer a favourable account of himself, wishes to MARRY. The intimations of any Lady, of unblemishable character, of an age not less than thirty, nor more than thirty-seven, and of an income at least equal to his own (as his rank requires such), having a similar wish, and condescending to favour him, will be received with due respect, and attended to with strict honour and inviolable secresy. Letters to be addressed, post paid, S. H., No. 8, Park-place, Kennington.

FIGURE 6.2 "Matrimony," *Morning Post*, December 19, 1822. Retrieved from https://www.mimimatthews.com/2016/01/04/alternative-courtship-matrimonial-advertisements-in-the-19th-century/(accessed March 22, 2019).

free partner choice were increasingly desired among the younger cohorts. The number of elopements and abductions increased, as young men and women were increasingly trying to avoid parental involvement in their partner choices.[29]

FROM LOVE TRAGEDIES TO HAPPY ENDINGS

The cultural shift from instrumental to romantic marriages based on free partner choice is also reflected in the Western literature of the time. Under the influence of such literary pioneers as Samuel Richardson and Jane Austen, romantic relationships were increasingly depicted in a positive way. Love had, of course, always been a theme of fiction, but it appears as if in former times the plot where two individuals followed their hearts—against the will of the family or the larger community, because they were, for instance, not of the same social class or religion or from rivalling families or groups, etc.—usually ended in a tragedy in the style of Shakespeare's Romeo and Juliet. Interestingly, this type of plot was also widely present in literature outside the Western world. In Arabic and Persian literature it is found in the genre known as "virgin love," for instance, in *Qays and Lubna* (seventh century), *Layla and Majnun* (twelfth century), and *Marwa and al-Majnun al-Faransi* (fifteenth century). In China it is represented by *Butterfly Lovers* (third century) and in India, for instance, by *Prithviraj Raso* (sixteenth century). Although the story line is often quite different, the love between two individuals ends in tragedy and the authors of the story seem to warn against (blindly) following romantic love and ignoring the wishes of the parents and larger family, as it would lead to nonrational decisions and would cause misfortune.

In eighteenth-century Western fiction tragedy still strongly dominated love stories. A rare but influential exception was Samuel Richardson's *Pamela* (1740), as the main character had a happy ending with her partner. The Romantic movement would put love increasingly at the center of the storyline, but it seems to have also reinforced the tragic element in the story line. One only has to think about Johann Wolfgang von Goethe's Sturm und Drang novel *Sufferings of the Young Werther* (1774), which ended in the suicide of Werther when he realized that his love Charlotte was unreachable for him and married to Albert. Another example is Jean-Jacques Rousseau's *Julie ou la nouvelle Héloïse* (1761) in which social class differences prevented middle-class preceptor Saint-Preux from marrying his upper-class love Julie.

FIGURE 6.3 Nineteenth-century Keshan carpet depicting a scene of Layla and Majnun. Public Domain via Wikimedia Commons.

Many of the European classics of the nineteenth century in which love has a central place have a tragic ending, such as Gustave Flaubert's *Madame Bovary* (1857) or Leo Tolstoy's *Anna Karenina* (1877). However, happy endings were increasingly coming to the stage and some were very successful, including Jane Austen's *Sense and Sensibility* (1811) and *Pride and Prejudice* (1813). Interesting to mention is also Charles Dickens's *Great Expectations* (1861), as the author provided initially a "classic" tragic ending, which he changed, upon recommendation by Edward Bulwer-Lytton, into a more open and arguably happy ending, before the book was published.[30]

Although there is not a straight line to draw from Jane Austen to the twentieth-century mass-market genre of the romance novel, championed by such authors as Barbara Cartland in England and Kathleen Woodiwiss in the United States, in which the happy ending is a compulsory way to terminate the love story, it is fair enough to argue that in the course of the nineteenth century the classic plot in which romantic love ended in tragedy received for the first time in history a—although mainly for literary reasons often highly criticized—counterpart in which romantic love gave way to a happy ending, a formula that would be very successfully picked up in the film industry by Hollywood in the course of the twentieth century. It is no coincidence that the above-described trend in fiction went hand in hand with the advent of the new societal ideal that love should be a condition for marriage, but it is most likely also related to the fact that women more often started to write novels and simultaneously formed an ever-growing group of readers thanks to the fact that more and more women enjoyed education, learning to read and write.

Changing attitudes toward partner choice and marriage are also elsewhere reflected in fiction. In Brazilian literature, critique of arranged marriages was expressed in the successful novel *Elzira, a morta virgem* (1883), authored by Pedro Vianna. In this novel Elzira encounters Amâncio on a festival and they fall heavily in love. As their relationship evolves they plan to get married, but this is strongly opposed by her family, especially by Elzira's mother, who wants to marry her off to a wealthy man. Elzira tries to convince her mother to give permission for her to marry the man she loves, but her mother refuses and because of this Elzira becomes heavily ill. When her parents finally give in, it is too late. Elzira dies as a virgin in the arms of her lover.[31]

In the Ottoman Empire criticism on arranged marriages as well as on polygyny started—under the influence of the Tanzimât reforms—to take shape from the middle of the nineteenth century onward, along with calls to improve the situation of women in society and within marriage and the family. In 1859, Ibrahim Şinasi wrote *The Poet's Wedding*, a satiric play, which criticized the tradition of marrying of women.[32] The same kind of criticism is found in the *The Love of Talât and Fitnat* (1871) by Şemseddin Sami, *Finest Stories* (1871) by Ahmed Midhat, *Awakening* (1876) by Namik Kemal, and *Night Entertainment* (1871) by Emin Nihat. These novels, written by an urban cultural elite in the Ottoman Empire, can be interpreted as a call for free partner choice and love-based marriages.[33] Whereas in previous novels, usually the unwillingness of the lovers to follow the will of the parents led to a tragedy, in these novels the parents who made the marriage arrangements were now explicitly depicted as the cause of the evil, just as was the case in the Brazilian novel *Elzira, a morta virgem*. As such the authors' societal criticism in love novels had shifted from the non-obeying children to the absolutist power of the parents and the lack of freedom among young individuals and women in particular.

Notwithstanding these and other literary charges against arranged marriages, such as Mohammed Husayn Haykal's *Zeinab* (1913)—widely considered as the first Egyptian novel—it was too early for novelists in Latin America and the Middle East to design a plot in which love would ultimately prevail, as such a plot would have been received as a mere opposition against the patriarchal hierarchy that bound society together: the family, community, and nation. Nevertheless, the criticism of arranged marriages as well as of polygyny and the position of women echoed an important cultural shift toward a society in which there was more room for love and in which a more equal relationship between spouses was desired. This was, however, the voice of a small cultural elite, and it did not foreshadow any significant change in larger society.

MARITAL LOVE AND INTIMACY

One wonders whether the trend toward freer partner choice and the introduction of the romantic marriage ideal was more often translated into true love between the spouses and into happier marriages. For a long time, it seemed that Victorian marriages were platonic, pragmatic, passionless, and cold,[34] but this picture has been considerably adjusted as historiography developed.[35] Peter Gay was one of the first who argued that the "official discourse" on sexuality and intimacy should not simply be equated with the experiences of individuals in the Victorian age.[36] Karen Lystra, on the basis of extensive collections of personal letters, showed that in the United States many nineteenth-century American couples were in fact soul mates, who shared intimacy and communicated in private on things which they would not share with parents, siblings, friends, colleagues, and neighbors.[37] The letters also showed that married individuals sincerely missed each other emotionally and physically at times that they were not together, as was, for instance, the case during the Civil War (1861–65), when husbands were fighting at the front. In the letters spouses exchanged information on hugging and kissing, but also on erotic and sexual matters. As emotions, desires, feelings, and sexual experiences were strictly kept secret from the outside world for a long time it looked as though the Victorians had cold relationships.

There is reason to believe that in fact marriages became more loving and intimate. As industrialization evolved, real income increased, the number of working hours per week was reduced and holidays were introduced. Increasing numbers of women started to withdraw from the labor market in order to rear their children and manage household affairs. As a result of these development, families had more leisure time, which they could spend in new ways and they increasingly did so together. The theater and the music hall became more popular and also more accessible to working-class couples. The latter, however, spent most of their spare time in associations and in taverns and pubs. Drinking in public spaces turned into a social activity, which both unmarried and married couples took part in. But families also went together for a walk on Sunday in the forest or the park, and more time was spent together at home as a result of the new domestic ideal.[38]

In the nineteenth century it became common—for those who could afford it—to go on a honeymoon; initially this was a trip that was made with the family (it often also involved visiting family members who had been unable to attend the wedding), but increasingly this special event was undertaken only by the couple, signifying a new desire for privacy and romance. In the United States, Niagara Falls became a main destination for newly-wed couples in the first half of the nineteenth century, as is illustrated by a popular 1841 song:

FIGURE 6.4 *Niagara Falls and Wedding Trip*. Library of Congress via Getty Images.

Oh the lovers come a thousand miles,
They leave their home and mother;
Yet when they reach Niagara Falls
They only see each other.

See Niagara's water rolling
See the misty spray
See the happy lovers strolling
It's everybody's wedding day.

To see the Falls they took a ride
On the steamship "Maid O' the Mist";
She forgot the Falls she was so busy
Being hugged and kissed.

See the mighty river rushing
Tween its rocky walls;
See the happy lovers strolling
By our Niagara Falls.

He said, "Is oo my darling?"
He said, "Whose darling is oo?"
He said, "Is oo my baby?"
And she always answered, "Goo-goo-goo."[39]

Not all couples in the Western world married in the nineteenth and early twentieth century for love and, of course, not all couples were happy. Moreover, a marriage that started off with love was no guarantee for a long satisfactory marital life. Love might fade away over time as the Flemish writer and poet Willem Elsschot expressed so vividly in the poem *Het Huwelijk* (the marriage), composed in 1910 in Rotterdam, the Netherlands. In this poem, the narrator describes how he regretted that he had married his wife as she grew older and lost her former beauty, how he wished that she would pass away, how he desired to kill her and to flee abroad with a new lover, but how he remained with her and the children. It is not only for the literary quality of this poem that this is one of the most cited works in Dutch literature but also because readers could identify themselves with the feelings expressed by Elsschot. As marriage evolved some individuals started to become dissatisfied with their relationship, and this was probably more problematic for those who had chosen their partner for life themselves and who had done so out of romantic love, as these individuals might have had higher expectations and, even more important, were responsible for their own destinies.

Although marriage became in many ways more popular than ever before—the number of singles in Western European countries decreased slowly but surely and so did average ages at first marriage[40]—the introduction of romanticism and the idea that a marriage should be based on love weakened the institution of marriage in the long run, as Stephanie Coontz has argued at length.[41] As love became the basis for marriage, the emotional standards of such relationships were raised, and cheating or domestic violence as well as the fading away of mutual love became reasons to end a marital relationship. In the United States and several Western European countries, including Sweden, Belgium, and the Netherlands, divorce rates showed a significant rise from the latter half of the nineteenth century on.[42] This was also related to the improved bargaining power of women within marriage. It is indeed striking that the majority of divorces were initiated by the wife.[43] Next, it was mostly the higher and middle classes who got divorced as they had the economic means to afford the legal procedure and were able to overcome the financial damage of terminating a marriage.[44] Of course, the lower classes experienced their conflicts in marriage too—often related to domestic violence, poverty, and alcohol abuse—but for them divorce was usually not (yet) an option. They had to continue their life in the way Elsschot had described or had to reinvent themselves as a couple.

While marriage in most non-Western societies of the nineteenth century did not start with love, it did not mean that love did not develop in the years after the wedding. Certainly, people who had never met each other before but got married, had sex with each other, had children, and shared fate and fortune could fall deeply in love with each other. They might also feel lucky and thankful that their parents or a matchmaker had brought them together. The degree to which this happened was dependent on the compatibility of the spouses but also, and maybe even more so, on other family members and especially the bride's mother-in-law. Let us have a look at the Persian Empire, which could serve as an example of the wider Middle East and North Africa.

In the Persian Empire, girls usually married during puberty and were by law able to refuse a marriage proposal but, in practice, they were often not even aware of this legal option and could therefore easily be bypassed. The men were usually in their twenties or thirties, and thus more experienced in life. It was the mothers who sought a match for their sons and daughters, with the approval of the fathers, who discussed and arranged the financial matters involved in the marriage. It was common that both partners did not know each other before the wedding, unless they were relatives. However, things quickly gained momentum as the marriage was consummated on the wedding night. On that very night a man had to demonstrate his virility, while a woman had to prove her virginity. Consequently two individuals who met each other for the first time in their life had to make love with each other and both had to prove something, which could be demonstrated to the wedding guests in the form of bloodstained sheets. This early challenge for the couple led not seldom to long-lasting marital traumas and some marriages ended, in fact, that very night, in cases where there were reasons to believe that the bride had not preserved her virginity until marriage.[45] The defloration ritual was also practiced in the Arab world. For Moroccan women from Casablanca it has been detailed by Soumaya Naamane Guessous.[46]

Upon the wedding night the wife usually moved into the extended household of her husband, his parents, and other relatives. From that moment on, her fate depended to a large degree upon her mother-in-law, who not only had power over her but also over her son. In practice, the mother-in-law could make or break the marriage. She could praise the young lady in front of her son, encourage him to be gentle and generous to her, but she could also tell her son to beat her, divorce her, and/or to marry a second, third, or fourth wife. As the mother-in-law had chosen the girl to become the wife of her son, she was probably well disposed toward her but that could change quite radically. In fact, mothers-in-law in the Middle East and North Africa have a reputation for making the life of their daughters-in-law difficult, while supporting that of their own daughters, and in fact they mingled in all private matters of their children, even those concerning their sex life. In this respect Janet Afary describes the following anecdote of a family who was sleeping on a hot summer night on the rooftop of their dwelling. The mother-in-law approached her son and daughter-in-law and asked: "Why are you holding each other so tight? Don't you see it is so hot? Move apart!" Subsequently she moved in the direction of her daughter and her son-in-law and woke them up with the question: "Why are you sleeping so far apart? Don't you see it is so cold? Get closer!" Upon which the daughter-in-law bitterly replied "Praise be to god. One roof and two weathers!"[47]

Given the often complicated nature between daughters and their in-laws, it is quite natural to see that cousin marriages were favored in the larger region, as these marriages guaranteed that all members involved treated each other with a certain amount of respect. It decreased the likelihood of violence, rejection, divorce, and polygyny. After all the new lady in the household belonged already to the family, and therefore had to be treated with dignity. Cousin marriages were so common that permission from the father's nephew had to be requested if a young lady was about to marry someone other than her cousin.[48]

Given the fact that husband and wife in arranged marriages did not know each other before the wedding, that the relationship was fundamentally unequal in terms of power and age, that there was only limited opportunity for intimacy between husband and wife, and that relatives constantly interfered in their relationship, we can only conclude that the conditions for love in arranged marriages in general, and in the Middle East and North Africa in particular, were on average considerably worse than in Western societies dominated by free partner choice and the prevalence of nuclear households. Having said that, of course, some people in the region found love, but it was usually not romantic love but rather a form of attachment as expressed by a twentieth-century Moroccan married couple:

> The wife: "It wasn't romance that brought us together, but the choice of our parents. However, soon respect and affection developed between us. You are a good husband, dear Mohammed, we lack nothing. You are a good father to the children, you allow them space, and in our neighborhood everybody respects you."

> The husband: "My wife, you are the pillar of my existence. You have always been honorable and god has blessed us with many children, whom we, god be praised, were allowed to keep all but one. Our house is a place of unity, the children are prudent and your hospitality is known by several generations."[49]

THE BEDROOM AS A BATTLEGROUND?

For centuries sexuality and reproduction had been tightly connected to each other. In the absence of contraceptives, sexual intercourse could at any moment lead to pregnancy but also to the transmission of venereal diseases. Although both men and women were at risk of the latter, the lack of modern forms of birth control was especially burdensome for women. Unmarried women had to fear that their lover would leave them pregnant and without any support, while facing the gossip and contempt of the neighborhood. The latter would in turn decrease their chances of finding a suitable partner for life. Married women faced successive pregnancies and deliveries at a time when both maternal and infant mortality were high.[50]

However, men and women were not completely at the mercy of human nature. Whereas in Western Europe couples' high ages at marriages limited the fertile period within marriage,[51] Middle Eastern and East Asian couples practiced a combination of abortion and infanticide to limit the number of their offspring.[52] Next, individuals—at least in Western Europe but possibly also in other parts of the world—seem to have been aware of the fact that sustained breastfeeding increased women's infertile period following a delivery, which allowed them to space births before the fertility transition actually took off.[53] Nevertheless, in premodern times people's means to control fertility were very limited.

During the nineteenth century the influence of human beings on their fertility increased considerably, as the structural decline in fertility rates in Western countries proves. France was the first country in the world that witnessed the fertility transition. A structural decline in French birth rates started in the late eighteenth century. Most other European countries, the United States, Canada, Russia, Australia, New Zealand, and Argentina followed in the course of the nineteenth century. The rest of the world would witness the change in reproduction only during the twentieth century but on average at a faster pace.[54] Where fertility decline started it was an irreversible process, in the sense that fertility would never reach pre-transitional levels again. Within countries, there were also considerable difference in the timing and pace of the fertility decline. In general the fertility transition started earlier in urban areas and among the elite; farmers and unskilled laborers were usually latecomers.[55]

Fertility declined in the nineteenth and early twentieth century thanks to a combination of what we nowadays call *traditional* methods of birth control, including coitus interruptus and abstinence during and around ovulation (calendar method). Although these methods were not very reliable, they increased the agency of individuals and offered an alternative to full abstinence for couples who did not want to have additional children. At the macro-level, traditional methods of birth control were sufficient to realize a significant decrease in total fertility. The nineteenth century also saw the spread of the rubber condom. It took, however, some time before these were used by the broader public, as they were associated with various forms of illicit love and especially prostitution.[56] For sex workers, the rubber condom was indeed a pertinent invention as it offered a means to protect themselves against sexually transmitted diseases.

Although the discussion about the determinants of the start, timing, and speed of the fertility decline go on, the key factors that drove the transition have been identified. First of all couples had to feel an incentive to limit the number of their offspring. A strong incentive was given by the decline in infant and child mortality, as it led in the absence of some form of birth control to larger families. Moreover, it became increasingly economically burdensome to have a large family. In premodern times children had started to work from a young age and therefore to contribute to the family budget. This changed gradually once laws were introduced that banned child labor and prescribed compulsory schooling.[57] Due to these changes, children turned from net-contributors to the family budget into net-receivers.[58] However, incentives to reduce the number of child births was not enough to effectuate a decline in fertility. Couples had to have the know-how of at least some form of birth control and its application had to be morally acceptable. With respect to the latter, religion often delayed the application of birth control when the economic incentives to limit offspring numbers were already felt.[59]

In the course of the nineteenth century information on birth control spread, and this was facilitated by such organizations as the Malthusian League, which aimed to educate the laboring population on family planning and to put it into practice in order to prevent over-population and poverty. The Malthusian League in Great Britain was established in 1877 after its founders—Annie Besant and Charles Bradlaugh—had been arrested, prosecuted, and exonerated for publishing an earlier pamphlet by Charles Knowlton that described and explained various methods of birth control.[60] Similar leagues were established in various European countries and gradually also in other world regions, and they all had the same aim: to provide information on population control and to realize family planning through a bottom-up approach. Although they especially targeted the laboring classes, they first reached the middle class. In a country like Italy, neo-Malthusianism started to reach the laboring classes at the dawn of the twentieth century, when advertisements on contraceptives in such leading working-class newspapers as *iAvanti!* were published.[61]

Whereas neo-Malthusians aimed to spread knowledge and utilization of birth control, the church and the state tried to prevent both, as the use of any kind of birth control was considered not to be in line with Christian doctrine but also because high fertility resulted in more soldiers, more tax payers, and more church members, which was at the center of the power of these institutions. The Catholic Church especially was a fanatic opponent of neo-Malthusianism as it forbade every interference in human reproduction to its believers apart from total abstinence and openly attacked neo-Malthusian organizations. For a long time the Catholic Church was highly successful. In a country like the Netherlands, Catholic priests did not hesitate to interfere with the reproductive affairs of their parishioners and praised and encouraged high fertility.[62] The result was that Catholics had higher birth rates compared to Protestants and even more so compared to seculars, and in the end their fertility decline was considerably delayed.[63]

While the church was powerful in the domain of marriage, sexuality, and fertility, the state became even more so, when neo-Malthusianism became increasingly mingled with social Darwinism and ideas about the selective breeding of human populations started to circulate under the influence of, amongst others, Sir Francis Galton and Karl Pearsons. These ideas were picked up later on by totalitarian states, such as Nazi Germany. As a result, the fertility of those nationals who were deemed especially fit was strongly stimulated—i.e., the white middle- and upper-class men and women—while those who were deemed unfit for reproduction—in the case of the lower classes this was often related to the idea that they were unproductive—including individuals with physical and mental disabilities, criminals, but also members of minority groups (especially on the basis of racial and religious grounds) were prohibited from marriage or underwent forced sterilization.[64] As such, these developments foreshadowed the horrors of the Second World War and the Holocaust.

The battle over bedroom practices by neo-Malthusians, the state, and the church affected the actual reproductive behavior of married couples in many ways. Increasing numbers wished to have smaller families and especially coitus interruptus was increasingly put effectively into practice as a way of spacing and stopping pregnancy. However, oral historical research on the first half of the twentieth century in Great Britain, makes the supposition that couples—especially those from the laboring classes—did not openly discuss reproductive matters during this phase of the fertility transition and that they kept regarding fertility as a largely unpredictable outcome in the absence of safe methods of birth control. In terms of sexuality and reproduction, women remained mostly passive agents, but middle-class women had more agency compared to working-class women. Whether or not and how to apply birth control was something that British wives largely left to their husbands before the sexual revolution of the 1960s.[65]

In developing countries a structural decline in fertility started only in the course of the twentieth century. However, this did not necessarily mean that fertility reached its maximum during the Age of Empires nor did it imply that married couples in the pre-transitional times had no influence on their family composition at all. Let us take the example of China, where, contrary to Western Europe, women married early and marriage was nearly universal. According to Thomas Malthus this led to extreme high fertility,[66] but as more recent empirical research has convincingly demonstrated, this was not the case. Total fertility in China was considerably higher than in Europe, but marital fertility was only about 75 percent of that of European couples, mainly due to larger birth intervals[67]

Although the academic discussion on what caused relatively low marital fertility in China continues,[68] it is clear that Chinese couples—in the absence of both traditional and modern birth control—influenced their family composition by ways of abortion, infanticide, and adoption.[69] Due to the strong preference for male offspring, female babies—in particular those who had at least one older sister—were at an increased risk of being prematurely killed by their parents or sold to another family, who were looking for a future bride for their young son. The latter practice of minor marriages was driven again by the shortage of marriageable girls in the Chinese population, which was in itself a consequence of sex-selective infanticide.

When comparing China and Europe in terms of reproductive life courses, Theo Engelen reached the conclusion that the longer intervals between marriage and first birth and between consecutive births, might very well have been also caused by the absence of love between marriage partners.[70] After all, Chinese couples entered marriage either as complete strangers or having been raised as brother and sister. Both types of marriage probably did not foster the sex drive in these spouses.

SEXUAL REPRESSION OR LIBERATION?

For a long time scholars have depicted the Victorian age as passionless and extremely prudish.[71] In the eyes of the Belgian moral philosopher and historian Jos van Ussel, the European middle class managed to successfully repress sexuality not only among its own members but also among the elite and the working class. Sex had become, what in the eyes of the Christian Church it had always been, a "necessary evil." Sex was the prerogative of married couples and for them it was only allowed if it was targeted toward procreation and performed in the proper position, i.e., in the missionary position with the man on top, underlining women's passivity. Married couples were supposed to limit sexual intercourse as much as possible, and marriage manuals described sex as an unenjoyable act and summoned women to tame the libido of their husbands, providing them with practical tips of how to kill their husbands' sexual desires. Dress codes prescribed that women should show as little as possible of their bodies in order to avoid any potential sexual excitement in men; for some a bare ankle was already deemed erotic. Too much sex was objectionable and deemed unhealthy, and whole campaigns were set up to suppress prostitution and other morally reprehensible behavior. With the same aim in mind, special anti-masturbation devices were developed. Sexual restraint was the ultimate expression of self-control. In the same vein Queen Victoria is supposed to have given her daughter the following advice for her wedding night: "Lie still and think about the empire."[72]

Sexual repression was not confined to the Western world, but spread also through colonialism into African and Asian societies. While European colonizers were obviously fascinated by the (imagined) sexual behavior of the colonized, as the large production of Orientalist paintings of naked and half-naked harem women testifies (Figure 6.5), they also wanted to control and alter their sexual behavior through, what Foucault called, bodily discipline and mass regulations.[73] Medical inspections of soldiers and prostitutes were ordered, children and adults were (re)dressed by missionaries, sexual practices were investigated by medical specialists, and new laws regarding marriage and sexuality were

FIGURE 6.5 Théodore Chassériau (1819–56), *Orientalist Interior—Nude in a Harem, c.* 1850, oil on panel. Public domain via Wikimedia Commons.

issued in order to change love, sex, and sexuality to European standards.[74] It goes without saying that this created lots of trouble for diverse groups in colonial societies, ranging from homosexuals and transsexuals to polygamists. In some of the colonial societies the discourse on sex fell silent—such as in the Middle East and North Africa—or the discourse was altered in such a way that it fitted the Western counterparts.[75] Mixed relationships between colonizers and colonized, which had been very common during premodern times when the colonizers were overwhelmingly male, became increasingly questionable.[76]

While there is consensus in the literature on the fact that as a result of colonialism various new forms of sexual repression entered non-Western societies, "the repressive hypothesis," as Foucault call it, has been increasingly called into question for nineteenth- and early twentieth-century Western societies.[77] Of course, there is plenty of source materials that confirm the Victorian age was prudish and passionless, and photographs from the latter half of nineteenth and the early twentieth century show indeed that European and North American women covered their bodies much more than would be the case later in the twentieth century, even at such places as the beach or the swimming pool, where that might have been simply inconvenient. However, there are also a lot of source materials, which paint another picture of nineteenth-century sex and sexuality. A first indication is provided by the small-scale, non-representative survey by Mosher from the 1890s to the 1910s, who questioned forty-five married American women about their sexual life. The women mostly had a higher level of education and were from the middle and upper classes. As it turns out, the women had—in the line of expectations—poor knowledge on sex and the human body prior to marriage, but the large majority of them indicated that they had feelings of lust, experienced orgasms during intercourse, and enjoyed sexual intercourse with their husbands. Last, but not least, a good deal of the women connected sexuality with love for their husbands and not only with reproduction.[78]

There is further evidence, such as public source materials like marriage guides, to prove that the nineteenth- and early twentieth-century Western world should not be simply classified as prudish and passionless. We only have to look at out-of-wedlock fertility. Late eighteenth- and early nineteenth-century Europe saw a strong rise in extramarital births, especially in the growing industrial cities of the time. According to Edward Shorter this was a sign of an early sexual revolution.[79] Although the literature on the topic has produced more convincing counter-arguments,[80] it is clear that European and North American working-class youth had sexual experiences before marriage in the form of night courting, *fensterln, kweesten*, and similar premarital sexual practices, which resulted in bridal pregnancies and births out of wedlock. Premarital sex was not a new phenomenon in Europe, but it led increasingly to unintended outcomes, as social control became weaker as a consequence of rural-to-urban migration, urbanization, and industrialization. Consequently pregnant girls—for example urban domestic servants with a rural background—often lacked the support of family and friends to force their boyfriends to marry them.[81] The men on the other hand might have lacked the financial means to marry the women they had impregnated and certain groups—for example soldiers—were not allowed to marry by law.[82] Alternatively couples could consider cohabiting, and in some cities— Stockholm is a good example—consensual unions became a real alternative to marriage.[83] However, it is also clear that a considerable proportion of the children who were born out of wedlock were not conceived within stable relationships but were the result of fleeting affairs and casual sex. In this respect it is telling that out-of-wedlock fertility in the Dutch city of Nijmegen peaked nine months after the yearly fair.[84]

In terms of sex and sexuality there was much more going on in the Victorian age that contradicts the idea of prudery and sexual restraint. A good example is the rise of the utopian communities in Europe and the United States, which aimed to create a new ideal social society. In order to reach this goal, not only labor and government were reorganized in the newly created micro-cosmos but also marriage and gender-relations were being redefined.[85] Equality between men and women was the credo, pleas for the abolition of monogamous marriage arose and all kind of experiments with sexual freedom took place. Robert Owen called in his *Lectures of the Priesthood in the Old Immoral World* for "marriages of nature." He condemned traditional marriage for having its basis in economic need and plead for free love instead.[86] In the Owenite communities free love was put into practice and women took joint care of household tasks and the nursing and rearing of children. These revolutionary ideas led to the collapse of some of these communities, but they inspired others to radically overthink sexuality, marriage, and the gender division in the household and society at large.[87] Charles Fourier was in many ways even more revolutionary as he also opened options for homosexual love (and pedophilia) within his envisioned Phalanstère where work, creativity, and sex were supposed to stimulate each other.[88]

There is further evidence that opposes the view that sex was increasingly oppressed through the whole Western world. Pornography developed along new lines with the introduction of photography and was sold—under the counter—in ever larger numbers. Moreover, controversial pornographic novels in which alternative forms of sex were the center of attention, saw the light. A famous one is Leopold von Sacher-Masoch's quasi-autobiographical novel *Venus in Furs* (1870) which puts sadomasochism at the center of attention. It is also interesting that the nineteenth century saw the first English translation of the *Kamasutra* (1883), the ancient Indian erotic sex manual. But changing sexual ideas were not only produced on paper. Homosexuals, lesbians, and transgender people became increasingly visible in urban areas and formed their own subcultures.[89]

FIGURE 6.6 *Man on all Fours in Red Jacket with Fully Clothed Woman Riding Him and Holding a Whip, c.* 1880. Hand colored photograph from the collection of Richard von Krafft-Ebing (1840–1902). Public Domain via Wikimedia.

Moreover, influential scholars such as Magnus Hirschfeld, Richard Von Krafft Ebing, and August Forel started to campaign against laws banning homosexual acts, which led, for instance, to the imprisonment of the famous Irish author Oscar Wilde. These and other related efforts led to the establishment of the World League for Sexual Reform in 1928, which aimed to liberalize sexual morals and practices on the basis of scientific insight.[90]

Maybe even more striking is that in major European and North American cities prostitution became more visible in the course of the nineteenth century.[91] Commercial sex workers—prostitutes, courtesans, but also many other women in a more hidden way, such as waitresses[92]—offered their services to a very diverse group of customers, including men from the highest and the lowest rungs of societies. For middle-class men it has been argued that commercial sex offered a compensation for a boring marital sex life, resulting from repressive Victorian norms.[93] However, like in former times, prostitution was also a way to meet the sexual needs of single men and married men away from home, including sailors, traders, and soldiers. While for the men it was a way to satisfy their sexual desires, for the women it was a way to earn a living at a time when women's opportunities in the labor market had become increasingly limited, as a result of the separation of spheres and the rise of the male breadwinner model. Although sex work was often looked down upon, courtesans could move in the highest circles of society, either through marriage or through their social network.[94]

Prostitution was an important theme in art and fiction of the time. In France three of the most famous paintings of the late nineteenth and early twentieth century depicted prostitutes: Édouard Manet's *Olympia* (1863), Henri de Toulouse-Lautrec's *Au Salon de la rue des Moulins* (1894) (Figure 6.7), and Picasso's *Les Demoiselles d'Avignon* (1907). Prostitution was also a central topic in some of the most read novels of the time, ranging from Honoré de Balzac's *Splendeur et misères des courtisanes* (1838) to Fjodor Dostoevsky's *Crime and Punishment* (1866). In practice prostitutes and courtesans were part of the life of

FIGURE 6.7 Henri de Toulouse-Lautrec (1864–1901), *Au Salon de la rue des Moulins*, 1894, oil on canvas. The Yorck Project (2002) 10.000 Meisterwerke der Malerei (DVD-ROM), distributed by DIRECTMEDIA Publishing GmbH. Public Domain via Wikimedia Commons.

artists, poets, and novelists, and in the cultural scene they were appreciated in many ways. For Charles Baudelaire art itself was a kind of prostitution.[95] Notwithstanding the fact that prostitutes were well integrated in society, serious attempts were undertaken to control and suppress prostitution and other forms of immoral behavior in the latter half of the nineteenth and early twentieth century.[96] This shows again that there was a large discrepancy between public doctrine and social reality. From the outside, sex and sexuality were being suppressed, while from the inside the urge and desire for sex was so large that it turned into an obsession.

CONCLUSION AND DISCUSSION

In the course of the nineteenth and early twentieth century Western societies started a transition from instrumental to romantic marriage partner choice, which would only be completed in the latter half of the twentieth century. Nevertheless, some signs of this transition were already observable in the nineteenth century, such as a trend toward age-homogamy, signaling increasing equality between marriage partners on the home front. The rise of the romantic marriage was related to industrialization and the establishment of social welfare provisions, which stimulated individualization and lowered parental authority and intergenerational dependency in the long run. As individuals and families had to worry less about the bare essentials of life, such factors as personality, educational background, and appearance were increasingly valued when choosing a partner. However, in practice socioeconomic considerations remained key during the Age of Empires, showing that the transition toward romantic marriages had only just begun and that more instrumental factors kept guiding the choice of a marriage partner. This is also reflected by the fact that the boundaries in the marriage market by social class, migration status, religion, and race remained rigid.

In Asian and African societies marriages continued to be arranged by parents and matchmakers, and economic and political considerations were at the heart of the decision-making process, but in several Latin American countries important cultural shifts toward free partner choice took place, which were translated in changes in actual behavior and backed up by changes in the law. As a result young people were increasingly able to make their own decision in the realm of marriage partner choice. In the Ottoman Empire critique on arranged marriages, polygyny, and the subordinate position of women within marriage and the family was voiced during the Tanzimât reforms, but the critique remained in the circles of the cultural urban elite of the empire.

The shift toward romantic marriage was reflected in Western literature in the sense that love stories no longer necessary needed to end tragically. The happy ending became an optional way to terminate a love story plot. However, again this process developed slowly and reached its height only in the course of the twentieth century with the mass genre of the romance novel and its successful adoption on screen by Hollywood. It was only then that love had become really a necessary condition for marriage. The rising critique on arranged marriages in Latin America and the Middle East was also voiced by authors of love stories. The tragic end remained a necessary component of the storyline of novels, poems, and plays on love, but in the new tales the youngsters who followed their heart were no longer held responsible for their unfortunate fate, but the finger was now pointed at the parents.

In the Western world the conditions for love within marriage improved as a result of increased living standards and leisure time, which married individuals increasingly spent together as a couple. This started straight after the wedding with a honeymoon for those who could afford one. Going to the theater, the music hall, or going to the pub were social activities, which were undertaken more and more by couples. There is also reason to believe that couples became more profoundly attached to each other. Love letters from the United States show that married couples had become soul mates, who truly missed each other and shared intimate information that they kept secret from the outside world. However, at the same time free partner choice based on love and affection also weakened the institution of marriage, which is signified by rising divorce rates. The expectations of marriage had risen and this led more often to disappointment, especially from the female perspective, as it was the wife who increasingly started to opt for divorce.

If we compare the conditions for love in Western and non-Western societies, we can only conclude that the conditions for love were better in the West. Free partner choice increased the likelihood that couples were compatible, and due to the prevalence of the nuclear family there was less interference from parents and the larger kin group in private matters of the couple. To make a marriage work in non-Western societies, such as China or the Persian or Ottoman empires, it was not only important that spouses got a long with each other but that all members of the family maintained good ties, which increased the likelihood of twists and trouble, as simply more people were involved. This was especially the case if they all shared one household. Married couples in non-Western societies shared intimacy, had sexual intercourse, and developed attachment toward each other, but on average there was less room for romance.

For centuries sexuality and reproduction had been tightly knit together, but as a result of the application of the calendar method and coitus interruptus the link between the two weakened, and fertility started to decline in Western countries. This was a reaction to declining infant and child mortality as well as the fact that the rearing of children became evermore expensive, while their contribution to the family budget decreased due to prohibitions on child labor and the introduction of compulsory schooling. Religion delayed the moral acceptance of family planning. The church, and especially the Catholic Church, tried to prevent its members from intervening in fertility, while neo-Malthusian organizations actively advocated to do so. Things became dangerous, when the state also started to mingle in the sexual and reproductive affairs of couples by the adoption of eugenics programs. While there were so many institution trying to control the sexual and reproductive behavior of couples, it is surprising that couples themselves remained largely silent on the matter and hardly discussed family planning amongst themselves. In line with the gender norms of the time, birth control was considered to be a male affair and women remained passive agents.

In terms of sex and sexuality the nineteenth and early twentieth century was a very complex age, as there were many dialectical processes going on. On the one hand there were forces—the church, the state, and the middle class—which tried to repress sex and sexuality—for instance the bans on brothels and the spread of anti-masturbation devices—and which gave the Victorian age its image of prudishness. These forces were real and influential in Western countries, but they might have been even more so in the colonial word. However, sex was, of course, not crushed, neither from the outside nor from the inside of society, and in certain ways sex was more present than ever before, and it was also being interrogated more, which in itself was also related to colonial experiences as encounters with other sexual cultures sparked curiosity. Such encounters, however, also helped to define and categorize sexual identities and different forms of sex, and as Foucault has shown this led to a powerful form of knowledge creation, which became strongly intensified with the introduction of the academic discipline of sexology toward the end of the nineteenth century. As a consequence, certain groups of individuals, for instance homosexuals and prostitutes, and certain behaviors, such as masturbation, were labeled as "perverse" and were increasingly pushed at the margin of society.

While the classification and repression of certain sexual identities and behaviors seems to have influenced both the colonizing and the colonial world, in the former more or less simultaneously important steps were being made from within those groups, which would ultimately lead to the liberation of some of those groups, including homosexuals. The process, however, had just started and would only accelerate during the sexual revolution of the 1960s. In the colonial world, by contrast, important liberties in terms of sex and sexuality that had existed in precolonial times were lost, and in certain regions, many of those liberties did not reappear. This was, for instance the case with more liberal attitudes toward homosexual activities in the Middle East and North Africa.

If we view the described developments in terms of love, sex, and sexuality in the Age of Empires from the different parts of the world, we can conclude that individuals had to balance economic considerations, sociocultural expectations, and personal desires and preferences. At the start of the epoch Western countries enjoyed on average more agency than individuals elsewhere in the world to shape their married life, and therefore they could follow their own personal desires and preferences more. However, financial matters and the expectations of the family, the church, and the community had priority over individuals wishes. As the nineteenth century evolved, living standards improved, the authority of the parents weakened, and individualization broke through. Consequently, the agency of individuals increased further. In most non-Western societies individuals' agency regarding love, sex, and sexuality had been highly limited and became, partially as a consequence of colonialism, even more limited. However, in those Latin American countries that enjoyed independence from their former European metropolises, important steps toward more individual freedom were taken.

Freedom in terms of sexuality existed nowhere in the world and definitely not in Europe and North America. However, most people in the nineteenth and early twentieth century seem to have made a balancing act between how they presented themselves in front of a suspicious outside world and how they acted within the private atmosphere of the homely bedroom, the hay barn, the backroom office, or the brothel. The spread of birth control practices enabled ever larger parts of the heterosexual population to keep the secrets of their sexual life to themselves, and therefore they did not violate the sociocultural expectations *en plain public*. However, the risks of premarital pregnancies and venereal diseases kept lurking in the absence of modern safe forms of anti-conception, and gays, lesbians, and transgender persons were in most corners of the globe never fully at ease, not even within their own community. It would take another half a century to see further major improvements in that respect.

CHAPTER SEVEN

Breaking Vows

Divorce in European and North American Literature of the Long Nineteenth Century

KARL LEYDECKER

In her study of divorce in the American novel, the American critic Kimberly Freeman noted that "divorce has been slighted in many histories of the novel, both of the novel in general and the novel in America."[1] A classic example of this can be found in Tony Tanner's seminal work on adultery in the novel, where he avoids any serious discussion of divorce by arguing that the three novels that he discusses in detail do not contain divorce and by speculating that: "it is as if the novelist realized that divorce was a piece of surface temporizing, a forensic palliative to cloak and muffle the profoundly disjunctive reverberations and implications of adultery."[2] But no argument is offered in support of this assertion, and as Tanner acknowledges, two of his own "novels of adultery," Rousseau's *Julie ou la nouvelle Héloïse* (Julie, or The New Eloise) and Goethe's *Die Wahlverwandtschaften* (Elective Affinities), do not even feature adultery.[3] Tanner is, however, at his most convincing when, in his concluding chapter, talking of the novel as a genre, he remarks: "Yet it is my contention that its [the novel's] real, if secret, interest has been aroused by the weak points in the family, the possible fissures, the breaches, the breakdowns."[4] Tanner in his study regards the exploration of the "fissures," "breaches," and "breakdowns" of marriage and the family as necessarily synonymous with a focus on adultery, however, as his very next sentence exemplifies: "Which is why the novel tends to be drawn, all but irresistibly, to the problems of adultery."[5] Tanner was not alone in being drawn to focus on adultery in the novel at the expense of divorce.[6] The Californian critic Joseph Allen Boone too in his classic exploration of the traditional marriage plot and the counter-traditional response to it in English and American fiction had surprisingly little to say about the counter-traditional potential of divorce.[7] His exploration of alternative narratives focuses predominantly on indeterminate endings within marriage and on the representation of female characters who choose to remain outside the marriage plot altogether. In this chapter, by contrast, I will foreground those narratives of for the most part female characters who seek to escape the marriage plot through divorce. A significant proportion of these narratives are by female writers, for as Boone notes "although men may and do critique marriage with acuity and sensitivity ... because women stand to benefit most immediately from the demystification of a system—and a story—that has worked to the benefit of men at their expense, it also makes sense that more women than men have actively engaged in a revision of the marriage plot."[8]

While in recent years critics have begun to address the deficit in focusing on divorce in relation either to individual authors or more broadly to the literatures of individual countries, this chapter is unique in attempting to address this critical deficit through a comparative analysis for the long nineteenth century from the French Revolution to the First World War as a whole across national and linguistic barriers. I will show that in the turbulent period around the time of the French Revolution, which coincided with a rise in the legal possibility and actual rates of divorce in several countries, divorce began for a brief period to be a subject for fiction in several Western countries. Then as revolution gave way to restoration, and in some countries possibilities of legal divorce were removed or restricted, so explicit depiction of divorce was much reduced in many Western literatures in the first half of the nineteenth century in particular. While it is difficult to be certain about the causes of this decline in the depiction of divorce, it is clear that there is a strong correlation between the general political climate and the willingness of authors to deal with radical topics such as divorce, so that as revolution gave way to reaction and the Romantic and early feminist movements ebbed away, so too did divorce decline as a topic of interest for writers. Yet while explicit depiction of divorce may have been relatively rare, I will argue that divorce haunts many of the canonical works of the nineteenth century as a potential if unrealized narrative possibility, often appearing in the margins of texts or in disguised form, prior to the reemergence of more open depictions of divorce especially toward the end of the century. Thus, divorce narratives form an important strand of the counter tradition to the marriage plot referred to by Boone, but which he did not discuss himself. Finally, it will be shown that as divorce gradually began to lose its explosive potential for romance plots at the turn of the twentieth century, several writers instead began to focus on the economic and social dimensions of divorce, rather than its implications for the fate of individuals.

In tracing the patterns of depiction of divorce in the long nineteenth century I will also argue that divorce is typically a subject that appealed more to female writers than their male counterparts, and that connections can be traced between the depiction of divorce and the ebb and flow of feminist movements across the West in the nineteenth century. Thus it can be argued that the marginalization of divorce in the critical tradition until recently, referred to by Freeman, can be viewed as a consequence of the wider marginalization of fiction by women.[9] Before turning to the representation of divorce in fiction, however, it will be useful briefly to summarize the legal position with regard to divorce that pertained in Britain, France, Germany, and the United States in the long nineteenth century, as for reasons of focus it is the literatures of these countries that will predominantly be the subject of discussion in this chapter. This will facilitate the tracing of the relationship between fictional representations of divorce and the legal and social realities across the century.

DIVORCE IN THE LONG NINETEENTH CENTURY

In the late eighteenth century there was a marked liberalization of divorce law in several Western countries. The most striking example of this was in France in the aftermath of the outbreak of the French Revolution in 1789. Between 1792 and 1804 France had extremely liberal divorce laws "that made divorce available for any reason whatsoever,"[10] and there were an estimated 30,000 divorces in France in those years (Figure 7.1).[11] With the introduction of the Napoleonic Code in 1804 divorce was, however, made more difficult to obtain—especially for women, who notoriously could now only obtain a divorce on the grounds of adultery if the husband committed adultery in the marital home—and was abolished completely in 1816. Meanwhile in the Protestant German states, where divorce had been permitted since the Reformation, a considerable liberalization also occurred in the second half of the eighteenth century, with Prussia's new Civil Code (*Allgemeines Landrecht*) in 1794 including twenty grounds for divorce, thereby marking the high point of liberal divorce legislation in the German states until the 1970s.[12] The important element in common between the civil code in Prussia and the revolutionary

FIGURE 7.1 French Revolution *Liberte du Mariage* (Queen of clubs/Dame de trefles), French playing card, *c.* 1793. Named *Pudeur* (modesty) but displaying the sign "Divorce" under the cap of liberty. Photograph by Culture Club via Getty Images.

divorce law in France was that both went far beyond divorce on the grounds of adultery, allowing divorce by mutual consent or on the grounds of incompatibility as perceived by either partner (albeit in Prussia the marriage had to be childless in all but exceptional circumstances for a divorce to be possible on these grounds, and one or both parties had to be found guilty of causing the divorce). In England, by contrast, divorce could only be obtained on the grounds of adultery on the part of the wife by an Act of Parliament, an expensive and very public process that rendered divorce extremely rare by comparison with revolutionary France and Protestant German states. Nevertheless, although the law in England remained unchanged in the late eighteenth century "after 1770 and again after 1790 ... contemporaries discerned a 'divorce epidemic' raging in England" as the number of divorces increased, albeit actual numbers remained small.[13] Meanwhile in the wake of American Independence in 1776 there was a "surge in divorce-related legislative activity and the spread of divorce throughout almost all of the United States at the end of the eighteenth century."[14] In New England in particular, the new laws passed by the individual states tended to be more liberal, introducing additional grounds for divorce beyond adultery (such as desertion, impotence, or cruelty), and at the same time tending to make divorce a judicial rather than a legislative matter, in what was a clear break with the situation in England.

If the late eighteenth century is characterized by this common pattern of liberalization of the law and growth in the incidence of divorce, albeit to very different extents in different countries, the development of divorce law and practice in Western countries in the course of the nineteenth century is much more heterogeneous. The Protestant German states continued to have liberal divorce laws throughout the nineteenth century, though the courts sought to make divorce more difficult to obtain in practice in the 1840s. Then, following German Unification in 1871, a new civil code for Germany (*Bürgerliches Gesetzbuch*) was finally introduced in 1900, which rendered divorce law more conservative, ending divorce by mutual consent or on the grounds of incompatibility. In Catholic France, by contrast, divorce was not legally possible from 1816 until the reintroduction of divorce in 1884, and even then the *Loi Naquet*, based as it was on the Napoleonic Code, was relatively restrictive in its grounds for divorce, though it did remove the double standard in that a husband's adultery did not need to take place in the marital home for it to be a ground for divorce. In England the major legal reform occurred in the 1850s with the passage of the Matrimonial Causes Act in 1857, which established civil divorce court proceedings, though divorce remained more accessible to men than women, with wives having to prove that their husbands had not only committed adultery but also cruelty or another serious offense, an inequality that persisted until the Matrimonial Causes Act of 1923. Finally as the historian Roderick Phillips noted "The United States of America assumes particular importance in the history of divorce in the nineteenth century," with divorce rates rising rapidly from the middle of the century.[15] Whereas there were 7,380 divorces in 1860, by 1910 there were 83,045, or 0.9 per thousand population.[16] Although divorce law was a matter for individual states, which liberalized at different rates, it was in the west of the country that "the legal and other foundations were laid for what would become the especially high divorce rates in the Midwest and West of the nation," leading to the United States becoming the divorce capital of the world, with no European nation in 1910 having a rate above 0.5 per thousand population and most below 0.2 per thousand.[17]

In sum, there is no clear pattern to the development of divorce laws and practice in the West in the long nineteenth century and certainly no linear narrative of gradual liberalization. On the contrary, both France and Germany had more liberal divorce laws at the end of the eighteenth century than at the end of the nineteenth century. While divorce was a legal possibility in most Western countries by the end of the nineteenth century, the main ground for divorce sanctioned by the legal codes in France and Germany as much as in England was adultery. It would be the United States that led the way in reintroducing the possibility that had pertained at the end of the eighteenth century in France and in the Protestant German states throughout the nineteenth century of divorce by mutual consent or because one partner desired to terminate an unhappy marriage. Yet for all the lack of similarity in the development of laws of divorce in the West in the nineteenth century, paradoxically there are nevertheless some striking patterns of similarity in the depiction of divorce in Western literature in the long nineteenth century that will be explored in this chapter.

DIVORCE IN FICTION AROUND 1800

For some critics, the prevailing subject of at least the English novel up to the middle of the nineteenth century was not the married state at all, but courtship, echoing the views expressed in this classic quotation from the English novelist William Thackeray's *Vanity Fair*:

> As his hero and heroine pass the matrimonial barrier, the novelist generally drops the curtain, as if the drama were over then; the doubts and struggles of life ended: as if, once landed in the marriage country, all were green and pleasant there: and wife and husband had nothing to do but to link each other's arms together, and wander gently downwards towards old age in happy and perfect fruition.[18]

This view became something of a critical commonplace in the wake of Stanford critic Ian Watt's influential *The Rise of the Novel* first published in 1957, which argued that marriage in novels marks the end of the narrative, with the courtship plot regarded as the dominant mode of English fiction.[19] The novels of Jane Austen at the beginning of the nineteenth century are generally regarded as the apotheosis of this tradition of courtship fiction. Yet as Watt himself acknowledged, the plot of one of the seminal early novels, Samuel Richardson's *Pamela; or Virtue Rewarded* (1740) goes beyond the marriage rites to focus on the married state itself,[20] and in recent times the traditional view of eighteenth-century fiction as predominantly focusing on courtship at the expense of marriage has been increasingly challenged, with a number of critics exploring the representation of marriage and its discontents.[21] This challenge has, however, rarely extended to an exploration of early representations of divorce in fiction that began to appear at the end of the eighteenth century.[22]

The Canadian critic Chris Roulston's contention with regard to English and French fiction that "while divorce could be theoretically imagined in polemical works, it was only rarely actualized within realist fiction" certainly holds true for much of the eighteenth century, and not just in England and France.[23] Nonetheless, pioneering female novelists writing in German in the wake of the publication of what is generally regarded as the first German language novel by a woman, Sophie von La Roche's *Geschichte des Fräuleins von Sternheim* (The History of Lady Sophia Sternheim) in 1771 did begin to explore the narrative possibility of divorce as early as the 1780s. Moreover, it is my contention that it is not by chance that depictions of divorce in German literature in the late eighteenth and early nineteenth century occur predominantly in fiction written by women, as this reflects not only the traditional importance of marriage in the lives of women but also the strikingly high incidence of divorce amongst women writers at this time. In a bibliography of novels and stories by women covering the period from 1771 to 1810, of the 103 writers featured whose biographical details were known, 27 percent were unmarried, but more surprisingly, 37 percent of those who did marry divorced at least once.[24] In other words, over a quarter of the writers were divorced at least once. Thus, not only does divorce feature prominently as a topos in German novels of the period written by women, but divorce can also be said to have been an important factor in the very establishment of a tradition of novel writing by women in Germany.

In looking briefly at divorce in early German novels predominantly by women, we will see the emergence of typical features that persist in fiction featuring divorce throughout the long nineteenth century and across Western literature. The most striking of these is the extraordinary caution that writers adopted in depicting divorce, indicating that even in a society where divorce was legally possible, and comparatively relatively widely practiced,[25] including by many of the writers themselves, there remained strong psychological impediments to the representation of divorce. Thus, the predominant theme in the novels of early German women novelists writing around 1800 is the suffering of wives trapped in loveless marriages of convenience, their happiness sacrificed to social convention. While these novels can be read as a cautious critique of the prevailing marriage system,[26] the most conservative of these novels are unable even to contemplate divorce as an option, or where it does occur, as for example in Meta Liebeskind's *Maria* (1784), it results from villainy and is in no way endorsed by the text as legitimate. Indeed, even though Marie's [*sic*] divorce from her husband is not her fault and seems to free her up to marry her ideal partner, the novel ends instead with her death. As so often in novels of the period by women, artificial, unconvincing, and self-imposed barriers to the union of well-suited couples in marriage by means of divorce are erected, so that renunciation is privileged over fulfillment in love.[27]

This avoidance of divorce even where it is clearly legally possible and even socially acceptable is not confined to novels by women, however. Goethe's *Die Wahlverwandtschaften*, as I have argued elsewhere at length, is a novel profoundly of and about divorce, with divorce being not only a compulsive topic of conversation for the characters but an omnipresent narrative possibility that haunts the text.[28] Yet Goethe's novel ultimately avoids divorce, ending instead with the death of Eduard and Ottilie, with the latter's death from that mystery illness to which so many women in nineteenth-century novels succumb seemingly the only narrative device available to forestall Eduard's intended divorce from his wife Charlotte to be united with Ottilie. Goethe's text exemplifies that even where divorce was both legally possible and socially acceptable, there could be profound psychological impediments to divorce, a phenomenon found throughout the nineteenth century. It set the tone of resignation that would predominate in German literature in the period following the Congress of Vienna in 1815 through to the turbulent 1840s.

A second typical feature of early German divorce novels is that where writers were able to break with the presumption against divorce, there is a relatively consistent set of circumstances that typically pertain for divorce to succeed and be represented as legitimate. The first of these is that the marriage in question should as a rule be childless, with duty to family always trumping aspirations toward self-fulfillment in love. Abandonment or neglect of children, by wives in particular, but not only wives,[29] is profoundly shocking to the nineteenth-century reader and frequently used as a narrative device to demonize female characters, perhaps most famously in Flaubert's *Madame Bovary* (1857), where a key marker of the destructiveness of Emma's adultery is her ill-treatment of her daughter Berthe and the latter's sad fate. The second is that the party seeking the divorce should be the innocent party, with their spouse represented in a negative light. Third, a divorcing woman should not become a free agent but pass rapidly from her husband into the arms of a more suitable match. Rare indeed are depictions of separation or divorce that lead to female autonomy and self-determination, though examples do exist, as for example in Marianne Ehrmann's *Amalie* (1788), where the eponymous central character after much renunciation eventually leaves her violent husband and lives as a single woman, rather than divorcing in order to remarry (albeit after many adventures she does eventually remarry at the end of the novel, and also typically her former husband is reported to have died in the interim). Fourth, where a divorce does occur in order to facilitate an ideal marriage between partners who are bound by an elective affinity, it is very typical that the new romantic relationship in some sense predates the marriage to the unsuitable partner. Thus, typically a courtship between ideally suited partners is thwarted by an outside intervention such as an arranged marriage engineered by parents, as for example in Regina Frohberg's *Verrath und Treue* (Betrayal and Loyalty, 1812).

These patterns can also be observed in French and English fiction that depicts divorce around 1800. For example, in the most famous French novel of the period to focus on divorce, Germaine de Staël's *Delphine* (1802), the divorce of Mme Lebensei that is presented very positively was from a cruel husband, and their marriage was childless. By the same token, Delphine feels unable to accept that Léonce, the man she loves, should divorce his wife Mathilde to facilitate their union, not least because Mathilde is pregnant and her behavior is not such as would warrant the fate of being divorced against her wishes. Moreover, even the subsequent deaths of Mathilde and her child do not lead to the marriage of Delphine and Léonce. For in ways that parallel *Die Wahlverwandtschaften*, psychological barriers eventually replace legal and social ones to the union of the star-crossed couple, with Léonce's words holding true for so many nineteenth-century narratives that contemplate divorce only to shy away from it: "Of all the torments, surely the most frightful, the most extraordinary is to find in our own hearts a feeling that separates us from the object of our tenderness, to harbor the obstacle in ourselves when all other obstacles have disappeared."[30]

In *Delphine* the spokesperson for the liberalization of divorce notes that "it is true that divorce will displease some people far more for being the result of a revolution they detest than for any other reason,"[31] and there is no doubt that the association of divorce with revolution was very strong in the minds of those writers, be they conservative or radical, whose works focused on divorce in England in the 1790s and the first decade of the nineteenth century. The passage of the revolutionary divorce law in France in 1792 had profound reverberations in England, not least because it coincided with an upsurge in petitions for divorce in England, and fueled what Katherine Binhammer called "the sex panic of the 1790s."[32] Divorce had certainly featured in English novels as far back as the 1750s, as for example in Sarah Fielding's *The History of the Countess of Dellwyn* (1759), which, in line with the legal reality of the time, presents divorce as a punishment for the adulterous wife. It is, however, around 1800 that the issue of divorce first becomes more prominent in the English novel, with conservatives and liberals responding in contrasting ways to the provocation of French revolutionary divorce.

The dominant mode of representation of divorce in English fiction around 1800 was undoubtedly as a punishment for adultery by the straying wife. For example, Eliza, the wife of Colonel Brandon's brother in Austen's *Sense and Sensibility*, committed adultery and was divorced by her husband, her fate being to "sink deeper into a life of sin," poverty, consumption, and death,[33] while the wife of the Earl of Glenhorn in Maria Edgeworth's *Ennui* (1809), after leaving her husband to be with her lover, is eventually rejected by him and "died in extreme poverty and wretchedness."[34] Indeed, Edgeworth demonized divorce explicitly as a dangerous import from France in her fiction, with *Leonora* (1806) a conscious reaction against de Staël's *Delphine*, which appeared when Edgeworth was staying in Paris in 1802. Lady Olivia left her husband, took a lover in France, then leaving her child there returned to England in an attempt to steal the husband of Leonora, the epitome of English domestic wifely virtue. Lady Olivia's behavior is all the more dastardly in that Leonora is pregnant and gives birth to a child at the time that her husband is lured away from her, but eventually Lady Olivia's scheme is foiled, Leonora's husband returns to her, and Lady Olivia is forced to flee to the Continent again.

If Edgeworth's depiction of divorce in her novels represents the conservative pole of reaction in English fiction to liberalization of divorce on the Continent, and especially France, then Mary Wollstonecraft's (Figure 7.2) remarkable *Maria or The Wrongs of Woman* (1798) is at the opposite end of the spectrum and a milestone in the history

FIGURE 7.2 John Opie (1761–1807), *Portrait of Mary Wollstonecraft, c.* 1797, oil on canvas. National Portrait Gallery via Getty Images.

of representations of divorce in Western fiction. Maria is literally imprisoned in her marriage to a libertine husband to prevent her escape, leading to her famous lament that "marriage had bastilled me for life."[35] This makes explicit that Wollstonecraft's campaign through her novel for legal reform of marriage and divorce is inspired by the Revolution in France, which commenced with the storming of the Bastille prison in Paris. In this novel, as so often, the presence of a child represents an obstacle to divorce, and it is only the death of her child after it is forcibly removed from her that "dissolved the only tie which subsisted between me and my, what is termed, lawful husband."[36]

The importance of *Maria* as a novel of divorce is amplified in that it is the first literary representation in the English novel of a criminal conversation or divorce trial. In its focus on the public interrogation of female sexuality it anticipates the divorce court journalism and literary culture arising from it that flourished following the passage of the Matrimonial Causes Act in 1857, explored so illuminatingly by Barbara Leckie.[37] During her imprisonment, Maria meets Darnford and becomes his lover. On her escape, her husband sues Darnford for adultery. At the trial, Maria pleads guilty in an effort to secure a legal divorce from her husband to marry Darnford, telling the court "I claim then a divorce."[38] The judge, however, rejects her demand, noting that "we did not want French principles in public or private life," and the conclusion of his judgment is a classic statement of the conservative position on divorce that would be echoed in debates throughout the nineteenth century: "too many restrictions could not be thrown in the way of divorce, if we wish to maintain the sanctity of marriage; and though they might bear a little hard on a few, very few individuals, it was evidently for the good of the whole."[39] For most of the nineteenth century, debates about divorce raged between conservatives who adopted this line and liberals who, in the wake of the French Revolution and the rise of Romanticism, believed that the rights of the individual to pursue happiness at the expense of the institution of marriage should take precedence.[40]

Wollstonecraft's unfinished novel breaks off at this point during the trial, but she did leave various brief notes of possible endings for the novel that were published when the novel appeared posthumously. Two of these mention a separation of bed and board rather than a full divorce, but the shortest of all the notes shows how strongly ingrained was the idea of divorce as disastrous for women in the psyche even of as radical a novelist as Wollstonecraft at this time: "Divorced by her husband—Her lover unfaithful—Pregnancy—Miscarriage—Suicide."[41] Had the novel ended in this way it would have mirrored the dominant paradigm of divorce as punishment for transgressive behavior by a wife, but interestingly Wollstonecraft also drafted one page of a possible alternative ending. Having swallowed poison, Maria awaits her death, thinking of her supposedly dead child, but then the child is brought to her, she vomits, and the draft concludes with her words, "I will live for my child!"[42]

Nor was Wollstonecraft alone amongst novelists writing in English around 1800 in being able to envisage the possibility of women surviving marital breakdown, with the central character in Mary Robinson's *The Natural Daughter* (1799) telling the story of a wife abandoned to her fate by her husband, who is able nevertheless to survive as a single woman and like Ehrmann's Amalie only marries again at the very end of the novel. An even more surprising example is Sarah Gooch's novel *The Contrast* (1795).[43] This tells the story of Lady Jane, who after entering a loveless marriage falls in love with Glencairn, but he withdraws from her in order not to endanger her marriage. Her husband, suspicious of her relations with another man, Lord Darnley, abandons her and attempts to secure a divorce from her. She not only then becomes Darnley's lover but also takes on a series of other lovers when Darnley tells her he has no intention of marrying her, and she appears destined to sink into poverty and sexual exploitation, like so many in her situation before and after her. Yet in a very surprising reversal, not least because early in the novel the narrator had set out the archetypal fate that awaits the abandoned wife,[44] she escapes this fate, in that when Glencairn returns from India several years later they are united as lovers, albeit discreetly, until after a year the news of her estranged husband's death allows them to marry.

The depiction of marital separation and divorce was, therefore, by no means uncommon in English as much as continental fiction around 1800. Indeed, even though England had very much more restrictive divorce laws than France or the Protestant German states at this time, it is hard to discern this from the way in which divorce is represented in fiction. Thus, even in Jane Austen, whose plots typically focus on courtship, not marriage, one comes across a kind of matter-of-fact treatment of divorce, as for example in the final chapter of *Mansfield Park*, where the narrator notes blandly "Mr Rushworth had no difficulty in procuring a divorce."[45]

Comparing the representation of divorce in novels by German, French, and English novelists around 1800 reveals that divorce became an important literary topic for women writers across Europe during this period. While many novelists, notably in England, adopted a conservative stance, depicting divorce as punishment for wifely adultery and depicting the miserable demise of women after divorce, the most important divorce novels of the period such as those by Ehrmann, de Staël, and Wollstonecraft are distinguished by their exploration of the possibility of divorce, and life after divorce, for innocent wives. These texts begin to challenge the paradigm of the suffering wife and tentatively to raise the possibility of divorce as a means to the pursuit of happiness for women. They constitute an attempt by women to secure for themselves the same opportunities that were becoming possible for men, with the English historian Lawrence Stone noting for this period in the English context "the shift of the function of Parliamentary divorce from the protection of property to the pursuit of happiness, defined as getting rid of an adulterous wife in order to remarry."[46] While Wollstonecraft in particular sought to challenge patriarchal marriage and divorce laws head on, and *Delphine* too contains important reflection on the legal issues surrounding divorce, one surprising observation is the comparative lack of focus on the legal aspects of, and barriers to, divorce. Indeed, divorce appears to be relatively accessible not only in Germany but also in England, even though divorce in England was in practice much rarer than the novels of the period would appear to suggest. What also emerges is the generally cautious and ambivalent approach to the subject of divorce even where there are apparently few barriers to divorce, a notable tendency being the substitution of psychological barriers for legal ones, often in the shape of a strong taboo on divorce where the marriage has produced children, as in *Delphine* and *Die Wahlverwandtschaften*. That caution would only increase after 1800 as divorce came to be strongly correlated with (French) revolution, not only in France but in English discussions of divorce not only in the novels of the period but also in Parliament.[47] Thus, by the first decade of the nineteenth century, a European-wide reaction to the brief period of literary as well as legal experimentation with divorce was underway, resulting in representations of divorce becoming relatively infrequent in Britain, France, and Germany from around 1815 until the 1840s in the German states, the 1850s in England, and the 1880s in France, whilst in the United States the first novel of divorce is generally considered to be William Dean Howells's *A Modern Instance* (1881).[48]

THE DOMINANT TRADITION: THE NOVEL OF ADULTERY AND THE AVOIDANCE OF DIVORCE

If adulterous wives are largely confined to the margins of the novels of Jane Austen and her contemporaries, this changed in the course of the nineteenth century as adultery moved from the margins to the center of narrative interest amongst male novelists, especially on the Continent. Here one thinks of Flaubert's *Madame Bovary* (1857), Zola's *Thérèse Raquin* (1867), Tolstoy's *Anna Karenina* (1877), and Fontane's *Effi Briest* (1895) or in North America *The Scarlet Letter* (1850) by Nathaniel Hawthorne. The common thread running through these novels and countless others besides is that they are novels of female adultery, to borrow the designation for such narratives coined by the British critic Bill Overton, who explored these fictions extensively.[49] These narratives focus on the disastrous consequences of adultery for their female protagonists and typically end with the death of the adulteress. Where divorce does occur, as in *Effi Briest*, it is depicted as a punishment for transgressive behavior by the wife, albeit Fontane's text invokes sympathy for Effi as her rule-bound Prussian society insists that she pays the price for her transgression of the marriage bonds long after her single act of adultery. Thus, even though, as Turner has shown, Tolstoy's original plan for *Anna Karenina* (1877) envisaged her getting a divorce, allowing her to marry Vronsky (the original title of the novel, "Two Marriages," is interpreted by Turner as referring to Anna's two marriages), this outcome was eventually avoided in favor of her suicide. Yet it is noteworthy that even in that early version divorce was not presented as the resolution of the plot, but rather Anna was still to have come to an unhappy end through suicide.[50]

If fictions of female adultery by male authors represent one dominant narrative tradition in the nineteenth century, another is composed of novels that look set to depict divorce, only for that outcome ultimately to be avoided. Goethe's *Die Wahlverwandtschaften* set the tone for such novels of renunciation, and a number of classic novels of the nineteenth century likewise either explicitly or implicitly suggest the need for and the possibility of divorce as a potential plot resolution, only to avoid it in the end. To take one classic example, the plot of Henry James's *The Portrait of a Lady* (1881) culminates in the question of whether Isabel Archer will divorce her husband Osmond to be united with Caspar Goodwood. As Melissa Ganz notes, "an argument in favour of divorce" remains "ever present but always implicit in the text," but finally Isabel rejects the possibility of divorce, and James would again set his face against divorce as the resolution of marital crisis in *The Golden Bowl* (1904).[51]

Another typical plot structure of nineteenth-century novels involves what might be termed the disguised depiction of divorce, with that disguise usually taking the form of the convenient death of one of the marriage partners so as to bring about the union of a couple that would otherwise only have been possible by means of divorce. Such novels were particularly prevalent in English fiction and are indicative both of the practical barriers to divorce especially prior to the 1857 Matrimonial Causes Act and of the psychological barriers to divorce or, where that was not possible, living in a quasi-marital union outside wedlock. Charlotte Brontë's *Jane Eyre* (1847) is perhaps the most celebrated example of a novel that compellingly makes the case for the necessity of divorce (in this case on the grounds of incurable madness), while at the same time avoiding the depiction of divorce in practice. Nevertheless, although Jane refuses to live outside wedlock with Rochester after their marriage ceremony is interrupted by the news that he is already married, they are eventually united in marriage after his deranged wife Bertha commits suicide. In similar vein, *The Tenant of Wildfell Hall* (1848) by Charlotte's sister Anne Brontë, simultaneously illustrates the plight of a wife unable to divorce her dissolute husband, whilst also ultimately bringing about a resolution of the situation through the death of the husband, which clears the way for Helen to marry Gilbert. Markers of the caution with which separation and divorce are presented include the fact that Helen fled from her husband not for her own sake but for the sake of her child, and also that she agrees to return to her husband to nurse him prior to his death. Other female writers of the time remained wedded to the plot of female renunciation, refusing the option of resolving the plot through the death of the husband. A poignant example is *Stuart of Dunleath* (1851) by the great campaigner for divorce reform Caroline Norton. Famously unable to secure a divorce herself, Norton's heroine in this novel separates from her husband but is psychologically unable to pursue the option of divorce for fear of appearing to be motivated by a desire to be united with the person with whom she is in love and instead dies.[52]

Possibly the most famous novel of disguised divorce is George Eliot's *Middlemarch* (1871–72), which masks its divorce plot by having Dorothea "divorce" her husband Causabon after his death. The terms of Causabon's will mean that she will lose her inheritance if she marries Will Ladislaw, so that in effect Causabon attempts to bind Dorothea indissolubly to him in marriage even after his death. At the end of the novel Dorothea decides to defy this attempt to keep her shackled to her deceased husband and renouncing her inheritance, she marries Ladislaw.

Thus, in many of the classic novels of the nineteenth century, by both male and female writers, the question of divorce is raised, often more implicitly than explicitly, but the depiction of divorce is ultimately avoided, with that avoidance taking a variety of forms: renunciation, the death of the adulteress, or the timely death of a highly unsuitable marital partner, which clears the way for the romantic union of an ideally suited couple. It is rather in the less canonical works of female writers around the middle of the nineteenth century that we see the reemergence of the kinds of plot lines involving divorce as a means of emancipation of women that we encountered around 1800.

RADICAL ALTERNATIVES: DIVORCE AND FEMALE EMANCIPATION

The 1840s were a period of political turmoil across continental Europe, culminating in a series of revolutions in 1848. In Prussia that political turmoil was closely connected with the subject of divorce, as the Prussian Kaiser Friedrich Wilhelm IV after his accession in 1840 appointed Friedrich Carl von Savigny in 1842 with a brief to curtail the relatively liberal grounds for divorce in the *Allgemeines Landrecht*. That attempt at legal reform failed in the face of liberal opposition, with the young Karl Marx publishing the leaked plans for law reform in the *Rheinische Zeitung* in 1844. It was against this turbulent political and legal backdrop that a new generation of women novelists writing in German, including Louise Aston (1814–71), Fanny Lewald (1811–89), and Ida Gräfin Hahn-Hahn (1805–80), often repeatedly addressed the issue of divorce in their novels, breaking with the tradition of renunciation that had prevailed in the restoration period from 1815. Thus, in her divorce novel *Eine Lebensfrage* ("A Vital Issue," or literally translated "A Question of Life and Death") of 1845 Fanny Lewald explicitly counters the rejection of divorce in Goethe's *Die Wahlverwandtschaften*, and "corrects" the ending of his novel by allowing the correct partners to be married following divorce.[53] The stance of Lewald's novel is that romantic love should triumph over the state's interest in the stability of marriage, with divorce portrayed as a safety valve that is necessary in order to bring together ideally suited partners kept apart by circumstances. This novel is a barometer of the rise of the ideology of romantic love in the course of the nineteenth century that would be the key to the long-term rise and social acceptability of divorce in the West.[54]

For all that, Lewald's position remains relatively conservative. Some German women novelists of the 1840s moved away from the relatively conservative idea of divorce as means to unite ideally suited lovers, which necessarily means that women continue to be defined in relation to marriage. Louise Aston, for example, who herself divorced her husband not once but twice, in *Aus dem Leben einer Frau* (From the Life of a Woman) published in 1847 depicts the escape from marriage of an oppressed wife in a manner reminiscent of novels by women in the late eighteenth century. In sharp contrast to Anne Brontë in *The Tenant of Wildfell Hall*, however, Aston leaves open the trajectory of the oppressed and escaping wife. Yet Aston's novel still ends with a reaffirmation of the centrality of marriage inasmuch as the narrator weighs in on the last page to say that the central character rescued the holiness of marriage by tearing it apart.[55] It is perhaps above all the novelist Ida Hahn-Hahn, like so many nineteenth-century women writers who wrote about divorce also a divorcée herself, who most radically breaks with the idea of the centrality of marriage for women and whose works explore in a surprisingly modern way what it means to be an autonomous woman after divorce, so that, for example, in *Der Rechte* (The Right One) (1842) the central character Catherine is twice divorced within the first fifty pages of a three hundred page novel.[56]

In England, by contrast, the majority of novels around the mid-century that featured divorce were to a greater or lesser extent conservative tales. At the most conservative end of the spectrum were plots that warned women against divorce, such as Lady Charlotte Bury's *The Divorced* (1837), which shows the utterly disastrous consequences of divorce and remarriage for the wife, or *East Lynne* (1861) by Mrs. Henry Wood in which a woman who is divorced by her husband on account of her adultery returns as the unrecognized governess of her own children. This narrative device provides ample opportunity to reinforce the message of the folly of her behavior. In her survey of English novels from 1837 to 1869 featuring divorce, Anne Humpherys notes that a key narrative issue is whether to allow the divorcing party to make a second, more fulfilling marriage after divorce.[57] Contrary to the German narratives discussed above, Humpherys notes that in the English novel of the time "the results of the divorce or even judicial separation, however, are always disastrous for the woman," as for example in William Makepeace Thackeray's *The Newcomes*.[58] English novelists were caught in the "contradiction between the intent to expose the legal injustice and the denial of any remedy," and there was an upsurge in novels about bigamy around the middle of the century as a means of evading the implication that divorce might be both morally and socially acceptable.

This is not to say that there are not isolated examples of novels in English from mid-century that offer more radical alternatives, as Humpherys notes. Thus, in *Mauleverer's Divorce: A Story of a Woman's Wrongs* (1858), a novel written during the passage of the Matrimonial Causes Act but set in the 1840s, Emma Robinson depicts two attempted divorces, with the one by a dissolute husband succeeding and the one by an oppressed wife failing. The novel is both a plea for reform of divorce law and deeply ambivalent about the effects of divorce on women, as the divorced wife is left in precarious economic and social circumstances.

The upsurge in fictions of marital breakdown and divorce in the 1840s in the German states, and around the passage of the Matrimonial Causes Act in 1857 in England, was, however, relatively short-lived. The period from around the middle of the century on until the 1880s is, like the period from 1815 to the 1840s, characterized by a relative dearth of representations of divorce. The same is true in France, where divorce was still not available legally until 1884, though one novel entitled *Un divorce* (1866) by André Léo, the pseudonym of Léodile Béra (1824–1900), also known as Mme de Champseix, did depict divorce by adopting the device of geographical displacement to Protestant Switzerland, though in the end there is a conservative twist to what is otherwise a liberal narrative in that the divorcing wife abstains from establishing a new relationship with the man she loves.[59] In the German states in particular, the representation of divorce in fiction comes to an abrupt halt by 1850 until Theodor Fontane's groundbreaking novel *L'Adultera*, published in book form in 1882. Indeed, this novel's exceptionally liberal depiction of divorce is all the more remarkable for appearing at a time when the topic of divorce was otherwise virtually completely absent from German fiction following the conservative reaction after the revolutionary period of the 1840s. For not only does the novel contain a depiction of divorce but Melanie, the adulteress of the title, in leaving her husband also breaks another taboo by abandoning her two daughters and yet survives to tell the tale, marrying her lover and eventually regaining the respect of society.

Appearing shortly before *L'Adultera*, the Norwegian playwright Henrik Ibsen's *A Doll's House* (1879), possibly the most famous play by certainly the greatest dramatist of the nineteenth century, is another groundbreaking text of marital breakdown, as at the conclusion of the play Nora leaves her husband, slamming the door behind her. The profoundly shocking nature of this ending is magnified by the fact that Nora leaves behind not only her husband but also her children, thereby breaking one of the strongest taboos in the literary representation of marital breakdown and divorce in the nineteenth century. In the succeeding decades, dramatists across Europe followed Ibsen in exploring marital crises, women's roles, marital breakdown, and divorce, and nowhere more so than in Germany and Austria, where Ibsen's popularity was greater and his influence more profound than anywhere else. During the 1880s and especially during the 1890s Germany was in the process of drawing up a new civil code that would unify family law for the whole of Germany following German Unification in 1871. This coincided with the rise of socialist and feminist movements in Germany and an extraordinary proliferation of public discourse about marriage and divorce. As I have argued at length elsewhere, much German and Austrian drama of the 1890s and early 1900s, taking its cue from Ibsen, focuses on the question of whether the characters will or will not separate or divorce—key examples being Gerhart Hauptmann's *Einsame Menschen* (1890), Max Halbe's *Mutter Erde* (1897), or in Austria Arthur Schnitzler's *Zwischenspiel* (1905).[60] What is striking about the exploration of divorce by German dramatists in the 1890s is the extent to which the representation of divorce in their plays in many ways played out the same conflicts explored by writers a century earlier. Playwrights dramatized the same tensions between on the one hand the aspirations of individuals, usually wives, trapped in loveless and typically childless marriages to unsympathetic husbands, to be united with their soul mates whom they have usually known since before the unhappy marriage, and on the other hand deep-rooted fears about female emancipation and the social effects of undermining the stability of marriage. As my detailed survey of such plays demonstrates, only a few works matched the radicalism of *A Doll's House* in depicting marriages that led to women freeing themselves from marriage altogether,[61] just as such outcomes were very rare a century earlier, with the effects of police censorship of the theater undoubtedly curbing the most radical depictions of the rottenness of the state of marriage, female emancipation, and the need for liberal divorce laws.

If Ibsen's play, albeit with a delay of around a decade, ushered in an upsurge in dramatic treatments of divorce, especially in Germany, in France it was the reintroduction in 1884 of the legal possibility of divorce that would bring about a profound change in the representation of marriage in French fiction, bringing to an end the era of the novel of adultery, a change that was quite consciously perceived by novelists at the time. As Zola, reflecting on the impending introduction of divorce in France, famously put it in his essay "Le divorce et la literature" of 1881, "there will be two repertoires: the repertoire before divorce and the one after; and the first will be scarcely more than a dramatic museum, where one goes to see bygone social behaviour, just as one goes to see works of art from the past at the Louvre."[62] The subsequent history of the novel in France bears out Zola's prediction. If, as we saw earlier, much of the nineteenth century is the age of the novel of adultery, and most especially in France in the wake of Flaubert's *Madame Bovary* (1857), and it is surely not by coincidence that following the legalization of divorce in France, this novelistic genre is generally regarded as having come to an end by the end of the nineteenth century at the latest, not only in France but more generally in Western literature.[63] Moreover, it would be less than a year after the legalization of divorce that one of the heavyweights of French fiction, Guy de Maupassant, would publish *Bel Ami*, a novel in which divorce features as a major plot element. As Nicholas White's study of divorce in French fiction has shown, in subsequent decades a particular focus of French divorce fiction would be the question of remarriage after divorce.[64]

It is clear that many novels of the second half of the nineteenth century are not as radical or progressive in their representation of divorce as those written during the revolutionary period at the end of the eighteenth century, with divorce if anything more of a taboo subject.[65] The furor surrounding the publication of Thomas Hardy's *Jude*

FIGURE 7.3 William Quiller Orchardson (1832–1910), *The First Cloud*, 1887, oil on canvas. National Gallery of Victoria, Melbourne.

the Obscure in 1895, which profoundly shocked Victorian readers though ultimately depicting the reversal of the divorces of Jude and Sue from their spouses, is testimony to this. Moreover, while the topic of divorce became more prominent in English fiction during the Edwardian period at the beginning of the twentieth century with the rise of a new wave of feminism and a new generation of women writers, as Jane Eldridge Miller has noted, "although adultery and divorce are discussed and contemplated in these novels, they are rarely realized," and indeed "most marriage problem novels go to great lengths to avoid associating their heroines with divorce, or with any kind of illicit sexuality."[66] This is very much not the case, however, in the American novelist Kate Chopin's seminal novel of female emancipation, *The Awakening* (1899), which both deals frankly with the issue of a woman's sexual desire but also directly challenges the notion of divorce as a mechanism to bring together ideally suited individuals. Rather, divorce is presented here as a form of emancipation from patriarchal control. Thus, although Edna Pontellier's awakening is triggered by her interaction with Robert, she does not

FIGURE 7.4 *Kate Chopin in Riding Habit*, 1876, portrait. Missouri History Museum via Wikimedia.

leave her husband specifically in order to be united with him. Instead, she moves out of the marital home and then has a sexual relationship with Alcée Arobin, even though she knows that she does not love him nor he her. Then in her last conversation with Robert she explicitly rejects the idea of divorce as a transfer of a woman from husband to lover: "I am no longer one of Mr. Pontellier's possessions to dispose of or not. I give myself where I choose. If he were to say, 'Here, Robert, take her and be happy; she is yours,' I should laugh at you both."[67] The ending of the novel, where Edna rejects the option of a union with Robert and instead enters the waves in an ambiguous act of suicide/liberation illustrates the difficulty even for the most radical writers of imagining life after divorce for women, a difficulty that runs like a red thread through nineteenth-century divorce fiction.

THE BANALITY OF DIVORCE AFTER 1900

In recent years a number of critics have posited a connection between divorce and the development of the narrative experimentation of modernism. Anne Humphreys, for example, comments that "the introduction of divorce into the conventional marriage plot resulted in a disruption of form that made the novel more multi-voiced, more diffuse, more open-ended—divorce, in other words, is a factor in the development of the modernist and postmodernist experiments in narrative form."[68] Jennifer Haytock, noting that "divorce is an often overlooked factor in the study of modernist writing," is particularly persuasive in arguing that divorce is a modernist phenomenon par excellence:

> Modernism presupposes a sense of separation—from inherited institutions, from God, from others, from oneself—that becomes real and concrete in the form of divorce, an event that breaks a union that is perceived by Christianity and Western culture (especially in the years leading up to the modernist movement) as permanent. Marriage itself becomes a locus for fractured identity, problems of communication, and loss of meaning in words.[69]

In her conclusion, Haytock goes so far as to argue that "divorce—the breaking of a perceived permanent relationship—becomes a metaphor for the modernist project."[70]

Yet despite these claims about the relationship between divorce and modernism, divorce was not in fact a subject that pre-occupied the writers of high modernism who engaged in the kinds of formal experimentation identified by these critics as quintessentially modernist. Rather, it was those less formally experimental writers of what Chris Baldick refers to as the "broader modern movement," such as Arnold Bennett and John Galsworthy in England, who were particularly concerned with the representation of divorce in fiction.[71] Whereas throughout the nineteenth century, divorce, whether depicted or avoided in fiction, was represented as a matter of high stakes, a potent disruptive, or liberating force for the individual and potentially the state, in the period after 1900 divorce begins to be represented not as high stakes but commonplace, even banal. This is perhaps best captured in Edith Wharton's story *Madame de Treymes* (1907) (Figure 7.5), where Fanny de Malrive's mother views the approaching divorce of her American daughter from a French aristocrat as nothing more than "an uncomfortable but commonplace necessity, like house-cleaning or dentistry."[72] Moreover, it is not only in American literature that divorce is depicted as prosaic. In Jakob Wassermann's *Laudin und die Seinen* (1925), the divorce lawyer Laudin is positively worn down by the volume of cases he has to deal with,[73] while in Arnold Bennett's *Whom God Hath Joined* (1906), divorce is similarly represented as a grubby, commonplace business.

FIGURE 7.5 Illustration opposite page 116 of the first book edition of Edith Wharton, *Madame de Treymes* (New York: Charles Scribner's Sons, 1907). Public Domain via Wikimedia Commons.

It is not just that divorce is increasingly no longer represented as a momentous event in this period. In contrast to earlier periods, divorce or its avoidance begins no longer to be presented primarily in terms of its importance in the context of romance plots that focus on individuals and their marriages. This is in marked contrast to many novels of the nineteenth century, and not just the second half of the nineteenth century, where the key question is typically how a marriage crisis will be resolved, with divorce often a potential, if not an actual, possibility that sustains much of the suspense of the plot. In fiction written during the modern period, what might be called the divorce question—in the sense of will there be a divorce or not—begins in some important works involving divorce to cease to be of central interest. In Bennett's *Whom God Hath Joined*, for example, the focus is not on divorce as a mechanism to bring together individuals in love nor on female liberation but, rather, the realities of the divorce court. As Janice Hubbard Harris summed up: "Element after element of the romance plot is refuted."[74]

It is not just the refuting of the romance plot that is distinctively new in the representation of divorce during this period, however. While earlier fiction had often criticized the weak economic position of women in marriage, which had frequently made divorce unattainable or undesirable for women, in the early twentieth century there is a focus for the first time on what we might term the economics of divorce more broadly and more particularly the role that divorce plays in the economy of the family. William Dean Howells's *A Modern Instance* (1882) can be regarded as a forerunner of this shift in focus, with marital breakdown and divorce in that novel being a product of the ill effects of capitalism on the marriage of Bartley and Marcia. As I have argued elsewhere, novels as diverse as Thomas Mann's *Buddenbrooks* (1900), John Galsworthy's *The Forsyte Saga* (1906–22), and Edith Wharton's *The Custom of the Country* (1913) all focus not on romance plots but on the effects of divorce on the family economy.[75] Thus, in *Buddenbrooks* divorce is represented merely as an occupational hazard of bourgeois daughters, and bourgeois families, with the focus being on its disastrous potential not so much for the individual as for the family dynasty. In this novel the grounds for Tony's first divorce from her husband Grünlich are not adultery, or desire by either of them to be with another partner, but rather the inability of the husband to provide for his wife due to his bankruptcy.[76] Meanwhile in John Galsworthy's *The Man of Property* (1906), the first novel in *The Forsyte Saga*, Soames seeks a legal divorce from his long estranged wife not because this "Man of Property" is driven by passion to remarry but because he wishes to secure an heir to his fortune. The focus here again is no longer the individual romance plot, or even divorce as a liberator of women from marital oppression, but the role of divorce in the family economy and the transmission of property, as Young Jolyon, reflecting on divorce, makes clear:

> "The core of it all," he thought, "is property, but there are many people who would not like it put that way. To them it is 'the sanctity of the marriage tie'; but the sanctity of the marriage tie is dependent on the sanctity of the family, and the sanctity of the family is dependent on the sanctity of property."[77]

But the novel that best illustrates both the way in which the representation of divorce has become separated from any romance plot, and the close relationship between divorce and economics during the modern period, is *The Custom of the Country* (1913) by Edith Wharton.[78] Wharton is undoubtedly the preeminent chronicler in fiction of the gradual social acceptance of divorce that would play out in the West over the course of the twentieth century. In this novel, divorce is presented predominantly as a wife's response to economic underperformance by the husband, with the central character, Undine Spragg, in all divorcing three times in the course of the novel. Mr. Dagonet's response to the news that Undine wants a divorce from his grandson perfectly encapsulates the break with the traditional divorce narrative that is the achievement of this novel, and which, it can be argued, is characteristic of the innovative dimension of divorce in the modern period: "I never yet saw a marriage dissolved like a business partnership. Divorce without a lover? Why, it's—it's as unnatural as getting drunk on lemonade."[79] In this novel, people no longer just marry for money, they divorce for money. Divorce is represented as a way of life, at least in parts of American society, so that a French duchess remarks at one point, in response to a query about Undine's husband: "'Her husband? But she's an American— she's divorced' ... as if she were merely stating the same fact in two different ways."[80] In similar vein, Charles Bowen in response to Raymond de Chelles's question: "Why does the obsolete institution of marriage survive with you?" replies: "Oh, it still has its uses.

One couldn't be divorced without it."[81] This is the world of modern divorce, the world of serial monogamy that would become the social norm in elite parts of society in the early twentieth century, especially amongst the Hollywood set and parts of the aristocracy, and, in a kind of trickle-down effect, gradually becoming something of the norm in all parts of Western society.

CONCLUSION

The depiction of divorce in fiction in the nineteenth century has recently finally begun to attract the critical attention it deserves. Its previous neglect can be partly accounted for by the fact that explicit depiction of divorce is found predominantly in the works of less canonical women writers, frequently having its roots in the autobiographical experiences of those women, for whom divorce was frequently the trigger that launched them on their literary careers. Yet a focus on divorce can do more than shed light on a neglected dimension of literary culture. For it can be argued that viewing the more traditional (predominantly male) canon through the lens of and in the context of divorce fiction predominantly by women reveals the extent to which the possibility of divorce, just as much as the depiction of adultery, haunted nineteenth-century fiction in general.

A comparative study of the type attempted here reveals both the patterns of similarity across national and linguistic boundaries as well as the specificities of each separate literary tradition. What has emerged is that the depiction of divorce in the long nineteenth century needs to be viewed against the context not only of the legal history of divorce but also the tides of political and social revolution, the rise of concepts of romantic love, and the uneven ebbs and flows of the women's movements of the nineteenth century. Intuitively it might be supposed that the emergence of divorce in the West in the long nineteenth century was a relatively continuous process of liberalization. In truth, however, the radicalism of both divorce legislation and depictions of divorce at the end of the eighteenth century might occasionally have been equaled at key points during the nineteenth century (notably during the 1840s in Germany and to a lesser extent the 1850s and 1860s in England) but rarely surpassed until the end of the nineteenth century. Then at the beginning of the twentieth century the frame of reference that had persisted throughout the long nineteenth century began to change, with some writers beginning to depict divorce no longer as revolutionary, or as a narrative device in a romance plot, but as banal. Edith Wharton became the preeminent chronicler of those shifting attitudes to divorce, as a remark from her novel *The Glimpses of the Moon* published in 1922 pithily captures: "People had long since ceased to take on tragedy airs about divorce."[82]

This shift coincided with the emergence of a new kind of narrative of divorce, in which the focus shifts away from the role of divorce in the fate of the individual and more toward the wider socioeconomic dimensions of divorce. In sketching the broad contours of the representation across a wide temporal and geographic canvas, some aspects of the rich story of divorce have necessarily not received the attention they deserve, including the complex interplay of divorce and religion, the interplay of wealth and class, and the effects of the general adoption of marriage as the predominant social structure by the working as well as the middle classes in the latter half of the nineteenth century in particular. It is to be hoped that nevertheless this survey will provoke critics and readers to approach Western literature of the long nineteenth century with a fresh perspective.

CHAPTER EIGHT

Representations of Marriage

The Intricate Development of Bourgeois Marriage in Western Europe

MARJA VAN TILBURG

INTRODUCTION

An illustration of nineteenth-century marriage in the Western world seems easy to sketch: picture husband and wife surrounded by their progeny in a homely setting. While the man stands firmly upright, the woman engages with the children. This arrangement conveys family values: all family members are carefully arranged around a table or next to a fireplace, thus communicating ordered relationships and clear roles. The décor draws our attention to the intimacy and comfort of the home, the proverbial haven in a heartless world.[1] It also conveys the wealth of the head of the family and the taste of the woman, both important assets in bourgeois culture. In terms of historiography, this image has been connected to long-term socioeconomic changes in Western societies. Scholars agree that the bourgeois family is tailored to meet the requirements of the market economy: parents invest in preparing their children for a fast-changing world, paying attention to psychological development as much as to social compliance. By separating public and private spheres, the husband is able to focus on his job and the wife can manage the household economically.[2] These features allow the middle classes to adapt to changing circumstances. Furthermore, historians consider this social group to be a driving force within European culture. As the historian Peter Gay pointed out in his voluminous study *The Bourgeois Experience*, it has been connected with the Protestant work ethic, Enlightenment innovation, and democracy. Thus, the bourgeoisie has been credited with an influence much greater than its numbers.[3]

This picture is nearly ideal: not only do the wives make all family members happy but they are also attuned to societal requirements such as preparing children for school and supporting the husband in his hard day's work. How do we analyze such an image? This chapter seeks to unravel its make-up by distinguishing between marriage as a societal institution and marriage as a relationship between a man and a woman, who seek sexual satisfaction and personal fulfillment. At this point, the picture begins to show cracks: the organizational aspects of nineteenth-century marriage were established at the turn of the nineteenth century. These display the influence of Enlightenment thinking on family, society, and progress. The emotional aspects, such as romantic love and maternal

FIGURE 8.1 Engraving of a Victorian family gathered around the table. From an original engraving in the *Girl's Own Paper* magazine, 1883. Lakeview Images/Alamy Stock Photo. Image ID: MMHNNY.

care, developed more slowly. In this context, the slow development of modern sexual identities comes to the fore. At the same time, it is important to stay focused. Marriage is what brings these uneven developments together. The representations of marriage from the period aim toward harmonization and the resolution of tension. Critical studies of the bourgeoisie, however, have tended to concentrate on the dissonant notes. Scholars have focused especially on the disciplining effects of the institution vis-à-vis women and children. Moreover, the implications have been interpreted above and beyond the familial context: those for women have been discussed with reference to women's emancipation or gender, and those for children have been analyzed in terms of the prolongation of childhood or individualization through education. This chapter will discuss these aspects as relevant from the perspective of marriage, while selecting and situating these in the larger picture of the couple trying to navigate the family in a fast-changing world.

This chapter consists of three parts. The first of these discusses marriage as represented in the advice literature for married and soon-to-be-wed couples. Traditionally, this genre aims at helping married couples manage the household in accordance with societal requirements such as household management and budget control. Marriage manuals from the turn of the 1800s show important innovations. The authors stress the joint responsibility of the couple for the family. Furthermore, they teach spouses how to discuss problems and negotiate decisions. Thus, the marriage manual targets the marital relationship.[4] This aspect has caught the attention of historians, who have interpreted this development as a movement from patriarchy to partnership. As a consequence, they have represented the new rapport between spouses as an end in itself.[5] The last part of the argument is incorrect, however. The advice literature presents cooperation as a requirement for a functional family. By prioritizing functionality, marriage manuals aim to help couples adapt to changing socioeconomic circumstances, without addressing developments such as urbanization and industrialization in so many words. This aim testifies to the influence of the Enlightenment and its mission to improve society through education.[6] Moreover, this approach proved useful for later generations: the format of the marriage manual remained the same throughout the long nineteenth century, which extends from the French Revolution to the First World War.[7]

The second part addresses the marital relationship. This topic attracted more attention as the nineteenth century progressed. Change was brought about by different cultural developments, as we shall see. It started with the strict division of tasks and responsibilities between the sexes, advocated by that very advice literature. This division was seemingly corroborated by scientific discoveries suggesting that men's and women's bodies were very different. In this context, the influential *philosophe* Rousseau ascribed men and women opposing but complementary identities.[8] As a consequence, everything pertaining to the social relations between the sexes came under scrutiny. Of course, this trend has been analyzed by many scholars. They have discussed their findings in terms of the social relationships between the sexes or as gender. In this section, the results of this research will be discussed from the perspective of the marital relationship. After all, in the institution of marriage each spouse has a specific role to play. Therefore, the rapport between husband and wife should be distinguished from the sexual asymmetry within bourgeois culture as a whole.

The third and last part of this chapter deals with the role that marriage plays in the disciplining of the individual. Given the critique of bourgeois culture as especially restrictive, this topic needs to be addressed. Once again, the scholarly literature poses a problem, this time because it has drawn inspiration from critical currents within European society such as the fin de siècle and the cultural revolution of the 1960s. Most analysts point out perceived dysfunctional aspects of bourgeois culture, particularly when it comes to gender and sexuality.[9] Because this section is meant to focus on the disciplining effects of marriage, representations of marriage are analyzed in the writings of two contemporary critics. The first is the late eighteenth-century English feminist Mary Wollstonecraft. For her, marriage was an instrument for the subjugation of women. The second is the late nineteenth-century German sexologist and activist Magnus Hirschfeld. He considered marriage unsuitable for many people, even for many heterosexuals. Both of them have been chosen here, because they wrote about marriage in fiction as well as nonfiction. In the oeuvres of both authors the different genres complement one another. Furthermore,

FIGURE 8.2 A Victorian/Edwardian family portrait. Duncan 1890 via Getty Images.

these writings reflect historical change, particularly the increasing attention paid to the marital relationship. Finally, in the context of this chapter, these writings also serve to counterbalance the prescriptive character of the advice literature.

This chapter should provide further insight on how marriage functions in the Western world. Throughout the long nineteenth century, marriage was considered to be the cornerstone of society. This assumption informed the policies of governments, churches, and charitable institutions in Europe as well as in the wider world.[10] At the same time, marriage was changing tremendously. This warrants the question: what marriage are we talking about?

MARRIAGE MANUALS' IDEAL INSTITUTIONS

The Enlightenment's mission to improve the functioning of European society attracted critiques as well as proposals for improvement. In this debate, many philosophers focused their attention on marriage. They pointed out connections between social welfare and the family.[11] Their writings inspired the authors of advice literature to breathe new life into the genre of the marriage manual. Traditionally, the marriage manual offered advice to married couples, and most of the guidelines pertained to the management of the household. The style was reminiscent of the Sunday sermon in church: guidelines were wrapped in moral exhortations. This reflected the Protestant origin of the genre: the first marriage manuals were published in Reformation circles in Germany and England.[12] In the late eighteenth century, this advice was extended to include more aspects of organization, including cost-effective housekeeping. It addressed every relationship in the household, even the rapport between employer and servant. All the while, it explained how a well-ordered household contributed to the general welfare. Furthermore, authors were also innovative in terms of the way they presented the advice. They offered explanatory exposés and related exemplary tales. These showed causal connections between the couple's efforts and marital bliss, suggesting that couples who followed the guidelines would be happy and successful. These causal connections enhanced the disciplining effect of the advice literature, as Foucault has demonstrated so eloquently.[13] Finally, toward the end of the eighteenth century, the genre began to proliferate. Due to the Enlightenment's engagement with education, more marriage manuals were published than ever.

These marriage manuals' new style stressed the societal responsibilities of the couple. Some authors explained the connection between family and society in so many words. According to the popular booklet *Hausbedarf für Verlobte und Neuverehelichte und solche, die es noch werden wollen* (Manual for fiancées and newlyweds, and those aspiring to marry), marriage has created order in society and fostered well-being among the people.[14] Its author C. F. T. Voigt adds that if the institution of marriage should fail, society would fall apart and people would live "in a savage tribe."[15] In this passage the German clergyman creates a contrast between a society consisting of families and a savage state. By doing so he presents marriage as a prerequisite for a civilized society. By creating this opposition, the author makes a strong statement. This stylistic device may have been chosen with an eye to the intended readership: he seems to be reaching out to a broad audience, including shopkeepers and artisans. Thus, this manual illustrates the Enlightenment's mission, as stated above, in content as well as in style.

Most authors address societal requirements in the discussion of the marital relationship. They present the joint effort to meet these demands as the essence of marriage. In the words of Voigt, marriage should persuade husband and wife to become better people. He stresses that only marriage can make a person really virtuous as well as truly happy.[16] The German pedagogue Cramer simply instructs spouses to help each other to become better people. They should consider virtue as a reward for coping with the hardships of life.[17] And the Dutch *philosophe* Bodisco stresses that true happiness lies in the effort to live virtuously. Spouses should not expect more from married life.[18] Thus, authors of marriage manuals entwine societal requirements around the representation of marriage. Their representations go beyond the early-modern perception of marriage. The difference lies in the more exacting definition of mutual support.

These authors elaborate on the essence of marriage in various ways: they sketch idealistic images, present fictional biographies of married couples, and offer precise guidelines. These narrative strategies have common themes: happy couples find satisfaction in their joint effort to take care of the family; mutual love and appreciation comes with the knowledge of having done one's utmost. To further their collaboration, husband and wife should respect the division of tasks and responsibilities. The man should never interfere with his wife's business. He is to discuss matters with his wife, should problems arise. The woman should not accept negligence on the part of her husband. She may confront him, albeit in a polite and respectful way. This partnership implies a break with the early-modern view of the paterfamilias who has to offer guidance to his wife and children. The most important difference pertains to the husband's role: he is to oversee the household rather than to rule it. In order to ensure spousal cooperation, the husband has to step back from this leading role.

Partnership is considered a prerequisite for a functioning family. The guidelines for the choice of partner demonstrate as much. Of course, these prioritize the ability to get along very well with each other. But they also stress the need for a clear sense of duty and a strong work ethic. The future spouse should be conscious of the possibility of flaws and be willing to correct these. Most authors communicate this advice through a series of contrasts between "true love" and misguided notions of love. Guides intended for a large audience tend to present a contrast between love and sexual desire. Voigt admonishes his readership to ask if "sensuous pleasures caused the mutual attraction."[19] He warns that if that is the case, the relationship will soon turn sour. The Dutch author Van Ouwerkerk de Vries opts for even stronger language: "If the urge of such a love is satisfied … the heart will be left empty and lonely."[20] At first glance, this type of phrasing seems to suggest that authors do not consider sexual desire to be part of the marital relationship. Close reading reveals, however, that this is not the case. They assume that each marital relationship starts off with mutual attraction. However, they consider sexual desire as insufficient grounds to marry: managing a household requires much more. In order to hammer this message home, they apply rhetorical devices and use strong language.

In sum, the new marriage manual presents the readership with a new perception of marriage. In this representation, societal requirements are met if the prospective couple has a clear understanding of the marital relationship. Moreover, it offers strategies that should help readers turn theory into practice. The most important of these involve the advice to consider the choice of a partner carefully and to establish a good relationship well before the wedding. All this implies that the choice of a partner has been made by the prospective couple rather than the parents. The free choice of partner was advocated in so many words, the rationale being that a happy couple would do the utmost for their family. More importantly, this coherent set of innovations would last for a long time. In retrospect, it is easy to see why: the new marital rapport allowed the man to focus on his career, the children to be given undivided attention, and the woman to manage the household as she saw fit. This allowed the individual family to adapt to changing circumstances, although these are not spelled out. This aspect, in turn, allowed for the dissemination of the new guidelines in society at large. As a consequence, the genre of the marriage manual did not change until well into the twentieth century.

In the context of this section, it is interesting to see how authors of Protestant and Catholic marriage manuals adapted to these innovations (Figure 8.3). After all, confessional currents remained strong in Western Europe throughout the long nineteenth century. They continued to challenge the secular approach of Enlightenment thought throughout this period. Close reading reveals that some authors follow the example of the liberal guides closely and address the impact of the family on society at large. For instance, the Protestant manual *Das Christliche Haus* (The Christian Household) presents the family as being "a world in itself and a living organism, but at the same time a member of the larger family of the nation as well."[21] This sentence refers back to the early-modern idea of the body of the state, best known from Hobbes's *Leviathan*. But it also alludes to the nineteenth-century idea of the nation, which was gaining ground as the century progressed. Furthermore, the German Lehmann makes the remark in a chapter about the working poor that he hopes to alleviate the poverty resulting from late nineteenth-

THE

FAMILY MONITOR:

OR A

HELP TO DOMESTIC HAPPINESS.

———

CHAPTER I,

THE DOMESTIC CONSTITUTION, AND THE MUTUAL
DUTIES OF HUSBANDS AND WIVES.

> " By thee
> Founded in reason, loyal, just and pure,
> Relations dear, and all the charities
> Of Father, Son, and Brother, first were known.
> Far be it that I should write thee, sin or blame,
> Or think thee unbefitting holiest place,
> Perpetual fountain of domestic sweets !"　　　MILTON.

A FAMILY ! How delightful the associations we form
with such a word ! How pleasing the images with
which it crowds the mind, and how tender the
emotions which it awakens in the heart ! Who can
wonder that domestic happiness should be a theme
dear to poetry, and that it should have called forth
some of the sweetest strains of fancy and of feeling ?
Or who can be surprised, that of all the sweets
which present themselves in the vista of futurity, to
the eye of those who are setting out on the journey
of life, this should excite the most ardent desires,
and engage the most active pursuits ? But alas ! of
those who in the ardor of youth, start for the pos-
session of this dear prize, how many fail! And why?
*Because their imagination alone is engaged in the sub-
ject :* they have no definite ideas of what it means,
nor of the way in which it is to be obtained. It is

FIGURE 8.3 First page of a nineteenth-century, Protestant marriage manual. University Library, Rijksuniversiteit Groningen; from EBSCO e-book collection.

century economic change. Clearly, he shares the Enlightenment assumption that society would fare better if individual families were to function better.

Most Protestant and Catholic authors prioritize religious teachings above societal aspects, presenting living according to God's command as the couple's first and foremost obligation. They refer to societal requirements in the discussion of the marital relationship. The Protestant manual *The Family Monitor, or a Help to Domestic Happiness* admonishes husband and wife to strive toward perfection. In this context the author, James, speaks of "true, Christian love."[22] This type of love implies fulfilling societal duties as well as religious ones. In this context, Catholic authors stress that marriage is a sacrament. At the wedding ceremony, the couple receives God's grace to help carry the burden of marriage. In the words of the Dutch priest Van Campen, husband and wife are to shoulder the yoke of marriage.[23] With this word "yoke," the author refers to a traditional image of marriage as burdensome. More often than not, the image presented the yoke as resting on the shoulders of a woman. By creating a connection between the yoke and the couple, this author presents the burden of marriage as a joint responsibility.

There is one important aspect in which the religious marriage manuals differ from the secular guides. Both Protestant and Catholic authors uphold the traditional patriarchal order of the family. Of course, they favor a constrained and responsible execution of patriarchal authority. For instance, the man is advised to motivate his dependents to improve themselves rather than to punish them. Nevertheless, they stress that the woman is to obey her husband. In this context, Protestant and Catholic authors present different rationales. Protestants refer to the story of Eve's Creation as presented in the Apostle Paul's letter on the rapport between the sexes.[24] Catholics communicate a double message: on one level, the man is to oversee the household and the woman is to obey. On a deeper level, husband and wife are equal in God's eye, suggesting that both have to abide by His command. They cite Paul's letter on the marital relationship.[25] From these varieties, it can be inferred that Protestant and Catholic authors use this topic to underline their respective religious views. Or formulated more pointedly, they use the rapport between husband and wife to create difference.

Throughout the long nineteenth century, marriage manuals present similar norms and values. From the perspective of the family, the lifestyles of different social and religious groups converge. At the same time, these groups create distinctions on the basis of the woman's role in the family. All in all, gender offers the greatest reason for contention and the greatest incentive for change, as we shall see in the next section.

SEPERATING SPHERES, ORCHESTRATING EMOTIONS

Despite the efforts of the advice literature to discipline married couples, marriage in the long nineteenth century was not just about societal aims and internal organization. With the passage of time, marriage became more and more about familial bliss and individual happiness. In particular, middle-class couples were in pursuit of intimacy and contentment. They connected this aspiration to a new cultural space: the home. Here, the man can relax after working long hours in a competitive environment. Here, the children can grow up in sheltered surroundings. And last but not least, the woman was to make this happen by creating a happy home.[26] Historians have highlighted the functional aspects of this lifestyle: it allowed the woman to attend to the housekeeping and manage the household frugally, giving her the time and the opportunity to make the most of their financial resources. This allowed well-off families to show off their status, an important asset in a competitive society. Next, it helped lower income families live the bourgeois lifestyle, with the women adopting new styles of cooking, sewing, and decorating.[27] Finally, it could help poor people make do with the little money they had, which was the preferred policy of governments and charitable institutions to alleviate poverty.[28] This functionalist approach has its limitations. Although it discusses the functioning of the family in society, it overlooks the reason why men and women grasped at the chance to develop new ways of life. Women especially attempted to make the most of their new responsibility in the family, adopting new attitudes on education and health. Of course, they built upon the above-mentioned division of tasks and responsibilities between husband and wife. But their efforts entailed a further elaboration of men's and women's sexual identities.

By the turn of the 1800s, along with the advice literature cited above, these new sexual identities had already come to the fore. Most marriage manuals present them as a matter of course, as if no further explanation is needed. A representative example can be found in the writing of the Dutch author and publisher Loosjes. Instead of a conventional marriage manual, he published two fictitious biographies: *De man in de vier tijdperken zijns levens* (The man in the four phases of his life) and *De vrouw in de vier tijdperken haars levens* (The woman in the four phases of her life). This narrative strategy offered myriad possibilities for pointing out the consequences choices made in youth have on later life. Indeed, the author describes how the choice of partner affects societal success as well as individual happiness. On a conscious level, this strategy enhanced the credibility of the advice. On a subliminal level, the story may influence the reader still more. After all, the two protagonists are presented as examples to emulate. Their biographies are presented in separate books. What better way to communicate that life is different for men and women?

Loosjes created the difference between the fictitious man and the fictitious woman in a very systematic way. The man is pictured as providing for his family, advising his young adult children, and socializing with members of the community. The woman is portrayed as living her life in a web of familial relationships. Every time she needs advice, she turns to her mother. In old age she advises her married daughter in the same way. Thus, the author suggests that women live their lives in a distinct social sphere and according to a distinct cultural tradition. Furthermore, the author describes men's and women's work differently. Whereas the man has a job, the woman has to make her family happy. The phrasing abounds with references to familial well-being and feminine goodness. The message that the sexes are different is also communicated in the illustrations. The guide for men has a large illustration on the frontispiece. It shows the man on his march through life: the boy is playing with toys; the adult male is writing at a desk. Moreover, the boy is depicted next to a small branch, while the adult is shown beside a large tree in full bloom. Thus, the march through life of the male is represented with reference to society and nature. The guide for women also has illustrations on the title page. Each picture has a female clad in a tunic, similar to the clothing in Antiquity. Each figure holds an object that bears a symbolic meaning: the adult woman holds an hourglass, a symbol of the passage of time, and the senior woman holds a large anchor, a symbol of hope. The women are sitting on a cloud, and the clouds are arranged in a circle around the title. From cover to cover, Loosjes conveys the message that women are different from men.

To all intents and purposes, Loosjes intended his guides for relatively well-off people. But the attention to sexual identities is not limited to advice literature for the middle class. Bodisco, mentioned above, wrote a marriage manual for the lower strata of society. His booklet has two chapters: the first lists the obligations of the marital couple and the second discusses why many couples fail to fulfill them. The first chapter has three parts: the first contains the rules of conduct for the husband, the second presents those of the wife, while the third and last chapter enumerates the couple's joint responsibilities, focusing on the rapports with children and servants. Furthermore, the section for the wife is written in a distinct style. The author applied the stylistic device of the metonymy in order to connect each activity to some virtue: domestic tasks are to be done carefully, and linens and woolens should be stacked neatly in the closet. Toward the end of this section, the lists of responsibilities abound with references to virtue: there should be cleanliness and tidiness in the house, and healthiness and moderation in the kitchen. This narrative strategy connects women's work to some greater encompassing virtue. This presentation of advice offers another example of creating a difference between the sexes.

FIGURE 8.4 *Victorian Woman Cooking and Chatting in her Kitchen*, from *Bleak House* by Charles Dickens (London: Chapman and Hall, *c.* 1870); illustrations by F. Barnard. Getty Images.

The preoccupation with the difference between the sexes noted above is not restricted to authors of advice literature. It is also a dominant theme in contemporary literature of the time. Women writers especially wove this theme into their stories of love and marriage. Many centered the plot on the struggle between the traditional approach to marriage and the new marital relationship. The clash is conveyed through the misunderstandings that occur between the female protagonist and her suitor. Jane Austen's *Pride and Prejudice* offers an example of this type of romance. The fictitious Elizabeth Bennet wants to marry for love. But her love interest, the rather stiff aristocrat Darcy, hesitates because of the lesser wealth and lower status of the Bennet family. In the story, Elizabeth confronts Darcy and agrees to marry him only after he has accepted her take on the matter. In this narrative, the female protagonist is the personification of the new perception of love.[29] Given her engagement with family and friends, Elizabeth also embodies the new type of woman.

This preoccupation with love and gender comes to the fore in other types of writing as well. It dominates the letters exchanged by young adult women, both from lower income families and from wealthy ones. All of them learned letter writing as children because of its importance to contemporary etiquette. As young adults, they also favored the medium because of the opportunity to express themselves among friends. Analyses of epistolary exchanges show young women confessing their infatuations to their friends. Moreover, these letters show them wondering what type of husband they want. Thus, letter writing helps young women become conscious of their personal preferences, even if the world only wants them to conform to the norm. At the same time, the writing itself helps them to understand themselves as women. From a historical perspective, young women are simultaneously gaining self-awareness both as individuals and as women.[30]

Women were not only trying to put their hopes and dreams into words but were also trying to turn theory into practice. This can be inferred from the innovations made in family life. From the turn of the 1800s on, middle-class families began to seek out larger houses with more rooms. The mistress of the house would then decorate them with an eye to specific family rituals. She especially wanted a separate room for relatively informal family gatherings. The trends in decorating suggested prioritizing comfort over decorum, thus contributing to a homely atmosphere.[31] At the same time, women stressed familial aspects, using memorabilia of the family such as souvenirs of the wedding. In this way, family members were reminded of their joint history. All the while, women tried to add a personal touch, such as embellishing rooms with cushions they'd made themselves. This presented visible tokens of the woman's efforts. And last but not least, the socializing of family members as a group was furthered, for example, by transforming meals into family rituals. They were supposed to act out being a family at least once a day. In these intricate ways, women created not only a new space for the family but also a new style of family life. Of course, in making these arrangements for the family, women took center stage.

While the above blueprint for the marital relationship was established early in the nineteenth century, people's aspirations for the family continued to grow. These aspirations brought about more specific rules and regulations for all members of the family. But the regulations for women were different: they were formulated with reference to women's identity. This association of women's behavior and femininity had a double effect: it represented the home as in need of a woman's touch. And it suggested that to qualify as a "true" woman, they had to become wives and mothers. In this context, it should be emphasized that men's work was not associated with men's sexual identity. Or, more precisely, the rules of conduct for men did not change, and connections to masculinity were not made. As a result, the advice literature of the nineteenth century presents a distinct asymmetry between the sexes, going well beyond the division of tasks and responsibilities between the sexes and the separation of public and private spheres.

To explore this asymmetry we will first take a closer look at the association of family with femininity. The best examples appear in conduct books for women, a type of advice literature that was mostly written by women. Even though the contents of these guides overlap with the marriage manual, the style seems far more exalted, as in the following example from a guide by the British author Mrs. Ellis:

> The customs of English society have so constituted women the guardians of the comfort of their homes, that, like the Vestals of old, they cannot allow the lamp they cherish to be extinguished ... without an equal share of degradation to their names.[32]

This passage presents an analogy between English women and Vestal Virgins. This analogy makes reference to civilization itself: the Romans expected their empire would fall, should the fire in the temple of Vesta go out. This analogy also refers to reputation: the woman who fails to take care of the home loses her good name. In this complex way, the author, Mrs. Ellis, suggests that the woman should safeguard the home as a sanctuary in order to keep society civilized.

Later in this conduct book, the connection between family and femininity is made in a more explicit and disconcerting way. The passage starts with an analogy between domestic duties and flowers:

> There are flowers that burst upon us, and startle the eye with the splendour of their beauty; we gaze until we are dazzled, and then turn away, remembering nothing but their gorgeous hues. There are others that refresh the traveller by the sweetness they diffuse—but he has to search for the source of his delight ...
>
> It is thus that the unpretending virtues of the female character force themselves upon our regard, so that the woman herself is nothing in comparison with her attributes; and we remember less the celebrated belle, than her who made us happy.[33]

This passage presents a contrast between two types of flowers and two types of attractiveness. While the former represents a dazzling beauty, the latter's appeal is acknowledged only as an afterthought. This sentence conveys to the reader that the woman's work, despite the good it does, may go unnoticed. The sting is in the last sentence. Here, the author makes a distinction between female character and the actual woman. The phrase "unpretending virtues" refers to a discussion of the required domestic skills appearing earlier in the chapter. This description shows the stylistic device of the metonymy, with domestic tasks being represented as virtues. Together, these stylistic devices suggest that domestic skills are part of womanhood. However, they are not necessarily part of the actual woman. The remark conveys the idea that femininity has to be acquired. Only the person who desires to take care of the family attains womanhood.

In contrast to the above theme of "mistress of the home," the theme of "motherhood" is not discussed much in nineteenth-century advice literature. Given the importance the middle classes attach to education, this prompts the question of why that is. Most likely the answer has to do with the situation itself, where nineteenth-century educational innovation took place outside the home: children went to school for much longer. Moreover, teenagers were increasingly looked after in special youth clubs.[34] In historiography, these trends have been interpreted as evidence of a new approach toward youth: young people were supposed to spend many years in a separate sphere before taking on adult responsibilities.[35] This interpretation tends to overlook the fact that youth clubs were organized following the rules and regulations of bourgeois custom. These offered primarily opportunities to pursue a specific interest with peers, such as literary societies or debating clubs. They also offered opportunities to practice management and leadership, thus preparing them for adult life. But whatever these trends brought about, they had little bearing on the care of children in the home.

In comparison to the elaborate and exalted descriptions of the wife in nineteenth-century advice literature, discussions about the husband appear traditional and functional. To begin with, authors of advice literature assume the basic aspects of manhood. For instance, they expect the man to marry and establish a family. Probably, this expectation goes back to a long-standing obligation to marry, which existed in European societies. After all, in traditional European societies a male person reached adulthood at marriage. To this assumption, Enlightenment authors added an important rationale: *philosophes* created contrasts between the married man and the single man. The former works hard to provide for his family, and as a result he fosters the general welfare of society. The latter is only pursuing hedonistic pleasures; he is a parasite on society.[36] To this assumption, the nineteenth-century advice literature adds even more elaborate rationales. These authors refer to aspects of social mobility and economic gain. A skilled wife provides services such

FIGURE 8.5 *Late Nineteenth Century Mother Surrounded by a Group of Five Children*, from *Our Own Magazine*, vol. 14, edited by T. B. Bishop (London: The Children's Special Service Mission, 1893). Getty Images.

as cooking and laundering, which the man otherwise would have to pay for. Moreover a capable woman can increase her husband's fortune by working hard and spending money frugally. An accomplished wife can further his status in the community. Thus, the capacity of a wife to create value is underlined. More than ever before, to be a man means to be married.

Next, authors point out changes that followed from the new marital relationship. They admonish the man to abide by the rules as much his wife. He should take the societal requirements of marriage seriously. He should consult his wife and consider her wishes before making any decisions. He should also accept her flaws in order to keep the relationship functioning. As a father he oversees the education of his children but does not participate in it. Some authors do present men as advising older daughters as to the choice of a partner. Most of the time, fathers are pictured as correcting young women's rosy expectations of young men. Here, the message has to do with being wise and knowing the ways of the world. Admonishments about developing a homely lifestyle are few and far between. The few authors touching upon this subject do so to point out the reasons for being economical. Their intention is to instill a frugal lifestyle among the lower strata of society. A first attempt made by Dutch authors at the turn of the 1800s ascribes their readership to spend evenings at home. A second wave of books published at the turn of the 1900s offers this advice with reference to alcoholic men wasting their earnings in bars.[37] Although these authors want men to spend time with their families, they offer few suggestions about socializing with the family.

Having unraveled the threads of femininity and masculinity, it is time to return to the initial question regarding the new marital relationship. As the above shows, the descriptions of women differ from those of men. Whereas nineteenth-century authors ascribe new meaning to women's work, they remain silent as to the meaning of men's work. While these authors present domestic duties as a way of spreading happiness, they only indicate a man's responsibility to provide. And while they paint the home as a place of intimacy and comfort, and picture the wife as its guardian angel, they place the husband at the edge of the family portrait. Taken together, these differences indicate a specific asymmetry: while the woman's role is interwoven with the cultural space of the home and bourgeois family life, the man is connected mainly to the institutional aspects of the family.

After analyzing gender in the marital relationship, one question remains unanswered: what about love? Is not the nineteenth century the age of Romantic Love? Didn't Romanticism propose the idea of love as destiny, an emotion that can be only felt for one person? Before that, did not the Enlightenment plead in favor of marriage based on a combination of mutual affinity and sexual attraction? Indeed, authors of advice literature do assume that couples marry for love. They warn that marriage needed to be based on affinity and affection, and liberal authors list mutual sexual attraction as well. These authors want to help the couple make the marriage work. The strict division of tasks and responsibilities between the sexes can be interpreted as being instrumental. The rules for negotiating them were meant to be helpful in establishing a more egalitarian rapport. Furthermore, historians and literary critics agree that the nineteenth-century middle classes did want to marry for love. These scholars only argue as to whether this ideal became a reality. Their findings have led them to believe that bourgeois culture resulted in a great deal of frustration, as the American historian Peter Gay pointed out in his extensive *The Bourgeois Experience*,[38] or that hypocrisy was at the heart of bourgeois culture, as the German philosopher Peter Sloterdijk argued in his *Kritik der Zynischen Vernunft*.[39]

If we evaluate these research results from the vantage point of the new marital relationship, two topics come to the fore: the choice of a marriage partner and the wife's disappointments. The above scholars have shown that young adult women take the choice of a partner very seriously. The American historian Dena Goodman has pointed out how women considered this topic at length in their correspondence. They seem to develop their own personalities by discussing their preferences with their friends.[40] Furthermore, women novelists engage with this topic. Their stories are plotted around meeting Mr. Right and establishing a relationship with him. These tales end with the protagonist exclaiming: "Reader, I married him!"[41] In comparison to these love stories, tales of marital life are told less often. Those that come to mind portray women who are unhappy in their marriage. Sometimes the reason is obvious to the protagonist, as in the mid-nineteenth-century British novel *Middlemarch*. The female protagonist Dorothea decides to marry an older clergyman. Fascinated by his research on ancient mythologies, she hopes to educate herself by assisting him. The author Mary Ann Evans, publishing under the pseudonym of George Eliot, suggests the marriage fails because of the husband's inability to treat his wife as an intellectual partner as well as a wife. Sometimes the reason for the woman's unhappiness is not apparent to the protagonist, as in the novel *Madame*

Bovary. The author Gustave Flaubert depicts her distracting herself by decorating the home. Both authors present their protagonists as left unsatisfied by their husbands and turning to other men. Therefore, many scholars have connected these protagonists' *ennui* to bourgeois sexuality. There may be some truth to this interpretation, even though Gay has shown that middle-class prudery is a myth.[42] In this context, it is more significant that these stories present difficult marital relationships. The difficulties seemingly mirror this sexual asymmetry: whereas these female protagonists hope to find a real partner in life, the male characters envisage a wife who fulfills her duties and who is content with spending the money he makes.

Reading nineteenth-century prescriptive texts and scholarly analyses of a wider range of source material, it is apparent that the Enlightenment's pattern for the marital relationship is based on new sexual identities. Many philosophers think women's generic talents are best applied at home. Middle-class women seize the opportunities available to make the most of their role in the family. Over time, their expectations of married life become very specific, especially in comparison to men's. Women seek love, friendship, and partnership, while men remain focused on tasks and responsibilities. This asymmetry comes on top of the new order in the house, which allows the wife more control over her work than before. Together, these changes suggest a strong connection between femininity and the home. Given women's engagement with these new aspects of their lives, such changes may even indicate a feminization of home life.

This analysis is based to a large extent on the scholarly literature that discusses the social relationships between the sexes. This chapter discusses only one of these relationships, namely the rapport between husband and wife. To avoid myopic interpretations, we will take a closer look at two contemporary critics of marriage.

DISSENTING VIEWS, ALTERNATIVE LIFESTYLES

So far, we have seen a new perception of the institution developing at the turn of the 1800s. And we have traced the rapport between spouses that unfolded from the mid-nineteenth century onwards. The gender regime implied here especially came under scrutiny toward the end of the long nineteenth century. This fin de siècle critique of bourgeois culture has been very influential, even to this very day. As shown, scholars of bourgeois culture have drawn inspiration from this critique. This is evident, for instance, in the tendency to perceive bourgeois culture as status-oriented or even hypocritical. This perspective might have resulted in a certain bias. To check this, this section will discuss contemporary critics of nineteenth-century marriage. Did they consider marriage problematic as well? And, if so, did they take issue with these perceived flaws?

For the British feminist Mary Wollstonecraft (1759–97) the new rapport between the spouses, as introduced by Enlightenment marriage manuals, did not go far enough. She persisted in the view that marriage served the patriarchal order. First, in European societies there was no place for women outside of marriage: women could scarcely make a living, let alone establish a household of their own. Second, once married, women were at the mercy of their husbands; they lacked the means to correct an abusive or exploitative husband. Her conviction stemmed from personal experience. She had spent her youth in small villages in England and Wales. Because her father had failed at his business, they were obliged to move every few years. In the end, the family was in dire straits. The parents' marriage was unhappy. Her mother behaved submissively, perhaps to ward off her husband's anger and violence. At the age of nineteen Mary took it upon herself to help her siblings cope. She started working as a lady-in-waiting in Bath, and later she established a school for girls in London. These were difficult years, especially when co-founder and best friend Fanny Blood left in order to marry. After a decade of tutoring children, she opted for a life as a translator and author. In Enlightenment circles in London, she found friends and eventually a partner for life in the philosopher William Godwin.

Wollstonecraft set out her views in *A Vindication of the Rights of Woman*. The publication opens with an analysis of society and the nature of humankind. After pointing out the importance of women's work for society at large, she argues for girls' education. Not only should women become better mothers of their children and better companions to their husbands, they should also develop themselves as human beings. In this context, she creates contrasts between a properly educated woman and the contemporary girl who is prepared for socializing, and thus for attracting the attention of a potential husband.[43] She critiques the fact that women should be attractive and charming rather than sensible and strong. But she does not mention the advantage of education for finding a job and gaining economic independence, which, given her personal history, comes as a surprise. In the final analysis, she seemingly accepts the prevailing rapport between the sexes, including man's superior talent.

To trace Wollstonecraft's views of marriage we will take a closer look at the posthumously published, unfinished novel *Maria, or the Wrongs of Woman*. Contemporary critics considered this text to be as much a philosophical treatise as a romance.[44] Here, the feminist presents the ideal relationship between a man and a woman. Maria and Darnford establish a spiritual bond, reading the same copy of Rousseau's *Héloïse* and exchanging views by writing comments in the margins. After having recognized each other as kindred spirits, they decide to meet. The opportunities for getting together are limited, locked up as they are in an asylum. Their love can blossom, however, because the guard Jemima is willing to act as go-between. When they become better acquainted, Darnford confesses to having led the hedonistic life of the typical aristocrat, frequenting public venues and pursuing sexual pleasure. His relationships with women have been restricted: "I could only keep myself awake in their company by making downright love to them." He was sexually initiated by women "of a class of which you can have no knowledge."[45] His relationship with Maria opens up a different world: "He never before knew what it was to love." As the story draws to its end, Mary and Darnford enjoy their first sexual encounter. The author puts this event on a par with marriage, with Maria receiving her lover "as her husband" and Darnford "pledg[ing] himself as her protector, and eternal friend."[46] The relationship between Maria and Darnford is contrasted with a representation of Maria's actual marriage with Mr. Venables, the person who had her locked up in the asylum. He decided to marry after Maria's uncle and mentor promised to give 5,000 pounds to help establish the household. He used the money to settle outstanding debts procured in business as well as in gambling. Once married, he keeps spending his spare time in pubs and clubs. He is secretive about his whereabouts and the debts he runs up. But from the antagonisms in the text, it can be inferred that he spends his time drinking, gambling, and womanizing. Clearly, the author has created contrasts between two types of marriage. The difference pertains to the essence of marriage: a bond of love or an institution of convenience. The difference comes to the fore in particular in the character of the husbands: while Darnford loves Maria, Mr. Venables exploits her.

So far, Wollstonecraft represents Maria's relationships with Darnford and Venables in accordance with the contemporary feminine ideal, as presented by most contemporary women novelists. But to that she adds a second theme, how marriage functions in contemporary society. This topic is addressed in a series of contrasts between Maria and the guard Jemima. At first glance, Maria's and Jemima's lives are very different. While the former has been brought up in a middle-class setting, the latter has a history of abuse and exploitation, by her father and stepmother first, and then by her employer later. She ends up living in the streets, prostituting herself to survive. Finally, she is rescued by a philanthropist, who offers her the job of guardian and a place to live with her child. But close reading reveals their situations to be rather similar. Maria is manipulated in a marriage arranged by her uncle and has lost her inheritance to her husband. The latter tries to prostitute her: to settle a debt he has promised a sexual encounter with her. The narrative shows both women suffering from exploitation by the very men who are supposed to protect them. The message is clear: marriage does not protect women from poverty and abuse.

In this last piece of writing, Wollstonecraft creates contrasts between ideal love and the actual relationships between women and men. In the former, the author presents a romance between kindred spirits. In the latter, she points out how marriage enables men to subjugate and exploit women. Abiding by the rules of patriarchal society does not bring women financial security or personal safety. Contrary to contemporary ideology, the "good" Maria is not better off than the "bad" Jemima. Only if women are attributed rights as individual human beings, following the example of the French *Déclaration des Droits de l'Homme,* may their situation improve. By bringing this solution to the fore, this feminist proves that she is a true Enlightenment philosopher: women need to be protected from the institution of marriage as it is.

A century later the German sexologist and activist Magnus Hirschfeld (1868–1935) reached a conclusion similar to that of Wollstonecraft: society offers only one option. This circumstance makes people decide to marry even if they are not sexually attracted to the other sex. His own sexual preference must have motivated him. Born into an Ashkenazi family, he followed in his father's footsteps and studied medicine. His social commitment was evident already in his student days, when he helped establish a society for Jewish students. After working for a few years as a physician in Magdeburg and Berlin, respectively, he began his research on sexual practices. This endeavor led to the founding of the Wissenschaftlich-humanitäre Komitee (Scientific Humanitarian Committee) and later the Institut für Sexualwissenschaft [Institute of Sexual Science]. His work helped him start the movement for gay rights. He found love, later in life, with a German student who became his assistant and with a Chinese student he met at a conference in Shanghai. He lived in a ménage-à-trois until his death.

This physician conducted research on people who deviated from the standard of heterosexuality, from a physiological as well as a psychological point of view. In his seminal publication *Sexualpathologie* he distinguished hermaphroditism, androgyny, transvestitism, homosexuality, and metatropism. He categorized these varieties as "intersexual," because to him they showed a combination of masculine and feminine characteristics.[47] Following this line of reasoning, he envisioned several sexual identities besides masculinity and femininity. Throughout the study, he stressed fluidity: creating fixed categories would be intellectually misleading.[48]

In this context, it should be noted that this scientist clung to the Enlightenment approach to gender: he perceived the sexes as having very different natures. He strayed from this approach in one respect. He assumed that a person does not necessarily have all the physiologically and psychologically characteristics of his or her sex. Thus, a person

FIGURE 8.6 Magnus Hirschfeld, 1868. INTERFOTO/Alamy Stock Photo. Image ID: BB69PM.

can be physiologically masculine and psychologically feminine. As a consequence, he distinguished between homosexual males who have masculine characteristics and those who have feminine traits. He assumed that opposites attract among homosexuals as well as among heterosexuals. Thus, a masculine homosexual male is likely to be attracted to a feminine male. In order to give a full analysis, he offered precise definitions of manhood and womanhood. In this context, he took issue with the—in his opinion, outdated—idea that men are active and women are passive. He proposed to characterize the "fully" male as aggressive and the "fully" female as receptive.[49] In the latter instance, his theory shares the Enlightenment assumption that men and women have opposite natures.

While Hirschfeld discussed human sexuality in general in *Sexualpathologie*, he addressed homosexual desire in his pamphlet *Sappho und Sokrates*. In the preface he mentioned receiving a letter from a patient asking help for people "who live under the double curse of nature and law."[50] The actual text starts with the remark that homosexual desire is real love, not mere sensuality. This is followed by a citation from Schopenhauer stating that homosexual desire is so common that it has to be natural. Being a physician he offered a physiological explanation for the phenomenon. In the third month of pregnancy, the embryo transforms from a hermaphrodite into a male or a female. In this complex process things can go wrong. The problem is with Western civilization. It is not attuned to human desire. The Ancient Greeks fared better: they offered an explanation of human desire in their mythology. To finish the exposé, the author cited Nietzsche's famous dictum that what is natural cannot be unethical.

Basically, the author argues for cultural space for people whose sexuality does not fit in with marriage. In his view the institution is suitable only for fully masculine men and fully feminine women. It can only cause problems for all other varieties. This argument targets the prevalent gender regime. This approach is characteristic of fin de siècle culture that developed new identities for men and women, summarized by the American literary critic Showalter as "sexual anarchy."[51] Furthermore, this current started the trend to prioritize personal desire above societal order, characterized by the American historian Coontz as love slowly but surely conquering marriage.[52]

This analysis shows these critics taking issue first and foremost with the dominant position of marriage in society. Of course, they target different aspects: whereas Wollstonecraft points out how the institution of marriage subjugates women, Hirschfeld criticizes the prevalent gender regime as being oppressive to both men and women. This difference proves how much the concept of marriage had changed: the societal institution had given way to a specific type of marital relationship.

CONCLUSION

The iconic bourgeois family was created in phases. First, specific family values were put in place, disciplining the married couple so as to manage the household in an orderly way, sensibly, and frugally. If spouses worked hard and cooperated well together, the family should thrive. To sustain the work ethic over a long period of time, the rapport between husband and wife was adapted. The couple needed to adhere to a strict division of tasks and responsibilities. Each spouse should respect the responsibilities of the other. If difficulties arose, the couple should negotiate instead of quarrel. These guidelines show the influence of Enlightenment thinking regarding the connection between family and society. Moreover, this advice was based on the Enlightenment assumption that if people can choose their partner freely, they will take responsibility as a matter of course.

These family values were based on modern sexual identities that were developed in the late Enlightenment. These ascribed different but complementary natures to men and women. The middle classes especially elaborated on women's role in the family: they were to transform the house into an oasis of calm in the midst of a raucous world. Middle-class women also engaged with relationships in the family: they developed new ideas regarding marital love and familial care. In the mid-nineteenth century, authors of advice literature tended to represent marriage as a set of relationships rather than an institution, and to situate the woman at the center. As a consequence, in representations of bourgeois families, women dominate the picture. Furthermore, women authors writing for women readers liked to connect homeliness to femininity. Women's writings suggest that the female sex simultaneously gained a sense of self and a modern concept of femininity. Together, these trends contributed to a specific sexual asymmetry: whereas women sought to establish meaningful relationships with husbands and children, men continued with the traditional, functional approach.

The scholarly literature on nineteenth-century bourgeois culture has elaborated on middle-class women's frustrations. Some have interpreted these with reference to a gap between Romantic Love and mundane reality. Some point out the perceived tendency of the middle class to present an orderly façade to the world. However, contemporary critics of bourgeois marriage do not allude to this supposed hypocrisy. At the beginning of the century, Mary Wollstonecraft blamed the dominant place of marriage in society, which left women damned if they did marry and damned if they did not. Toward the end of the century Magnus Hirschfeld pointed a finger at the prevalent gender regime, which did not suit many men and women. These authors critiqued oppressive aspects of bourgeois marriage. Their differences of opinion reflect the intricate transformation of marriage from a societal institution to a specific set of relationships bound by specific sexual identities.

NOTES

Introduction

1. Sabean 1997; Ehmer 2002; Coontz 2005.
2. Kok and Mandemakers 2010; Szołtysek 2015.
3. Puschmann, Paping, and Matthijs 2016.
4. Lis and Soly 1979, cited in Deneweth, Gelderblom, and Jonker 2014: 80.
5. Coontz 2005; Puschmann in this volume.
6. Engelen and Wolf 2005a; Goode 1970; Goody 1990; Lundh and Kurosu 2014a.
7. Therborn 2004; Szołtysek et al. 2017.
8. Therborn 2004: 17.
9. Ibid.: 13.
10. Engelen and Wolf 2005b; Wolf 2005.
11. We have to acknowledge, though, that the nineteenth century initially meant a weakening of the position of women vis-à-vis men in Europe. In the wake of the French Revolution citizenship was defined exclusively as male, excluding women from the political arena. Moreover, the rise of the male breadwinner model also led to more inequality between men and women. See Timm and Sanborn 2016.
12. Wolf 2005.
13. Klep 2004.
14. See Kok, in this volume.
15. Goody 2000. Of course, there were notable exceptions to the rule of monogamy in the West, such as the Mormons in the United States.
16. De Moor and Van Zanden 2010.
17. Klep 2005.
18. Wolf 2005.
19. Ibid.; Therborn 2004.
20. Therborn 2004.
21. Ibid.
22. Cuno 2015.
23. Dalton and Cheuk Leung 2014.
24. Todd 2011.
25. Naamane Guessous 2007.
26. Fauve-Chamoux and Ochiai 2009.
27. Ochiai 2009.
28. Reher 1998.
29. Peletz 1987.
30. Bulten, Kok, Lyna and Rupesinghe 2018.
31. See also Kaser, this volume.
32. Thornton 2005.

33. Puschmann and Solli 2014.
34. Le Play 1855; Le Play 1872; Tönnies 1887.
35. For an overview of the discussion see Puschmann 2015 and Puschmann and Solli 2014.
36. Van Leeuwen and Maas 2010.
37. Janssens, this volume.
38. Laslett 1969; Macfarlane 1986, 1987; Hartman 2004.
39. Ruggles 1987, xvii.
40. Laslett 1969; Livi-Bacci 2017.
41. Sewel 2009.
42. Sewell 2009; Lucassen 2004; Puschmann 2015.
43. Puschmann et al. 2014.
44. Puschmann et al. 2015.
45. Marchand 2016.
46. Puschmann 2015.
47. Matthijs 2002.
48. Fitch and Ruggles 2000; Störmer et al. 2018.
49. Janssens 1997, Janssens this volume.
50. Bras 2011.
51. Matthijs 2006.
52. Socolow 2000: 77.
53. Jefferson and Lokken 2011.
54. Maubrigades 2017.
55. McDonald 1975; Wanhalla 2014.
56. Hunter 2017.
57. Fitch and Ruggles 2000.
58. Consensual unions had been very uncommon in Europe, while illegitimacy declined quickly from the middle of the nineteenth century after a remarkable high, which had started in the latter half of the eighteenth century. See Puschmann in this volume.
59. Cited in Perrot 1993: 252.
60. See also Kaser in this volume.
61. Puschmann 2011.
62. Pomeranz 2000.

Chapter 1

1. *Merriam-Webster*, s.vv. "courtship," accessed March 23, 2019, https://www.merriam-webster.com/dictionary/courtship; "courting," accessed March 26, 2019, https://www.merriam-webster.com/dictionary/courting.
2. Matthijs 2002.
3. Goode 1959: 41.
4. Schlegel 1991.
5. Skinner 1997: 54.
6. Therborn 2004; Therborn 2011.
7. Also Kok 2017.
8. Thornton 2005; Allendorf 2013; Ginsborg 2014.
9. Tambiah 1979: 119.
10. Goody 1990: 98, 104.
11. Cartier 1996.

12. Wolf and Huang 1980.
13. Bossen and Gates 2017.
14. Cartier 1996: 225.
15. Idema 1996: 69, translated by Jan Kok
16. Yan 2002: 32.
17. Sa 1985: 294; Engelen and Hsieh 2007: 90.
18. Wolf and Huang 1980: 177.
19. Sommer 2000: 97ff.
20. Siu 1990.
21. Stockard 1989; Topley 1975.
22. Wolf and Huang 1980: 73.
23. Jordan 2006.
24. Wolf and Huang 1980: 74.
25. Beillevaire 1996a.
26. Ibid.
27. Mann 2005: 52
28. Ochiai 2011: 403.
29. Mann 2005: 54.
30. Therborn 2004: 61.
31. Beillevaire 1996b.
32. Lardinois 1996b, the following is based on Kok 2017.
33. Goody 1990: 185.
34. Therborn 2004: 41.
35. Krishnan 1977: 274.
36. Goody 1990: 210.
37. Lardinois 1996a: 578.
38. Goody 1990: 275.
39. Weitbrecht 1875: 94, 100.
40. Sarkar 1993: 52.
41. Lardinois 1996a.
42. Tambiah 1989: 425; Goody 1990: 182.
43. Goody 1990: 256–258, 287, 311; Lardinois 1996a.
44. Allendorf 2013.
45. Lardinois 1996b: 292.
46. Monger 2004: 160.
47. Goody 1990: 364; see also Kok 2017.
48. Fargues 1996: 348.
49. Fargues 1996.
50. Therborn 2004.
51. Goody 1990: 379.
52. Larguèche 2011: 145.
53. Kozma 2011: 80; see also Al-Khowli 2006, on shari'a records.
54. Duben and Behar 2002: 99.
55. Wolf 2005.
56. Coontz 2005: 135.
57. See Szołtysek 2012.
58. Haines 1996.
59. See, for instance, on the merchant elite of Rotterdam, De Nijs 2001.

60. Van Cruyningen 2000: 272.
61. Gillis 1985: 24ff.
62. De Jager 1980: 45.
63. Van Leeuwen, Maas, and Miles 2005.
64. Hondius 2001: 59.
65. Engel 1990.
66. Ibid.: 698.
67. Ibid.
68. See also Leinarte (2017: 63–65) on parents and clergy obstructing "romantic" marriages in Lithuania.
69. Engel 1990: 702.
70. Ibid.: 704.
71. Wikman 1937.
72. Flandrin 1980: 34; Ekirch 2006; Sellers 1991: 241.
73. Baudouin 1906.
74. Kok, Bras, and Rotering 2016.
75. Sundt [1857] 1993.
76. Kok 2005.
77. Sundt [1857] 1993: 60.
78. Kok 2005.
79. Kok, Bras, and Rotering 2016.
80. See Engel 1990 on Russia; Anderson and Anderson 1962 on Ukraine.
81. Engel 1990: 703.
82. Alter 1988; Szreter and Fischer 2010; Kok, Bras, and Rotering 2016.
83. Maines 1992: 407; Davies 2006; Lloyd 1991.
84. Cited in Coontz 2005: 78; see also Albertine 1992.
85. Ward 1990: 96ff.
86. Coontz 2005: 162.
87. Ibid.: 169.
88. Gillis 1985; Matthijs 2002.
89. Borscheid 1986: 167.
90. Head-König 1993; Guinnane and Ogilvie 2014.
91. King 1999.
92. Cited in Coontz 2005: 200; see also Bailey 2004.
93. De Jager 1980: 59–62.
94. Montemurro 2006.
95. Coontz 2005: 167.
96. Therborn 2004, the following is based on Kok 2017.
97. Dozon 1996.
98. Murdock 1959.
99. Dozon 1996: 313.
100. Tambiah 1989: 423.
101. For example Kioli, Were, and Onkware 2012.
102. Delius and Glaser 2002: 33–34.
103. Hunter 2005.
104. Ibid.
105. Worthman and Whiting 1987.
106. Schapera 1933; Delius and Glaser 2002.

107. Low 2000: 119.
108. Therborn 2004.
109. Dozon 1996: 322.
110. Radcliffe 1950: 47.
111. Orchardson 1931.
112. Mann 1981.
113. Quoted in Dewaraja 1981.
114. Reid 1988.
115. Skinner 1997.
116. Therborn 2004: 54.
117. Loos 2008: 32.
118. Therborn 2004: 53.
119. Pieris 1956: 197.
120. Ibid.: 203.
121. Ryan 1952: 363.
122. Pieris 1956: 200.
123. Pieris 1956: 201.
124. Kok 2017.
125. Bernand and Gruzinski 1996.
126. Ibid.: 190.
127. Potthast-Jutkeit 1997b.
128. Kuznesof 1991: 246.
129. Therborn 2004:35.
130. Ibid.: 36.
131. Martinez-Alier 1974: 103ff.
132. Shumway 2001.
133. Goode 1959.
134. Terian 2004.
135. Monger 2004: 12, 82, 113ff.
136. Ibid.: 82.

Chapter 2

1.   Parrinder 2003: 43–5.
2.   Courtright 2006: 226.
3.   Riesebrodt 2013: 1–10.
4.   El-Menouar 2014: 68.
5.   Brown 2009: 91–2.
6.   Browning, Green, and Witte 2006: xxii–vii.
7.   Ibid.
8.   Garrett 1994: 12.
9.   Burguière and Lebrun 1997: 119.
10. Ibid.: 121.
11. Esposito 2002: 143.
12. Tucker 2008: 38–39.
13. Puschmann and Matthijs 2015: 15–16.
14. Parrinder 2003: 157–158.
15. Korotayev 2000: 395–403.

16. Cowan 2003: 571–576.
17. Tadmouri et al. 2009: 1–2.
18. Sholkamy 2003: 71–76.
19. Mitterauer 1997: 14–6; De Moor and Van Zanden 2010: 3–7.
20. Kaser 2000: 142–166, 192–193.
21. Potthast-Jutkeit 1997a: 65–66; 74–76.
22. Garrett 1994: 16; Witte and Nichols 2005: 19–20.
23. Burguière and Lebrun 1997: 124–127; Parrinder 2003: 232.
24. Constantelos 1985: 22–23. In the patristic and contemporary Orthodox Christian tradition, there are sharply divergent views on marriage and the place of sex within marriage. In the scriptural and patristic traditions, there are those who hold that marriage's only purpose is procreation. On the other hand, there are those who share a view much more compatible with the covenant idea of marriage: they hold that marriage is a multifaceted interrelationship of husband and wife in the unity of their person, in which marital conjugal relations are not only for procreation but also for expressing the loving unity of the couple. In the history of the development of marriage in Eastern Christianity, a struggle between these two orientations has taken and continues to take place (Harakas 2005: 95).
25. Calivas 1997: 48–54; Englert 1955: 105–106.
26. Parrinder 2003: 193–195.
27. Mashhour 2005: 571–575.
28. Parrinder 2003: 193–195.
29. Davies 1981: 139–144.
30. Mashhour 2005: 568–571; Tucker 2008: 56.
31. Parrinder 2003: 193–195.
32. Ibid.: 219
33. Van Poppel 1995; Engelen 2017.
34. Parrinder 2003: 219–220; Johnson 2005: 124.
35. Parrinder 2003: 219–220; Stan 2010: 39.
36. Johnson 2005: 127–128; Parrinder 2003: 230–232.
37. Ebrey 2006: 368.
38. Ibid.
39. Therborn 2004: 41–42.
40. Courtright 2006: 229–230.
41. Misra 1997: 129; Jain 2003: 134–135.
42. Therborn 2004: 62–64.
43. Thornton and Lin 1994: 359.
44. Parrinder 2003: 84–89.
45. Shang 2003: 228.
46. Jain 2003: 135–136.
47. Thornton and Lin 1994: 47.
48. Linck 1997: 108.
49. The first society in China to oppose foot-binding was founded in the Canton province in 1883. Anti-foot-binding societies spread in eastern China in the late nineteenth and early twentieth centuries (Therborn 2004: 64).
50. Cartier 1997: 273–278.
51. Moaddel 1998: 110, 126–128.
52. Esposito 2002: 145.
53. Tucker 2008: 66–69.

54. Brown 2009.
55. Weinzierl 1997: 256.
56. Van Poppel and Derosas 2006: 1–2.
57. Weinzierl 1997: 246–247, 252–256.
58. Freeze 1990: 709.
59. Therborn 2004: 84.
60. Nishihara 2000: 88.
61. Beillevaire 1997: 306–311.
62. Neuss-Kaneko 1990: 59–63.
63. Ma 1987: 674–675.
64. Ibid.; Therborn 2004: 86–87; Goossaert 2005: 3–6.
65. Esposito 2002: 151.
66. Therborn 2004: 88.
67. Moaddel 1998: 124.
68. Ibid.: 127.
69. Bernand and Gruzinski 1997: 244.
70. Borges 1992: 154, 165, 169.
71. Bonfield 2002: 129–132.
72. Berger 2006: 10–11; Kaplan 2007: 60–61.
73. Therborn 2004: 78.
74. Witte 2012: 310–311.
75. Bonfield 2002: 114–115.
76. Ibid.: 150.
77. Ibid.: 144.
78. Therborn 2004: 28–29.
79. Ibid.: 68.
80. Tucker 2008: 20, 70–72, 75.
81. Therborn 2004: 88.
82. Kaser 2008: 261.
83. Puschmann 2011: 21–22.
84. Potthast-Jutkeit 1997a: 71.
85. Potthast-Jutkeit 1997: 22–24.
86. Borges 1992: 46.
87. Falen 2008: 52.
88. Adamo 2011: 1–6.
89. Falen 2008: 52–56.
90. Ibid.
91. Grau, Hanak, and Stacher 1997: 141–142; Parrinder 2003: 137–139.
92. Parrinder 2003: 140–141.
93. Hunt 1991: 474–475.
94. Therborn 2004: 18, 49–51.
95. Chowdhry 1990: 259–265; Lardinois 1997: 343–346; Therborn 2004: 44–45.
96. Grey 2011: 107, 111, 115.
97. Lardinois 1997: 343–346; Therborn 2004: 45.
98. Parrinder 2003: 16.
99. Lardinois 1997: 352.
100. Therborn 2004: 45.

Chapter 3

1. Douglas 2015.
2. Chanock 1989.
3. Waddington and Van Hoecke 1998.
4. Witte 2012.
5. Phillips 1988: 180.
6. Vergniaud, quoted by Desan 2004: 57.
7. Glendon 1977: 56.
8. Civil Code 1804: Articles 63 and 75.
9. Glendon 1977: 57.
10. Moses 2017.
11. Novak 2000: 1070.
12. Vlaardingerbroek 1995–96; Torfs 2005.
13. Sachsen-Gessaphe 1989.
14. Rodriguez 2014.
15. Caulfield 2017.
16. Antokolskaia 2011.
17. Ibid.: 105; Rheinstein 1953; Garipova 2017.
18. Bonfield 2002: 143–144.
19. Seymour 2006: 13.
20. Nemes 2009: 333.
21. Quoted in ibid.: 335.
22. De Ussel 1991.
23. Sancifiena-Asurmend 2014.
24. De Ussel 1991; Sancifiena-Asurmend 2014.
25. Rheinstein 1953.
26. De Ussel 1991.
27. Logan 2008: 470.
28. Witte 2012.
29. *Dalrymple v. Dalrymple* (1811) 2 Hag Con 54; 161 ER 665.
30. Mair 2014.
31. Probert 2009.
32. For a detailed account see Harding 2019.
33. By the Marriage Notice (Scotland) Act 1878.
34. An Act to remove Doubts as to the Validity of certain Marriages had and solemnized within the British Territories in India, 1818, 58 Geo. III, c. 84, s. 1. Certain conditions applied, including that the ministers had been "appointed by the United Company of Merchants of England trading to the East Indies to officiate as Chaplains within the said Territories."
35. Hansard, May 13, 1851 vol 116 col 935.
36. An Act for Marriages in India, 14 and 15 c. XL: s 9.
37. Ibid: s 1.
38. An Act to Provide a Form of Marriage in Certain Cases, 1872.
39. See Mody 2002; Majumdar 2009, Chatterjee 2010; Newbigin 2013.
40. 9 Geo IV c 83 s 24.
41. 5 Geo IV no. 2.
42. Dodd 2018.
43. An Act to regulate the Celebration of Marriages in Newfoundland, 57 Geo III, c 51.

44. The Marriages Confirmation (Newfoundland) Act 1824, ss 3–4.
45. See An Act to Extend the Provisions of the Marriage Act of Upper Canada to Ministers of All Denominations of Christians, 1847: 10 & 11 Vict c 18; An Act to Amend the Laws Relating to the Solemnization of Matrimony in Upper Canada, 1857: 20 Vict c 66.
46. Elliott 2003–04.
47. 21 & 22 Geo III c. 25.
48. *R v Millis* (1843–44) 10 Cl & F 534; 8 ER 844. See further Probert 2008.
49. "The *Yelverton* Marriage Case" (1861) 11 Law Mag & L Rev Quart J Juris 3rd Ser 215.
50. Sörgjerd 2012: 44.
51. Sörgjerd 2012.
52. Simotta 1995–96.
53. Tucker 2008; Scharffs and Disparte 2010.
54. Welchman 2007: 12.
55. Tucker 2008: 70.
56. Barkey and Gavrilis 2016: 30.
57. Barkey and Gavrilis 2016.
58. Ibid.: 884.
59. Derrett 1968; Newbigin 2013.
60. Ibid.: 32–35; Chatterjee 2010: 539.
61. Benton 2001: 139.
62. Ipaye 1998: 34.
63. De Koker 1998: 324.
64. *In Re Bethell* (1887) 38 Ch D: 220.
65. Ibid.: 229.
66. Ibid.: 224.
67. Ibid.: 236.
68. Kabeberi-Macharia and Nyamu 1998; De Koker 1998.
69. Chanock 1989; De Koker 1998.
70. Chanock 1989; De Koker 1998.
71. Kabeberi-Macharia and Nyamu 1998.
72. Quoted in Seuffert 2003: 206.
73. *Armitage v Armitage* (1866) LR 3 Eq 343.
74. Seuffert 2003: 186.
75. *Ruding v Smith* (1821) 2 Hag Con: 371; 161 ER 774: 385.
76. *Ruding*, 394; *Kent v Burgess* (1840) 11 Sim 361; 59 ER 913, 376.
77. Probert 2017.
78. Westermarck 1891: 417.
79. Grossberg 1988: x.
80. Cott 2000.
81. Probert 2008, 2009.
82. Bowman 1996: 721.
83. Lind 2008.
84. Bowman 1996: 722.
85. Grossberg 1985.
86. Keller 1994: 18.
87. *In re Estate of McLaughlin v. McLaughlin*, 4 Wash. 570; 30 P. 651 (1892).
88. Todorova 2000.

Chapter 4

1. Lundh and Kurosu 2014a: 25.
2. Bourdieu and Passeron 1977.
3. Levi-Strauss 1969.
4. EAP is an international collaboration that compares relationships between economic conditions, household organization, and demographic behavior, using household register data from eighteenth- and nineteenth-century communities in Europe and Asia (MIT Book Series: *Eurasia Population Family History*).
5. Bengtsson et al. 2004.
6. Engelen 2005.
7. Lyon 2013.
8. Ehmer 2002: 292.
9. Dribe and Lundh 2014: 247.
10. Raghuvanshi 1969.
11. Dribe, Manfredini, and Oris 2014: 109.
12. Probert in this volume.
13. Fuess 2012: 176–177.
14. Tsuya and Kurosu 2014; Chen, Campbell, and Lee 2014; Han 2004. It is also stimulating to consider Wolf's assertion here that nuptiality is not the key to the differences between Europe and the rest of the world, but that the difference lies in parental authority (Wolf 2005: 221).
15. Skinner 1997: 62.
16. Saito (1998) discusses the views of M. Mitterauer and J. Hajnal.
17. Saito 1998.
18. Aruga 1943; Otake 1982.
19. Hirschman and Teerawichitchainan 2003.
20. Reid 2014. This relates to the arguments of Saito (2014) and Dyson and Moore (1983) in regard to the relationship between female autonomy and demographic behaviors.
21. Chen, Campbell, and Lee 2014: 462.
22. Engelen and Hsieh 2007: 56.
23. Wolf and Huang 1980.
24. Gamage 1982.
25. Wolf and Huang 1980.
26. Gamage 1982.
27. Dribe, Manfredini, and Oris 2014.
28. Wolf and Huang 1980: 57.
29. Dribe, Manfredini, and Oris 2014.
30. The household registers used for the EAP comparison (Tsuya et al. 2010) do not record exact dates and those infants who were born and passed away during the interval of the two consecutive registers are not recorded. Therefore it is important to emphasize here that it is the first "recorded" child.
31. Tsuya and Kurosu 2010.
32. Engelen and Hsieh 2007: 134.
33. Kok et al. 2006; Campbell and Lee (2010) survey and succinctly summarize the debate on Chinese low fertility.
34. Engelen and Hsieh 2007.
35. Ibid.: 166.

36. Emori 1998.
37. Wolf and Huang 1980; Kok, Yang, and Hsieh 2006.
38. Agarwala 1957.
39. Ibid.
40. Raghuvanshi 1969: 95–98.
41. Phillips 1988; Van Poppel 1997; Matthijs 2008.
42. Kurosu 2011; Hirschman and Teerawichitchainan 2003; Jones 1981; Boomgaard 1989: 145.
43. Kurosu 2007.
44. Fuess 2004.
45. Takagi 1987; Kurosu 2011.
46. Son 2010.
47. Dribe, Manfredini, and Oris 2014.
48. Hajnal 1965.
49. For example, Kertzer and Hogan 1991: 157; Reher 1991; Lundh et al. 2014b. Engelen and Wolf (2005b: 20) clarify various debates by sorting the claims by (1) "geography," that Europe is unique or almost unique to the world; (2) "niche," that a man has an independent livelihood before marrying; and (3) "equilibrium," that nuptiality regulated the relationship between economic well-being and population growth in Europe.
50. Engelen and Hsieh 2007: 54.
51. For example, for Europe, Ehmer 2002; Kertzer and Hogan 1991; Reher 1991; Szołtysek 2015. For Asia, Hayami 1987; Kurosu, Tsuya, and Hamano 1999; Chuang and Wolf 1995; Agarwala 1957. A stark contrast between early marriage in north and east India, in contrast to late marriage in the south, is shown in Table 4.1.
52. Lundh et al. 2014b.
53. Boomgaard 1989: 140–141; Reid 1987: 38.
54. Wang, Campbell, and Lee 2010.
55. See figures 3A and 3B in Lundh et al. 2014b.
56. Table I, Krishnan 1977.
57. Dribe and Lundh 2005.
58. Chen, Campbell, and Lee 2014: 459.
59. Raghuvanshi 1969.
60. Majumdar 2004.
61. Dribe and Lundh 2005; Van Leeuwen and Maas 2002. There was also a tendency for women to marry upward, while men married downward.
62. Van de Putte et al. 2009.
63. Yagi 2001: 577.
64. Lee, Wang, and Ruan 2001; Wolf and Huang 1980.
65. Chen, Campbell, and Lee 2014: 464.
66. O'Hanlon 2017.
67. Ibid.
68. Goody 1983.
69. For example, Kingdom of Naples, Brittany in France, Neckarhausen in southwestern Germany (Ehmer 2002: 294–295).
70. Ehmer 2002: 294–296.
71. Ibid.: 292–297.
72. Shaw and Raz 2015: 1.
73. Ibid.: 9.
74. Campbell and Lee 2008.

75. Lyon 2013.
76. Oto 1996: 55.
77. Goody 2000: 33–34.
78. Reid 2014: 19.
79. Chen, Campbell, and Lee 2014: 462–463.
80. Park 2008.
81. Prince Peter 1955: 180.
82. Ibid.: 180.
83. Levine and Sangree 1980: 391.
84. Ji, Xu, and Mace 2014.
85. Leach 1955.
86. Anderson 2007.
87. Goody 1973: 2–3; 49–52.
88. Lundh and Kurosu 2014a: 31.
89. Dribe and Lundh 2014: 216.
90. Bengtsson 2014: 149.
91. Derosas et al. 2014.
92. Yagi 2001: 25.
93. Otake 1977: 145.
94. Chen, Campbell, and Lee 2014: 462–463.
95. Ahmad 2010.
96. Mathur 1995.
97. Skinner 1997; Zhao 1997.
98. Tsuya and Kurosu 2010.
99. Dupâquier et al. 1981; Kurosu, Lundh and Breschi 2014.
100. Park 2008.
101. Kurosu, Lundh, and Breschi 2014.
102. Van Poppel 1995; Matthijs 2003.
103. Kurosu, Lundh, and Breschi 2014: 223.
104. Kurosu, Lundh, and Breschi 2014.
105. See Puschmann and Solli (2014) for an overview of these studies in Europe.
106. Bengtsson et al. 2004.
107. Lundh 2002: 427.
108. Kurosu, Lundh, and Breschi 2014: 216.
109. Shorter 1975; Stone 1993: 36.
110. Ehmer 2002: 321.
111. Matthijs 2006.
112. Ehmer 2002: 300.
113. Janssens 1997.
114. Matthijs 2006.
115. Phillips 1988.
116. Vikström, Van Poppel and Van de Putte 2011: 113.
117. Lee and Wang 2009.
118. O'Hanlon 2017.
119. Lyon 2013.
120. Majumdar 2004.
121. Hayami 1992.
122. Reid 2014.

Chapter 5

1. Pomeranz 2000.
2. Osterhammel 2014.
3. Broadberry, Fremdling, and Solar 2010.
4. Beckert 2014.
5. Osterhammel 2014.
6. Ibid.
7. Sen 1998.
8. Cameron and Neal 2003.
9. Osterhammel 2014.
10. Janssens 2003.
11. Dennison and Simpson 2010.
12. Levine 1985.
13. Cohen 1970.
14. Saito 2000; Tsuya and Kurosu 2014.
15. Saito 2000; Lundh and Kurosu 2014c.
16. De Vries 2008.
17. Klep 2004.
18. Rowntree 1901.
19. Alter and Clark 2010.
20. Hajnal 1965.
21. Szołtysek 2015.
22. Lynch 1991.
23. Janssens 1993.
24. Gillis 1985.
25. Alter 1988; Janssens 2014.
26. Lynch 1986.
27. Spagnoli 1983.
28. Oris, Alter, and Servais 2014.
29. Janssens 1993; Puschmann and Solli 2014.
30. Störmer et al. 2018.
31. Haines 1996.
32. Scott and Tilly 1975.
33. Berg 1998.
34. Anderson 1971; Schwarzkopf 2007.
35. Cameron and Neal 2003.
36. Janssens 2014.
37. Clark 1995.
38. Alter 1988.
39. Devos 2000.
40. Boomgaard 1981.
41. Van Nederveen Meerkerk 2017.
42. Booth 2016.
43. Sen 1998.
44. Ibid.
45. Seccombe 1993.
46. Janssens 2014.

47. Humphries and Weisdorf 2015.
48. O'Dowd 1994; Wikander 1998.
49. Humphries and Sarasua 2012.
50. Seccombe 1993.
51. Clark 1995; Rose 1992.
52. Fraundorf 1979.
53. Humphries and Sarasua 2012.
54. Humphries and Weisdorf 2015.
55. Horrell and Humphries 1998.
56. Van den Eeckhout 1993.
57. Gálvez-Muñoz 1998.
58. Hanagan 1998.
59. Safa 1995.
60. Sen 1998.
61. Thompson 1963.
62. De Herdt 2001.
63. Nardinelli 1990.
64. Horrell and Humphries 1995.
65. Humphries 2013.
66. Cunningham and Viazzo 2001.
67. Goldin 1979.
68. Horan and Hargis 1991.
69. Nardinelli 1980.
70. Cunningham 2000.
71. Saito 2001.
72. Camps I Cura 2001.
73. Baines and Johnson 1999.
74. Haines 1979.
75. Camps I Cura 1998, 2001.
76. Saito 2000.
77. Caldwell 2005.
78. Seccombe 1993.

Chapter 6

1. Lystra 1989: 3; Mann 2011: xv.
2. Freedman 1982: 201.
3. Jankowiak and Fischer 1992.
4. Fisher 1998, 2017.
5. McBride 2010: 384.
6. Halperin 1989: 258.
7. Ferrante 2015: 207.
8. Coontz 2005: 15.
9. Coontz 2004: 977.
10. Coontz 2005: 7.
11. Durães et al. 2009: 6.
12. Majumdar 2004: 912.
13. Lindsey 2011.

14. Kozma 2011.
15. De Moor and Van Zanden 2010: 6.
16. Kok and Mandemakers 2008.
17. Kok in this volume.
18. Wolf 1995.
19. Coontz 2005: 145–160.
20. Klep 2011.
21. Coontz 2005: 146; Klep 2011: 23–25.
22. Putnam 2015: 135–190.
23. Van de Putte et al. 2009.
24. Van Leeuwen and Maas 2002; Van de Putte 2003; Puschmann et al. 2015.
25. Ekamper, Van Poppel, and Mandemakers 2011.
26. Wienholts 2018.
27. Vries 2018.
28. Haworth 2012.
29. Karandashev 2017: 158.
30. Eigner 1970.
31. El Far 2014: 235–236.
32. Kandiyoti 1991: 25.
33. Duben and Behar 2002: 91.
34. Marcus 1966.
35. Zisowitz Stearns and Stearns 1985.
36. Gay 1984–98: 468.
37. Lystra 1989.
38. Shorter 1975: 224–225.
39. Quoted in McKinsey 1984: 171.
40. Hajnal 1965; Watkins 1981.
41. Coontz 2006.
42. Amato and Irving 2005: 44; Phillips 1991: 164. Matthijs, Baerts, and Van de Putte 2008: 241; Van Poppel 1992: 473.
43. Amato and Irving 2005: 44.
44. Matthijs, Baerts, and Van de Putte 2008: 264.
45. Afary 2009: 29.
46. Naamane Guessous 2007.
47. Afary 2009: 32–33.
48. Lindholm 2002: 55.
49. Van Wijk 1986; Quoted in Obdeijn, De Mas and Pel 2012: 219. Translated by Paul Puschmann.
50. Engelen and Wolf 2011.
51. Engelen and Kok 2003; Engelen and Puschmann 2011.
52. Lee and Wang 2009; Afary 2009.
53. Van Bavel 2004.
54. Livi-Bacci 2017.
55. Dribe et al. 2017.
56. Jütte 2008: 152.
57. Janssens in this volume.
58. Caldwell 1980: 225; Engelen and Hillebrand 1986: 490.
59. Engelen 1997.

60. D'arcy 1977: 429.
61. Masjuan and Martinez-Alier 2004: 18.
62. Schoonheim 2005.
63. Engelen 1997; Engelen 2009.
64. Lucassen 2010.
65. Fisher 2006: 210; Szreter and Fisher 2010: 230.
66. Malthus [1798] 1960.
67. Engelen 2006: 11; Wolf and Engelen 2008.
68. See especially Campbell, Feng, and Lee 2004; Wolf and Engelen 2008; Lee and Wang 2009; Tsuya et al. 2010.
69. Relatively low marital fertility was most likely also a consequence of poverty and undernutrition, as it caused (temporary) sterility. The dangerous practice of abortion without professional caretakers heightened maternal mortality and also increased the risk of (permanent) sterility.
70. Engelen 2006; 20–21; Engelen and Hsieh 2007.
71. Marcus 1966; Cominos 1972; see also Zisowitz Stearns and Stearns 1985.
72. Lystra 1989: 58.
73. Frühstück 2003; Foucault 1990.
74. Timm and Sanborn 2016.
75. Ze'evi 2006.
76. Timm and Sanborn 2016: 133.
77. Foucault 1990: 11.
78. Degler 1974.
79. Shorter 1971; 1973.
80. For an early critique see Tilly, Scott, and Cohen 1976.
81. Kok 2005.
82. Levine 1977.
83. Matovic 1986.
84. Van den Boomen and Puschmann 2018.
85. Timm and Sanborn 2016: 80–81.
86. Owen 1840.
87. Timm and Sanborn 2016: 81.
88. Beecher 1986: 220–240.
89. Timm and Sanborn 2016: 99–105.
90. Ibid.: 216.
91. Wood Hill 1993.
92. Ross 2015.
93. Timm and Sanborn 2016: 106.
94. Kota 2014.
95. Bernheimer 1997: 1, 73.
96. Bartley 2000.

Chapter 7

1. Freeman 2003: xi.
2. Tanner 1979: 18.
3. Ibid.: 113 and 179.
4. Ibid.: 371.

5. Ibid.
6. See for example Black 1975; Armstrong 1976; Segal 1992; Sinclair 1993; Overton 1996; White and Segal 1997; White 1999.
7. Boone 1987.
8. Ibid.: 224.
9. In her important study of Charles Dickens, Kelly Hager offers an alternative explanation for the fact that critics have ignored works that feature what she terms the failed-marriage plot: "critics—both victorian and victorianist—may (have) be(en) reluctant to admit them to the canon because they need to believe in the myth of marriage" (Hager 2010: 32).
10. Phillips 1988: 179.
11. Pasco 2009: 131.
12. Blasius 1992: 27–33.
13. Horstman 1985: 15. Horstman's table of parliamentary divorces in England before 1800 lists 126 divorces between the first case in 1672 and 1799, but of these, 32 were between 1771 and 1779, and 41 between 1790 and 1799 (16–18), meaning that well over half of all divorces granted in England over 130 years were granted in those two decades. Lawrence Stone notes that "the 12 petitions for divorce received in 1799 (10 of which were successful) were the highest number ever handled in a single year, before or after"—by which he means up to the 1857 Matrimonial Causes Act, which ended the need for divorce to be secured by an Act of Parliament (Stone 1990: 325).
14. Phillips 1988: 155.
15. Ibid.: 439.
16. Ibid.: 463.
17. Ibid.
18. Thackeray [1847–48] 1968: 310.
19. Watt 2001: 138.
20. Ibid.: 149.
21. See for example Overton 2002; Ganz 2005; Roulston 2010; DiPlacidi and Leydecker 2018.
22. Exceptions include Gerig 2008. The following discussion of the representation of divorce in European fiction around 1800 draws on Leydecker 2007, 2011a.
23. Roulston 2010: 48.
24. Gallas and Runge 1993: 12.
25. There are no reliable figures for the numbers of divorces in Prussia around 1800, but Blasius notes that there were on average over 3,000 divorces a year there between 1836 and 1841 (Blasius 1992: 36).
26. Schieth 1990: 122.
27. Gallas 1990: 74.
28. For a full discussion see Leydecker 2011b.
29. In *Die Wahlverwandtschaften*, the news of Charlotte's pregnancy becomes a barrier to Eduard divorcing her to be united with Ottilie at a key moment in the text.
30. Staël [1802] 1995: 442.
31. Ibid.: 308.
32. Binhammer 1996.
33. Austen [1814] 1983: 155.
34. Edgeworth [1809] 1992: 314.
35. Wollstonecraft [1798] 2005: 76.
36. Ibid.: 119.
37. Leckie 1999 and 2007.

38. Wollstonecraft [1798] 2005: 120.
39. Ibid.: 121.
40. See Leydecker 1996 for a full account of these debates in Germany.
41. Wollstonecraft [1798] 2005: 123.
42. Ibid.: 124.
43. The novel was published in England under the pseudonym E. S. Villa-Real in 1795, with an American edition being published under the name E. S. Villa-Real Gooch the following year.
44. "A woman's fame depends less on her own character, than it does on that of her husband. If he discards her, the world will also, without enquiring why he has done so ... Alas! Her day will soon set in darkness–her breaking heart will be overwhelmed by the storms of adversity, until in some obscure corner of the earth she dies unknown—unpitied—and unlamented!" (Gooch 1796: 52).
45. Austen [1814] 1983: 449.
46. Stone 1990: 329.
47. Ibid.: 332.
48. "Howells is credited with the first 'serious' attempt at a literary portrayal of divorce" (Freeman 2003: xii), though as Norma Basch notes, there were (as in England) some literary portrayals, notably in the works of T. S. Arthur, of the dangers of divorce for women in American sentimental fiction around the middle of the century (Basch 1999: 176–185).
49. Overton 1996, 2002.
50. Turner 1987.
51. Ganz 2006: 156.
52. On Norton, see Poovey 1988: 51–88.
53. For a full discussion of Lewald's novel, see Leydecker 2005.
54. On the rise of romantic love and marriage, see Coontz 2005; Puschmann in this volume.
55. Aston [1847] 1982: 154.
56. For a full discussion of German women novelists of the 1840s, see Möhrmann 1977.
57. Humpherys 1999: 44.
58. Ibid.: 45.
59. For an extensive discussion of this novel see White 2013: 85–92.
60. See Leydecker 1996, 2002, 2013a, 2013b.
61. Leydecker 2002.
62. Zola [1881] 1966–69, XIV, 543–547, English translation quoted from Overton 2002, 188. See also Maupassant 1980.
63. As indicated by the titles of Overton 1996 and 2002.
64. White 2013.
65. In parallel with the restraint in the treatment of divorce in novels in the later decades of the nineteenth century, the Scottish painter William Quiller Orchardson (1832–1910) in the 1880s specialized in depicting marital crises in an understated fashion.
66. Miller 1994: 70.
67. Chopin [1899] 2000: 119.
68. Humpherys 1999: 42. See also Leckie 1999: 105, where she identifies four characteristics of Victorian divorce court journalism—"the disruption of narrative causality and linearity, the unreliability of the narrative itself, the multiple points of view, and the question of narrative closure"—which "stand in opposition to the dominant aspects of the eighteenth- and nineteenth-century marriage-plot tradition, but they also match several innovations now associated with modernism."
69. Haytock 2002: 217.

70. Ibid.: 228.
71. See Baldick 2004: 1–14 (quotation from 5) for a discussion of the wider modern movement, of which, according to Baldick, high modernism was one element.
72. Wharton [1907] 1996: 36. While it might be argued that the fact that divorce is in fact avoided in *Madame de Treymes* (just as it is in Wharton's best-known novel *Age of Innocence*, published in 1920 but set in the 1870s) gives the lie to the alleged commonplace nature of divorce, as Haytock notes: "In Wharton's writing about the 1920s, divorce is no longer scandalous and in fact has an established place in society" (Haytock 2002: 219).
73. Wassermann 1987: especially part 1, chapters 7–8, 29–39.
74. Harris 1996: 125.
75. Leydecker 2015.
76. Mann [1900] 1986: 215.
77. Galsworthy [1906] 2001: 206.
78. For a full discussion of Wharton's novel see MacComb 2000: 121–170.
79. Wharton [1913] 2000: 212.
80. Ibid.: 245.
81. Ibid.: 174.
82. Wharton [1922] 2006: 258.

Chapter 8

1. The phrase is borrowed from Lash 1977.
2. Fryckman and Löfgrenn 1987.
3. Gay 1984–98, 1: 31–35.
4. All information regarding nineteenth-century advice literature is discussed in Tilburg 1998.
5. This argument was first made by Mitterauer and Sieder 1977; more recently, it has also been advanced by Gordon and Nair 2003: 71–73.
6. Pagden 2013: 5–7, 16–18.
7. For several reasons providing figures is difficult. One manuscript could be published by different booksellers, and the practice of editing a single manuscript for different audiences still existed. With the internationalization of the book market, marriage manuals circulated widely: in this period, the Dutch market offered translations of French, Belgian, German, British, and American titles.
8. This was demonstrated first by Laqueur 1990, and more recently by O'Brien 2005: 3–7.
9. Weeks 1981; Showalter 1990.
10. Gillen and Ghosh 2007: 181–188.
11. Connections between marriage, society, and civilization have been discussed by early Enlightenment philosophers such as Hobbes and Locke. Several Enlightenment theories regarding cultural diversity are based on the varieties of marriage and family, as in Montesquieu's *De l' esprit des lois* (1748) and Buffon's *Histoire naturelle* (1749–88). Enlightenment theories regarding societal development and civilization elaborate on the theme of marriage as well, as in Rousseau's *Discours sur l'origine de l'inégalité* (1754) and Adam Smith's *Wealth of Nations* (1776).
12. Groenendijk 1984: 44–46.
13. Foucault 1966.
14. The translations of the citations from the German and the Dutch advice literature are mine [MT].

15. Voigt 1821: 3–4.
16. Ibid.: 2–6.
17. Cramer 1781: 23, 47.
18. Bodisco 1795: 15.
19. Voigt 1821: 42.
20. Ouwerkerk de Vries 1795: 162.
21. Lehmann 1877: 47.
22. James 1828: 102.
23. Van Campen 1866: 127–129.
24. I Cor. 11:9.
25. Eph. 5.28–29.
26. Vickery 2009: 16–24.
27. Branca 1975.
28. Donzelot 1979.
29. This analysis follows Armstrong 1987: 96–160.
30. Goodman 2009: 274–307.
31. Vickery 2009: 12–13, 16–24, 83–105, 231–256.
32. Ellis 1839, 1: 24–25.
33. Ellis 1839, 1: 29.
34. Kett 1977; Springhall 1986.
35. This argument was made first by Demos and Demos 1969: 632–638.
36. Vickery 2009: 77–79.
37. Regt 1984: 148–50, 209–218.
38. Gay 1984–98, 1: 31–35.
39. Sloterdijk 1983.
40. Goodman 2009: 274–307.
41. The phrase is borrowed from Beer 1974.
42. Gay 1984–98, vol. 1.
43. Taylor 2005: 32–33.
44. Bour 2013: 584.
45. Wollstonecraft [1798] 1975: 44–45.
46. Ibid.: 138.
47. Hirschfeld 1918: 205.
48. Ibid.: 206.
49. Ibid.: 200–212.
50. Ramien [Hirschfeld] 1896: ii.
51. Showalter 1990.
52. As argued by Coontz 2005.

BIBLIOGRAPHY

Adamo, David T. (2011), "Christianity and the African Traditional Religion(s): The Postcolonial Round of Engagement," *Verbum et Ecclesia*, 32 (1): 1–10.

Afary, Janet (2009), *Sexual Politics in Modern Iran*, Cambridge: Cambridge University Press.

Agarwala, S. N. (1957), "The Age at Marriage in India," *Population Index*, 23 (2): 96–107.

Ahmad, Nehaluddin (2010), "Female Feticide in India," *Issues in Law & Medicine*, 26 (1): 13–29.

Albertine, Susan (1992), "Heart's Expression: The Middle-Class Language of Love in Late Nineteenth-Century Correspondence," *American Literary History*, 4 (1): 141–164.

Al-Khowli, Ramadan (2006), "Observations on the Use of Shari'a Court Records as a Source of Social History," in Amira El-Azhary Sonbol (ed.), *Beyond the Exotic: Women's Histories in Islamic Societies*, 139–151, Syracuse, NY: Syracuse University Press.

Allendorf, Keera (2013), "Schemas of Marital Change: From Arranged Marriages to Eloping for Love," *Journal of Marriage and Family*, 75 (2): 453–469.

Alter, George (1988), *Family and the Female Life Course: The Women of Verviers, Belgium, 1849–1880*, Madison: University of Wisconsin Press.

Alter, George and Gregory Clark (2010), "The Demographic Transition and Human Capital," in Stephen Broadberry and Kevin H. O'Rourke (eds.), *The Cambridge Economic History of Modern Europe*, Vol. 1, *1700–1870*, 43–69, Cambridge: Cambridge University Press.

Amato, Paul R. and Shelley Irving (2005), "Historical Trends in Divorce in the United States," in Mark A. Fine and John H. Harvey (eds.), *Handbook of Divorce and Relationship Dissolution*, 41–58, London: Routledge.

Anderson, Michael (1971), *Family Structure in Nineteenth-Century Lancashire*, Cambridge: Cambridge University Press.

Anderson, Robert T. and Gallatin Anderson (1962), "Ukrainian Night Courting," *Anthropological Quarterly*, 35 (1): 29–32.

Anderson, Siwan (2007), "The Economics of Dowry and Bride Price," *Journal of Economic Perspectives*, 21 (4): 151–174.

Antokolskaia, Masha (2011), "Family Law and Religion: The Russian Perspective, Past and Present," in Jane Mair and Esin Örücü (eds.), *The Place of Religion in Family Law: A Comparative Search*, 97–116, Antwerp: Intersentia.

Armstrong, Judith (1976), *The Novel of Adultery*, Basingstoke: Macmillan.

Armstrong, Nancy (1987), *Desire and Domestic Fiction: A Political History of the Novel*, New York: Oxford University Press.

Aruga, Kizaemon (1943), *Nihon no Kazoku-seido* (Family System and Tenant Farming in Japan), Tokyo: Miraisha.

Aston, Louise ([1847] 1982), *Aus dem Leben einer Frau*, Stuttgart: Akademischer Verlag.

Austen, Jane ([1814] 1983), *Mansfield Park*, Harmondsworth: Penguin.

Bailey, Beth (2004), "From Front Porch to Back Seat: A History of the Date," *Magazine of History*, 18 (4): 23–26.

Baines, Dudley and Paul Johnson (1999), "Did they Jump or were they Pushed? The Exit of Older Men from the London Labour Market," *Journal of Economic History*, 59 (4): 949–971.

Bairoch, Paul (1982), "International Industrialization Levels from 1750 to 1980," *Journal of European Economic History*, 11 (2): 269–333.

Baldick, Chris (2004), *The Oxford English Literary History*, Vol. 10: *1910–1940: The Modern Movement*, Oxford: Oxford University Press.

Barkey, Karen and George Gavrilis (2016), "The Ottoman Millet System: Non Territorial Autonomy and its Contemporary Legacy," *Ethnopolitics*, 15 (1): 24–42.

Bartley, Paula (2000), *Prostitution: Prevention and Reform in England, 1860–1914*, London: Routledge.

Basch, Norma (1999), *Framing American Divorce: From the Revolutionary Generation to the Victorians*, Berkeley: University of California Press.

Baudouin, Marcel (1906), *Le Maraîchinage, coutume du pays de Monts (Vendée)*, Paris: Maloine.

Beckert, Sven (2014), *Empire of Cotton: A Global History*, New York: Vintage Books.

Beecher, Jonathan (1986), *Charles Fourier: The Visionary and His World*, Berkeley: University of California Press.

Beer, Patricia (1974), *Reader I Married Him: A Study of the Woman Characters of Jane Austen, Charlotte Brontë, Elizabeth Gaskell and George Eliot*, London: Macmillan.

Beillevaire, Patrick (1996a), "Japan: A Household Society," in André Burguière, Christiane Klapisch-Zuber, Martine Segalen, and Françoise Zonabend (eds.), *A History of the Family*, Vol. 1: *Distant Worlds, Ancient Worlds*, 523–565, Cambridge, MA: Harvard University Press [First published 1986 in French].

Beillevaire, Patrick (1996b), "The Family: Instrument and Model of the Japanese Nation," in André Burguière, Christiane Klapisch-Zuber, Martine Segalen, and Françoise Zonabend (eds.), *A History of the Family*, Vol. 2: *The Impact of Modernity*, 242–267, Cambridge, MA: Harvard University Press [First published 1986 in French].

Beillevaire, Patrick (1997), "Die Familie: Instrument und Modell der japanischen Nation," in André Burguière, Christiane Klapisch-Zuber, Martine Segalen, and Françoise Zonabend (eds.), *Geschichte der Familie—Neuzeit*, 305–342, Frankfurt: Campus Verlag.

Bengtsson, Tommy (2014), "The Influence of Economic Factors on First Marriage in Historical Europe and Asia," in Christer Lundh, Satomi Kurosu, et al. (eds.), *Similarity in Difference: Marriage in Europe and Asia, 1700–1900*, 145–192, Cambridge, MA: MIT Press.

Bengtsson, Tommy, Cameron Campbell, James Z. Lee, et al. (2004), *Life under Pressure: Mortality and Living Standards in Europe and Asia, 1700–1900*, Cambridge, MA: MIT Press.

Benton, Lauren (2001), *Law and Colonial Cultures: Legal Regimes in World History, 1400–1900*, Cambridge: Cambridge University Press.

Berg, Maxine (1998), "What Difference Did Women's Work Make to the Industrial Revolution?" in Pamela Sharp (ed.), *Women's Work: The English Experience 1650–1914*, 149–171, London: Arnold.

Berger, Michael S. (2006), "Judaism," in Don S. Browning, M. Christian Green, and John Witte Jr. (eds.), *Sex, Marriage, & Family in World Religions*, 1–76, New York: Columbia University Press.

Bernand, Carmen and Serge Gruzinski (1996), "Children of the Apocalypse: The Family in Meso-America and the Andes," in André Burguière, Christiane Klapisch-Zuber, Martine Segalen, and Françoise Zonabend (eds.), *A History of the Family*, Vol. 2: *The Impact of Modernity*, 161–215, Cambridge, MA: Harvard University Press [First published 1986 in French].

Bernand, Carmen and Serge Gruzinski (1997), "Die Kinder der Apokalypse: Die Familie in Mittelamerika und in den Anden," in André Burguière, Christiane Klapisch-Zuber, Martine Segalen, and Françoise Zonabend (eds.), *Geschichte der Familie—Neuzeit*, 195–268, Frankfurt: Campus Verlag.

Bernheimer, Charles (1997), *Figures of Ill Repute: Representing Prostitution in Nineteenth-Century France*, Durham, NC: Duke University Press.

Binhammer, Katherine (1996), "The Sex Panic of the 1790s," *Journal of the History of Sexuality*, 6 (3): 409–434.

Black, Michael (1975), *The Literature of Fidelity*, London: Chatto & Windus.

Blasius, Dirk (1992), *Ehescheidungen in Deutschland im 19. und 20. Jahrhundert*, Frankfurt am Main: Fischer.

Bodisco, Martinus (1795), *Verhandeling over de verpligtingen van eenen braaven huisvader, en zulk eene huismoeder in 't gemeen burgerlijk leven*, Verhandelingen, uitgegeeven door de Maatschappij tot Nut van 't Algemeen IV, Amsterdam: H. Keijzer, C. de Vries and H. van Munster.

Bonfield, Lloyd (2002), "European Family Law," in David I. Kertzer and Marzio Barbagli (eds.), *Family Life in the Long Nineteenth Century 1789–1913*, 109–154, New Haven, CT: Yale University Press.

Boomgaard, Peter (1981), "Female Labour and Population Growth on Nineteenth-Century Java," *Review of Indonesian and Malayan Affairs*, 15 (2): 1–31.

Boomgaard, Peter (1989), *Children of the Colonial State: Population Growth and Development in Java, 1795–1880*, Amsterdam: Free University Press.

Boone, Joseph Allen (1987), *Tradition Counter Tradition: Love and the Form of Fiction*, Chicago: University of Chicago Press.

Booth, Anne (2016), "Women, Work and the Family: Is Southeast Asia Different?" *Economic History of Developing Regions*, 31 (1): 167–197.

Borges, Dain (1992), *The Family in Bahia, Brazil, 1870–1945*, Stanford, CA: Stanford University Press.

Borscheid, Peter (1986), "Romantic Love or Material Interest: Choosing Partners in Nineteenth-Century Germany," *Journal of Family History*, 11 (2): 157–168.

Bossen, Laurel and Hill Gates (2017), *Bound Feet, Young Hands: Tracking the Demise of Footbinding in Village China*, Stanford, CA: Stanford University Press.

Bour, Isabelle (2013), "A New Wollstonecraft: The Reception of the Vindication of the Rights of Woman and of The Wrongs of Woman in Revolutionary France," *Journal of Eighteenth-Century Studies*, 36 (4): 575–587.

Bourdieu, Pierre and Jean-Claude Passeron (1977), *Reproduction in Education, Society and Culture*, London: Sage.

Bowman, Cynthia Grant (1996), "A Feminist Proposal to Bring Back Common Law Marriage," *Oregon Law Review*, 75 (3): 709–780.

Branca, Patricia (1975), *Silent Sisterhood: Middle Class Women in the Victorian Home*, London: Croom Helm.

Bras, Hilde (2011), "Intensification of Family Relations? Changes in the Choice of Marriage Witnesses in the Netherlands, 1830–1950," *TSEG/Low Countries Journal of Social and Economic History*, 8 (4): 102–135.

Broadberry, Stephen, Rainer Fremdling and Peter Solar (2010), "Industry," in Stephen Broadberry and Kevin H. O'Rourke (eds.), *The Cambridge Economic History of Modern Europe*, Vol. 1, *1700–1870*, 164–186, Cambridge: Cambridge University Press.

Brown, Callum G. (2009), *The Death of Christian Britain: Understanding Secularization, 1800–2000*, London: Routledge.

Brown, Melissa J. (2007), "Ethnic Identity, Cultural Variation, and Processes of Change: Rethinking the Insights of Standardization and Orthopraxy," *Modern China*, 33 (1): 91–124.

Browning, Don S., M. Christian Green and John Witte Jr. (2006), "Introduction," in Don S. Browning, M. Christian Green, and John Witte Jr. (eds.), *Sex, Marriage, & Family in World Religions*, xvii–xxix, New York: Columbia University Press.

Bulten, Luc, Jan Kok, Dries Lyna, and Nadeera Rupesinghe (2018), "Contested conjugality? Sinhalese Marriage Practices in Eighteenth-Century Dutch Colonial Sri Lanka," *Annales de Démographie Historique*, 135 (1): 51–180.

Burguière, André and François Lebrun (1997), "Der Priester, der Fürst und die Familie," in André Burguière, Christiane Klapisch-Zuber, Martine Segalen, and Françoise Zonabend (eds.), *Geschichte der Familie—Neuzeit*, 119–194, Frankfurt: Campus Verlag.

Caldwell, John C. (1980), "Mass Education as a Determinant of the Timing of Fertility Decline," *Population and Development Review*, 6 (2): 225–255.

Caldwell, John C. (2005) "On Net Intergenerational Wealth Flows: An Update," *Population and Development Review*, 31 (4): 721–740.

Calivas, Alkiviadis C. (1997), "Marriage: The Sacrament of Love and Communion," in Anton C. Vrame (ed.), *Intermarriage: Orthodox Perspectives*, 34–61, Brookline, MA: Holy Cross Orthodox Press.

Cameron, Rondo and Larry Neal (2003), *A Concise Economic History of the World: From Paleolithic Times to the Present*, New York: Oxford University Press.

Campbell, Cameron and James Z. Lee (2008), "Villages, Descent Groups, Households, and Individual Outcomes in Rural Liaoning, 1789–1909," in Tommy Bengtsson and Geraldine P. Mineau (eds.), *Family and Kin as Immediate Providers of Well-being for Its Members*, 73–101, Netherlands: Springer.

Campbell, Cameron and James Z. Lee (2010), "Fertility Control in Historical China Revisited: New Methods for an Old Debate," *The History of the Family*, 15 (4): 370–385.

Campbell, Cameron D., Wang Feng and James Z. Lee (2004), "Pretransitional Fertility in China," *Population and Development Review*, 28 (4): 735–750.

Camps I Cura, Enriqueta (1998), "Transitions in Women's and Children's Work Patterns and Implications for the Study of Family Income and Household Structure: A Case Study from the Catalan Textile Sector (1850–1925)," *The History of the Family. An International Quarterly*, 3 (2): 137–153.

Camps I Cura, Enriqueta (2001), "Family Strategies and Children's Work Patterns: Some Insights from Industrializing Catalonia, 1850–1920," in Hugh Cunningham and Pier Paolo Viazzo (eds.), *Child Labour in Historical Perspective, 1800–1985: Case Studies from Europe, Japan and Colombia*, 57–71, Florence: UNICEF.

Cartier, Michel (1996), "The Long March of the Chinese Family," in André Burguière, Christiane Klapisch-Zuber, Martine Segalen, and Françoise Zonabend (eds.), *A History of the Family*, Vol. 2: *The Impact of Modernity*, 216–241, Cambridge, MA: Harvard University Press [First published 1986 in French].

Cartier, Michel (1997), "Der Langer Marsch der Familie in China," in André Burguière, Christiane Klapisch-Zuber, Martine Segalen, and Françoise Zonabend (eds.), *Geschichte der Familie—Neuzeit*, 269–303, Frankfurt: Campus Verlag.

Caulfield, Sueann (2017), "From Liberalism to Human Dignity: The Transformation of Marriage and Family Rights in Brazil," in Julia Moses (ed.), *Marriage, Law and Modernity: Global Histories*, London: Bloomsbury Academic.

Chanock, Martin (1989), "Neither Customary nor Legal: African Customary Law in an Era of Family Law Reform," *International Journal of Law and the Family*, 3 (1): 72–88.

Chatterjee, Nandini (2010), "English Law, Brahmo Marriage, and the Problem of Religious Difference: Civil Marriage Laws in Britain and India," *Comparative Studies in Society and History*, 52 (3): 524–552.

Chen, Shuang, Cameron Campbell, and James Z. Lee (2014), "Categorical Inequality and Gender Difference: Marriage and Remarriage in Northeast China, 1749–1913," in Christer Lundh, Satomi Kurosu, et al. (eds.), *Similarity in Difference: Marriage in Europe and Asia, 1700–1900*, 393–498, Cambridge, MA: MIT Press.

Chopin, Kate ([1899] 2000), *The Awakening and Other Stories*, ed. Pamela Knights, Oxford: Oxford University Press.

Chowdhry, Prem (1990), "An Alternative to the Sati Model: Perceptions of a Social Reality in Folklore," *Asian Folklore Studies*, 49 (2): 259–274.

Chuang, Ying-chang and Arthur P. Wolf (1995), "Marriage in Taiwan, 1881–1905: An Example of Regional Diversity," *Journal of Asian Studies*, 54 (3): 781–795.

CICRED (1974), *The Population of Sri Lanka*, Colombo: Department of Census and Statistics.

Clark, Anna (1995), *The Struggle for the Breeches: Gender and the Making of the British Working Class*, Berkeley: University of California Press.

Cohen, Myron L. (1970), "Developmental Process in the Chinese Domestic group," in Maurice Freedman (ed.), *Family and Kinship in Chinese Society*, Stanford, CA: Stanford University Press.

Cominos, Peter T. (1972), "Innocent Femina Sensualis in Unconscious Conflict," in Martha Vicinus (ed.), *Suffer and be Still: Women in the Victorian Age*, 155–172, Bloomington: Indiana University Press.

Constantelos, Demetrios J. (1985), "Marriage in the Greek Orthodox Church," *Journal of Ecumenical Studies*, 22 (1): 21–27.

Coontz, Stephanie (2004), "The World Historical Transformation of Marriage," *Journal of Marriage and Family*, 66 (4): 974–979.

Coontz, Stephanie (2005), *Marriage, a History: How Love Conquered Marriage*, London: Penguin.

Coontz, Stephanie (2006), "The Origins of Modern Divorce," *Family Process*, 46 (1): 7–16.

Cott, Nancy (2000), *Public Vows: A History of Marriage and the Nation*, Cambridge, MA: Harvard University Press.

Courtright, Paul B. (2006), "Hinduism," in Don S. Browning, M. Christian Green, and John Witte Jr. (eds.), *Sex, Marriage, & Family in World Religions*, 226–298, New York: Columbia University Press.

Cowan, Edith (2003), "Consanguineous Marriage and Childhood Health," *Developmental Medicine and Child Neurology*, 45 (8): 571–576.

Cramer, H. M. A. (1781), *Unterhaltungen zur Beförderung der häuslichen Glückseligkeit*, Berlin: Himburg.

Cunningham, Hugh (2000), "The Decline of Child Labour: Labour Markets and Family Economies in Europe and North America since 1830," *Economic History Review*, 53 (3): 409–428.

Cunningham, Hugh and Pier Paolo Viazzo, eds. (2001), *Child Labour in Historical Perspective, 1800–1985: Case Studies from Europe, Japan and Colombia*, Florence: UNICEF.

Cuno, Kenneth (2015), *Modernizing Marriage: Family, Ideology, and Law in Nineteenth- and Early Twentieth-Century Egypt*, New York: Syracuse University Press.

D'arcy, Frank T. (1977), "The Malthusian League and the Resistance to Birth Control Propaganda in Late Victorian Britain," *Population Studies*, 31 (3): 429–448.

Dalton, John T. and Tin Cheuk Leung (2014), "Why Is Polygyny More Prevalent in Western Africa? An African Slave Trade Perspective?" *Economic Development and Cultural Change*, 62 (4): 599–632.

Davies, Andrew (2006), "Youth, Violence, and Courtship in Late-Victorian Birmingham: The Case of James Harper and Emily Pimm," *The History of the Family*, 11 (2): 107–120.

Davies, Eryl W. (1981), "Inheritance Rights and the Hebrew Levirate Marriage: Part 1," *Vetus Testamentum*, 31 (2): 138–144.

De Herdt, René (2001), "Child Labour in Belgium," in Hugh Cunningham and Pier Paolo Viazzo (eds.), *Child Labour in Historical Perspective, 1800–1985: Case Studies from Europe, Japan and Colombia*, 23–40, Florence: UNICEF.

De Jager, Jef L. (1980), *Volksgebruiken in Nederland. Een nieuwe kijk op tradities*, Utrecht: Het Spectrum.

De Koker, Jeanne (1998), "African Customary Family Law in South Africa: A Legacy of Many Pasts," in J. Eekelaar and T. Nhlapo (eds.), *The Changing Family: Family Forms and Family Law*, 321–340, Oxford: Hart.

De Moor, Tine and Jan Luiten van Zanden (2010), "Girl Power: The European Marriage Pattern and Labour Markets in the North Sea Region in the Late Medieval and Early Modern Period," *The Economic History Review*, 63 (1): 1–33.

De Nijs, Thimo (2001), *In veilige haven. Het familieleven van de Rotterdamse gegoede burgerij 1815–1890*, Nijmegen: SUN.

De Ussel, Julio Iglesias (1991), "Family Ideology and Political Transition in Spain," *International Journal of Law & Family*, 5 (3): 277–295.

De Vries, Jan (2008), *The Industrious Revolution: Consumer Behaviour and the Household Economy 1650 to the Present*, New York: Cambridge University Press.

Degler, Carl (1974), "What Ought To Be and What Was: Women's Sexuality in the Nineteenth Century," *American Historical Review*, 79 (5): 1467–1490.

Delius, Peter and Clive Glaser (2002), "Sexual Socialisation in South Africa: A Historical Perspective," *African Studies*, 61 (1): 27–54.

Demos, John and Virginia Demos (1969), "Adolescence in Historical Perspective," *Journal of Marriage and the Family*, 31 (4): 632–638.

Deneweth, Heidi, Oscar Gelderblom, and Joost Jonker (2014), "Mircofinance and the Decline of Poverty: Evidence from the Nineteenth-Century Netherlands," *Journal of Economic Development*, 39 (1): 79–109.

Dennison, Tracy and James Simpson (2010), "Agriculture," in Stephen Broadberry and Kevin H. O'Rourke (eds.), *The Cambridge Economic History of Modern Europe*, Vol. 1: *1700–1870*, 147–163, Cambridge: Cambridge University Press.

Derosas, Renzo, Marco Breschi, Alessio Fornasin, Matteo Manfredini, and Cristina Munno (2014), "Between Constraints and Coercion: Marriage and Social Reproduction in Northern and Central Italy," in Christer Lundh, Satomi Kurosu, et al. (eds.), *Similarity in Difference: Marriage in Europe and Asia, 1700–1900*, 296–348, Cambridge, MA: MIT Press.

Derrett, J. Duncan M. (1968), *Religion, Law and the State in India*, London: Faber & Faber.

Desan, Suzanne (2004), *The Family on Trial in Revolutionary France*, Berkeley: University of California Press.

Devos, Isabelle (2000), "Te jong om te sterven. De levenskansen van meisjes in België omstreeks 1900," *Tijdschrift voor Sociale Geschiedenis*, 26: 55–75.

Dewaraja, Lorna S. (1981), *The Position of Women in Buddhism*, Kandy: Buddhist Publication Society.

DiPlacidi, Jenny and Karl Leydecker, eds. (2018), *After Marriage in the Long Eighteenth Century: Literature, Law and Society*, London: Palgrave Macmillan.

Dodd, Ian (2018), "Marriage Law in Colonial New South Wales: C. H. Currey Revisited," *Journal of Australian Colonial History*, 20: 1–22.

Donzelot, Jacques (1979), "The Poverty of Political Culture," *Ideology and Consciousness*, 5: 71–86.

Douglas, Gillian (2015), "Who Regulates Marriage? The Case of Religious Marriage and Divorce," in Russell Sandberg (ed.), *Religion and Legal Pluralism*, Farnham: Ashgate.

Dozon, Jean-Pierre (1996), "Africa: The Family at the Crossroads," in André Burguière, Christiane Klapisch-Zuber, Martine Segalen, and Françoise Zonabend (eds.), *A History of the Family*, Vol. 2: *The Impact of Modernity*, 301–338, Cambridge, MA: Harvard University Press [First published 1986 in French].

Dribe, Martin and Christer Lundh (2005), "Finding the Right Partner: Rural Homogamy in Nineteenth-Century Sweden," *International Review of Social History*, 50 (S13): 149–177.

Dribe, Martin and Christer Lundh (2014), "Social Norms and Human Agency: Marriage in Nineteenth-Century Sweden," in Christer Lundh, Satomi Kurosu, et al. (eds.), *Similarity in Difference: Marriage in Europe and Asia, 1700–1900*, 211–260, Cambridge, MA: MIT Press.

Dribe, Martin, Marco Breschi, Alain Gagnon, Danielle Geauvreau, Heidi A. Hanson, Thomas Maloney, Stanislao Mazzoni, Joseph Molitoris, Lucia Pozzi, Ken R. Smith, and Hélèna Vézina (2017), "Socioeconomic Status and Fertility Decline: Insights from Historical Transitions in Europe and North America," *Population Studies*, 71 (1): 3–21.

Dribe, Martin, Matteo Manfredini, and Michel Oris (2014), "The Roads to Reproduction: Comparing Life Course Trajectories in Preindustrial Eurasia," in Christer Lundh, Satomi Kurosu, et al. (eds.), *Similarity in Difference: Marriage in Europe and Asia, 1700–1900*, 85–116, Cambridge, MA: MIT Press.

Duben, Alan and Cem Behar (2002), *Istanbul Households: Marriage, Family and Fertility 1880–1940*, Cambridge: Cambridge University Press.

Dupâquier, Jacques, Etienne Hélin, Peter Laslett, Massimo Livi-Bacci, and Sølvi Sogner (1981), *Marriage and Remarriage in Populations of the Past*, London: Academic Press.

Durães, Margarida, Antoinette Fauve-Chamoux, Llorenc Ferrer, and Jan Kok (2009), "Introduction: Historicizing Well-being from a Gender Perspective," in Margarida Durães, Antoinette Fauve-Chamoux, Llorenc Ferrer, and Jan Kok (eds.), *The Transmission of Well-being: Gendered Marriage Strategies and Inheritance Systems in Europe (17th–20th Centuries)*, 1–52, Bern: Peter Lang.

Dyson, Tim and Mick Moore (1983), "On Kinship Structure, Female Autonomy, and Demographic Behavior in India," *Population and Development Review*, 9 (1): 35–60.

Ebrey, Patricia (2006), "Confucianism," in Don S. Browning, M. Christian Green, and John Witte Jr. (eds.), *Sex, Marriage, & Family in World Religions*, 367–450, New York: Columbia University Press.

Edgeworth, Maria ([1809] 1992), *Castle Rackrent and Ennui*, London: Penguin.

Ehmer, Josef (2002), "Marriage," in David Kertzer and Mario Barbagli (eds.), *The History of the European Family*, Vol. 2: *Family Life in the Long Nineteenth Century, 1789–1913*, 282–321, New Haven, CT: Yale University Press.

Eigner, Edwin M. (1970), "Bulwer-Lytton and the Changed Ending of Great Expectations," *Nineteenth-Century Fiction*, 25 (1): 104–108.

Ekamper, Peter, Frans van Poppel, and Kees Mandemakers (2011), "Widening Horizons? The Geography of the Marriage Market in Nineteenth and Early-Twentieth Century Netherlands," in Emily R. Merchant, Glenn D. Deane, Myron P. Gutmann, and Kenneth M. Sylvester (eds.), *Navigating Time and Space in Population Studies*, 115–160, Dordrecht: Springer.

Ekirch, A. Roger (2006), *At Day's Close: Night in Times Past*, New York: W. W. Norton & Co.

El Far, Alessandra (2014), "Popular Editions and Best-sellers at the End of the Nineteenth-century in Brazil," in Ana Cláudia Suriani Da Silva and Sandra Guardini Vasconcelos (eds.), *Books and Periodicals in Brazil, 1768–1930: A Transatlantic Perspective*, 230–244, Abingdon: Routledge.

Elliott, R. Douglas (2003–04), "The Canadian Earthquake: Same-Sex Marriage in Canada," *New England Law Review*, 38 (3): 591–620.

Ellis, Mrs. [Ellis-Stickney, S.] (1839), *The Family Monitor*, Vol 1: *The Women of England, Their Social Duties and Domestic Habits*, 2nd edn., London: Fisher.

El-Menouar, Yasemin (2014), "The Five Dimensions of Muslim Religiosity: Results of an Empirical Study," *Methods, Data, Analyses*, 8 (1): 53–78.

Emori, Itsuo (1998), *Kon'in no Minzoku: Higashi Ajia no Shiten kara* (Marriage Folklore: An East Asian Perspective), Tokyo: Yoshikawa Kobunkan.

Engel, Barbara A. (1990), "Peasant Morality and Pre-Marital Relations in Late 19th Century Russia," *Journal of Social History*, 23 (4): 695–714.

Engelen, Theo (1997), "The Fertility Decline in the Dutch Province of Limburg, 1880–1960: On Understanding Historical Actors in a Constrained Environment," *History of the Family*, 2 (4): 405–424.

Engelen, Theo (2005), "The Hajnal Hypothesis and Transition Theory," in Theo Engelen and Arthur P. Wolf (ed.), *Marriage and the Family in Eurasia: Perspectives on the Hajnal Hypothesis*, 51–73, Amsterdam: Aksant.

Engelen, Theo (2006), *De erfenis van Thomas Malthus betwist*, Nijmegen: Inaugural Lecture at Radboud University.

Engelen, Theo (2009), *Van 2 naar 16 miljoen Nederlanders. Demografie van Nederland, 1800—nu*, Amsterdam: Boom.

Engelen, Theo (2017), "What the Seasons Tell Us: The Monthly Movement of Marriages, Economic Modernization, and Secularization in the Netherlands, 1810–1940," *Historical Life Course Studies*, 4: 165–180.

Engelen, Theo and Arthur P. Wolf (2005a), *Marriage and the Family in Eurasia: Perspectives on the Hajnal Hypothesis*, Amsterdam: Aksant.

Engelen, Theo and Arthur P. Wolf (2005b), "Introduction: Marriage and the Family in Eurasia," in Theo Engelen and Arthur Wolf (eds.), *Marriage and the Family in Eurasia: Perspectives on the Hajnal Hypothesis*, 15–36, Amsterdam: Aksant.

Engelen, Theo and Arthur P. Wolf (2011), "Maternal Depletion and Infant Mortality," in Theo Engelen, John R. Shepherd, and Yang Wen-Shan (eds.), *Death at the Opposite Ends of the Eurasian Continent: Mortality Trends in Taiwan and the Netherlands, 1850–1945*, 275–288, Amsterdam: Aksant.

Engelen, Theo and Hans Hillebrand (1986), "Fertility and Nuptiality in the Netherlands, 1850–1960," *Population Studies*, 40 (3): 487–503.

Engelen, Theo and Jan Kok (2003), "Permanent Celibacy and Late Marriage in the Netherlands, 1890–1960," *Population* [English edition], 58 (1): 1–29.

Engelen, Theo and Ying-hui Hsieh (2007), *Two Cities, One Life: Marriage and Fertility in Lugang and Nijmegen. Life at the Extremes*, Amsterdam: Aksant.

Engelen, Theo and Paul Puschmann (2011), "How Unique is the Western European Marriage Pattern? A Comparison of Nuptiality in Historical Europe and the Contemporary Arab World," *The History of the Family*, 16 (4): 387–400.

Englert, Clement (1955), "Eastern Orthodox Theology," *Proceedings of the Catholic Theological Society of America*, 10: 97–124. https://ejournals.bc.edu/ojs/index.php/ctsa/issue/view/245.

Esposito, John L. (2002), *What Everyone Needs to Know about Islam*, Oxford: Oxford University Press.

Falen, Douglas J. (2008), "Polygyny and Christian Marriage in Africa: The Case of Benin," *African Studies Review*, 51 (2): 51–75.

Fargues, Philippe (1996), "The Arab World: The Family as Fortress," in André Burguière, Christiane Klapisch-Zuber, Martine Segalen, and Françoise Zonabend (eds.), *A History of the Family*, Vol. 2: *The Impact of Modernity: A Natural History of Mating*, Cambridge, MA: Harvard University Press [First published 1986 in French].

Fauve-Chamoux, Antoinette and Emiko Ochiai, eds. (2009), *The Stem Family in Eurasian Perspective: Revisiting House Societies, 17th–20th Centuries*, 287–324, Bern: Peter Lang.

Ferrante, Joan (2015), *Sociology: A Global Perspective*, Stamford, CT: Cengage Learning.

Fisher, Helen (1998), "Lust, Attraction, and Attachment in Mammalian Reproduction," *Human Nature*, 9 (1): 23–52.

Fisher, Helen (2017), *Anatomy of Love: A Natural History of Mating, Marriage, and Why We Stray*. New York: W. W. Norton & Company.

Fisher, Kate (2006), *Birth Control, Sex, and Marriage in Britain, 1918–1960*, Oxford: Oxford University Press.

Fitch, Catherine A. and Steven Ruggles (2000), "Historical Trends in Marriage Formation," in Linda Waite, Christine Bachrach, Michelle Hindin, Elizabeth Thomson, and Arland Thornton (eds.), *Ties that Bind: Perspectives on Marriage and Cohabitation*, 59–88, Hawthorne: Aldine de Gruyter.

Flandrin, Jean-Louis (1980), "Repression and Change in the Sexual Life of Young People in Medieval and Early Modern Times," in Robert Wheaton and Tamara K. Hareven (eds.), *Family and Sexuality in French History*, 27–48, Philadelphia: University of Pennsylvania Press.

Foucault, Michel (1966), *Les mots et les choses*, Paris: Gallimard.

Foucault, Michel (1990), *The History of Sexuality*, Vol. 1: *An Introduction*, New York: Pantheon Books.

Fraundorf, Martha Norby (1979), "The Labour Force Participation of Turn-of-the-Century Married Women," *Journal of Economic History*, 39 (2): 401–418.

Freedman, Estelle B. (1982), "Sexuality in Nineteenth-Century America: Behavior, Ideology, and Politics," *Reviews in American History*, 10 (4): 196–215.

Freeman, Kimberly A. (2003), *Love American Style: Divorce and the American Novel, 1881–1976*, New York: Routledge.

Freeze, Gregory L. (1990), "Bringing Order to the Russian Family: Marriage and Divorce in Imperial Russia, 1760–1860," *Journal of Modern History*, 62 (4): 709–746.

Frühstück, Sabine (2003), *Colonizing Sex: Sexology and Social Control in Modern Japan*, Berkeley: University of California Press.

Fryckman, Jonas and Orvar Löfgrenn (1987), *Culture Builders: A Historical Anthropology of Middle Class Life*, New Brunswick, NJ: Rutgers University Press.

Fuess, Harald (2004), *Divorce in Japan. Family, Gender and the State 1600–2000*, Stanford, CA: Stanford University Press.

Fuess, Harald (2012), "Marriage and Divorce in Meiji Japan: The Transition to Modern Society as Seen from a Different Socio-Cultural Perspective," in Satomi Kurosu (ed.), *Marriage, Divorce, and Re-Marriage as Seen from Historical Demography*, 157–189, Hikarigaoka: Reitaku University.

Gallas, Helga (1990), "Ehe als Instrument des Masochismus oder 'Glückseligkeits-Triangel' als Aufrechterhaltung des Begehrens," in Helga Gallas and Magdalene Heuser (eds.), *Untersuchungen zum Roman von Frauen um 1800*, 66–75, Tübingen: Niemeyer.

Gallas, Helga and Anita Runge, eds. (1993), *Romane und Erzählungen deutscher Schriftstellerinnen um 1800: Eine Bibliographie mit Standortnachweisungen*, Stuttgart and Weimar: Metzler.

Galsworthy, John ([1906] 2001), *The Forsyte Saga*, Vol. 1: *The Man of Property*, Harmondsworth: Penguin.

Gálvez-Muñoz, Lina (1998), "Breadwinning Patterns and Family Exogenous Factors: Workers at the Tobacco Factory of Seville during the Industrialization Process, 1887–1945," in Angélique Janssens (ed.), *The Rise and Decline of the Male Breadwinner Family?*, 87–128, Cambridge: Cambridge University Press.

Gamage, Siri (1982), "The Marriage Pattern of Sri Lanka," *Economic Review*: 24–26.

Ganz, Melissa (2005), "Moll Flanders and English Marriage Law," *Eighteenth-Century Fiction*, 17 (2): 157–182.

Ganz, Melissa (2006), "'A Strange Opposition': The Portrait of a Lady and the Divorce Debates," *Henry James Review*, 27 (2): 156–174.

Garipova, Rozaliva (2017), "Married or Not Married: On the Obligatory Registration of Muslim Marriages in Nineteenth-Century Russia," *Islamic Law and Society*, 24: 112–141.

Garrett, William R. (1994), "Religio-Cultural Foundations of Western and Eastern Family Systems in a Global Age," *International Journal on World Peace*, 11 (4): 11–36.

Gay, Peter (1984–98), *The Bourgeois Experience, Victoria to Freud*, Vol. 1: *Education of the Senses*, New York: Oxford University Press.

Gerig, Maya (2008), *Jenseits von Tugend und Empfindsamkeit: Gesellschaftspolitik im Frauenroman um 1800*, Cologne: Boehlau Verlag.

Gillen, Paul and Devleena Ghosh (2007), *Colonialism and Modernity*, Sydney: University of New South Wales Press.

Gillis, John R. (1985), *For Better, For Worse: British Marriages, 1600 to the Present*, Oxford: Oxford University Press.

Ginsborg, Paul (2014), *Family Politics: Domestic Life, Devastation and Survival, 1900–1950*, New Haven, CT: Yale University Press.

Glendon, Mary Ann (1977), *State, Law and Family: Family Law in Transition in the United States and Western Europe*, Amsterdam: North-Holland Publishing Company.

Goldin, Claudia (1979), "Household and Market Production of Families in a Late Nineteenth-Century American City," *Explorations in Economic History*, 16 (2): 111–131.

Gooch, E. S. Villa-Real (1796), *The Contrast*, Wilmington, DE: Joseph Johnson.

Goode, William J. (1959), "The Theoretical Importance of Love," *American Sociological Review*, 24 (1): 38–47.

Goode, William J. (1970), *World Revolutions and Family Patterns*, New York: The Free Press; London: Collier-Macmillan.

Goodman, Dena (2009), *Becoming a Woman in the Age of Letters*, Ithaca, NY: Cornell University Press.

Goody, Jack (1973), "Bridewealth and Dowry in Africa and Eurasia," in Jack Goody and Stanley J. Tambiah (eds.), *Bridewealth and Dowry*, 1–58, Cambridge: Cambridge University Press.

Goody, Jack (1983), *The Development of the Family and Marriage in Europe*, Cambridge: Cambridge University Press.

Goody, Jack (1990), *The Oriental, the Ancient and the Primitive: Systems of Marriage and the Family in the Pre-Industrial Societies of Eurasia*, Cambridge: Cambridge University Press.

Goody, Jack (2000), *The European Family: An Historico-Anthropoligical Essay*, Oxford: Blackwell Publishers.

Goossaert, Vincent (2005), "State and Religion in Modern China: Religious Policy and Scholarly Paradigms." Available online: https://halshs.archives-ouvertes.fr/halshs-00106187 (accessed December 22, 2016).

Gordon, Eleanor and Gwyneth Nair (2003), *Public Lives: Women, Family and Society in Victorian Britain*, New Haven, CT: Yale University Press.

Grau, Ingeborg, Irma Hanak, and Irene Stacher (1997), "'The Marriage Rite is Never Completed': Die Entwicklung in Afrika südlich der Sahara," in Michael Mitterauer and Norbert Ortmayr (eds.), *Familie im 20. Jahrhundert: Traditionen, Probleme, Perspektiven*, 137–164, Frankfurt: Brandes & Apsel.

Grey, Daniel J. R. (2011), "Gender, Religion, and Infanticide in Colonial India, 1870–1906," *Victorian Review*, 37 (2): 107–120.

Groenendijk, L. F. (1984), *De nadere reformatie van het gezin: De visie van Petrus Wittewrongel op de christelijke huishouding*, Dordrecht: Van den Tol.

Grossberg, Michael (1985), "Crossing Boundaries: Nineteenth-Century Domestic Relations Law and the Merger of Family and Legal History," *Law & Social Inquiry*, 10 (4): 799–847.

Grossberg, Michael (1988), *Governing the Hearth: Law and the Family in Nineteenth-Century America*, Chapel Hill: University of North Carolina Press.

Guinnane, Timothy W. and Sheilagh Ogilvie (2014), "A Two-Tiered Demographic System: 'Insiders' and 'Outsiders' in three Swabian Communities, 1558–1914," *History of the Family*, 19 (1): 77–119.

Hager, Kelly (2010), *Dickens and the Rise of Divorce: The Failed-Marriage Plot and the Novel Tradition*, Farnham: Routledge.

Haines, Michael R. (1979), "Industrial Work and the Family Life Cycle, 1889–1890," *Research in Economic History*, 4: 289–356.

Haines, Michael R. (1996), "Long-Term Marriage Patterns in the United States from Colonial Times to the Present," *The History of the Family*, 1 (1): 15–39.

Hajnal, John (1965), "European Marriage Patterns in Perspective," in David V. Glass and David E. C. Eversley (eds.), *Population in History: Essays in Historical Demography*, 101–146, London: Edward Arnold.

Halperin, David (1989), "Is There a History of Sexuality?," *History and Theory*, 28 (3): 257–274.

Han, Hee-sook (2004), "Women's Life during the Chosŏn Dynasty," *International Journal of Korean History*, 6 (1): 113–160.

Hanagan, Michael (1998), "Family, Work and Wages: The Stéphanois Region of France, 1840–1914," in Angélique Janssens (ed.), *The Rise and Decline of the Male Breadwinner Family?*, 129–151, Cambridge: Cambridge University Press.

Harakas, Stanley S. (2005), "Covenant Marriage: Reflections from an Eastern Orthodox Perspective," in John Witte Jr. and Eliza Ellison (eds.), *Covenant Marriage in Comparative Perspective*, 92–123, Grand Rapids, MI: Eerdmans Publishing Co.

Harding, Maebh (2019), *From Catholic Outlook to Modern State Regulation: Developing Understandings of Marriage in Ireland*, Antwerp: Intersentia.

Harris, Janice Hubbard (1996), *Edwardian Stories of Divorce*, New Brunswick, NJ: Rutgers University Press.

Hartman, Mary (2004), *The Household and the Making of History: A Subversive View of the Western Past*, Cambridge: Cambridge University Press.

Haworth, Daniel S. (2012), "'To do as I will:' Marriage Choice and the Social Construction of Female Individuality in Nineteenth-Century Guanajuato, Mexico," *Latin Americanist*, 57 (3): 51–81.

Hayami, Akira (1987), "Another Fossa Magna: Proportion Marrying and Age at Marriage in Late Nineteenth-Century Japan," *Journal of Family History*, 12 (1): 57–72.

Hayami, Akira (1992), *Kinsei Nobi-chiho no jinko, Keizai, Shakai* (Population, Economy and Society in Early Modern Japan: A Study of the Nobi Region), Tokyo: Sobunsha.

Haytock, Jennifer (2002), "Marriage and Modernism in Edith Wharton's Twilight Sleep," *Legacy*, 19 (2): 216–229.

Head-König, Anne-Lise (1993), "Forced Marriages and Forbidden Marriages in Switzerland: State Control of the Formation of Marriage in Catholic and Protestant Cantons in the Eighteenth and Nineteenth Centuries," *Continuity and Change*, 8 (3): 441–465.

Hirschfeld, Magnus (1918), *Sexualpathologie: Ein Lehrbuch für Ärzte und Studierende*, Bonn: A. Marcus and E. Webers Verlag.

Hirschman, Charles and Bussarawan Teerawichitchainan (2003), "Cultural and Socioeconomic Influences on Divorce during Modernization: Southeast Asia, 1940s to 1960s," *Population and Development Review*, 29 (2): 215–253.

Hondius, Dienke (2001), *Gemengde huwelijken, gemengde gevoelens. Hoe Nederland omgaat met etnisch en religieus verschil*, Den Haag: SDU Uitgevers.

Horan, Patrick M. and Peggy G. Hargis (1991), "Children's Work and Schooling in the Late Nineteenth-Century Family Economy," *American Sociological Review*, 56: 583–596.

Horrell, Sarah and Jane Humphries (1995), "'The Exploitation of Little Children': Child Labor and the Family Economy in the Industrial Revolution," *Explorations in Economic History*, 32 (4): 485–516.

Horrell, Sarah and Jane Humphries (1998), "The Origins and the Expansion of the Male Breadwinner Family: The Case of Nineteenth-Century Britain," in Angélique Janssens (ed.), *The Rise and Decline of the Male Breadwinner Family?*, 25–64, Cambridge: Cambridge University Press.

Horstman, Allen (1985), *Victorian Divorce*, London: Crook Helm.

Humpherys, Anne (1999), "Breaking Apart: The Early Victorian Divorce Novel," in Nicola Diane Thompson (ed.), *Victorian Women Writers and the Woman Question*, 42–59, Cambridge: Cambridge University Press.

Humphries, Jane (2013), "Childhood and Child Labour in the British Industrial Revolution," *The Economic History Review*, 66 (2): 395–418.

Humphries, Jane and Carmen Sarasua (2012), "Off the Record: Reconstructing Women's Labor Force Participation in the European Past," *Feminist Economics*, 18 (4): 39–67.

Humphries, Jane and Jacob Weisdorf (2015), "The Wages of Women in England, 1260–1850," *Journal of Economic History*, 75 (2): 405–447.

Hunt, Nancy R. (1991), "Noise over Camouflaged Polygamy, Colonial Morality Taxation, and a Woman-Naming Crisis in Belgian Africa," *Journal of African History*, 32 (3): 471–494.

Hunter, Mark (2005), "Courting Desire?: Love and Intimacy in Late 19th and Early 20th Century Kwazulu-Natal. Passages: A Chronicle of the African Humanities, New Series 2." Available online: http://hdl.handle.net/2027/spo.4761530.0010.016 (accessed June 6, 2017).

Hunter, Tera W. (2017), *Bound in Wedlock: Slave and Free Black Marriage in the Nineteenth Century*, Cambridge: Cambridge University Press.

Idema, Wilt L. (1996), *Vrouwenschrift. Vriendschap, huwelijk en wanhoop van Chinese vrouwen, opgetekend in een eigen schrift*, Amsterdam: Meulenhoff.

Ipaye, Oluwatoyin A. (1998), "The Changing Pattern of Family Structure in Nigeria: Issues, Problems and Strategies for Family Support," in J. Eekelaar and T. Nhlapo (eds.), *The Changing Family: Family Forms and Family Law*, 33–46, Oxford: Hart.

Jain, Sandhya (2003), "The Right to Family Planning, Contraception and Abortion," in Daniel C. Maguire (ed.), *Sacred Rights: The Case for Contraception and Abortion in World Religions*, 129–143, Oxford: Oxford University Press.

James, John Angell (1828), *The Family Monitor, or a Help to Domestic Happiness*, Birmingham: Benjamin Hudson.

Jankowiak, William R. and Edward Fischer (1992), "A Cross-Cultural Perspective on Romantic Love," *Ethnology*, 31 (2): 149–155.

Janssens, Angélique (1993), *Family and Social Change. The Household as a Process in an Industrializing Community*, Cambridge: Cambridge University Press.

Janssens, Angélique (1997), "The Rise and Decline of the Male Breadwinner Family? An Overview of the Debate," *International Review of Social History*, 42 (S5): 1–23.

Janssens, Angélique (2003), "Economic Transformation, Women's Work and Family Life," in David I. Kertzer and Marzio Barbagli (eds.), *The History of the European Family: Family Life in the Twentieth Century*, Vol. 3, 55–110, New Haven, CT: Yale University Press.

Janssens, Angélique (2014), *Labouring Lives: Women, Work and the Demographic Transition in the Netherlands, 1880–1960*, Bern: Peter Lang.

Jefferson, Ann and Paul Lokken (2011), *Daily Life in Colonial Latin America*. Santa Barbara, CA: Greenwood.

Ji, Ting, Jing-Jing Xu and Ruth Mace (2014), "Intergenerational and Sibling Conflict under Patrilocality," *Human Nature: An Interdisciplinary Biosocial Perspective*, 25 (1): 66–79.

Johnson, James T. (2005), "Marriage as Covenant in Early Protestant Thought: Its Development and Implications," in John Witte Jr. and Eliza Ellison (eds.), *Covenant Marriage in Comparative Perspective*, 124–152, Grand Rapids, MI: Eerdmans Publishing Co.

Jones, Gavin W. (1981), "Malay Marriage and Divorce in Peninsular Malaysia: Three Decades of Change," *Population and Development Review*, 7 (2): 255–278.

Jordan, David K. (2006), "The Traditional Chinese Family & Lineage." Available online: http://pages.ucsd.edu/~dkjordan/chin/familism.html (accessed April 4, 2017).

Jütte, Robert (2008), *Contraception: A History*, Cambridge: Polity Press.

Kabeberi-Macharia, Janet and Celestine Nyamu (1998), "Marriage by Affidavit: Developing Alternative Laws on Cohabitation in Kenya," in J. Eekelaar and T. Nhlapo (eds.), *The Changing Family: Family Forms and Family Law*, Oxford: Hart.

Kandiyoti, Deniz (1991) End of Empire: Islam, Nationalism and Women in Turkey. In Deniz Kandiyoti (Ed.), Women, Islam and the State, 22–47, Houndmills & London: MacMillan

Kaplan, Zvi J. (2007), "The Thorny Area of Marriage: Rabbinic Efforts to Harmonize Jewish and French Law in Nineteenth-Century France," Jewish Social Studies, 13 (3): 59–72.

Karandashev, Victor (2017), *Romantic Love in Cultural Contexts*, Springer e-book.

Kaser, Karl (2000), *Macht und Erbe. Männerherrschaft, Besitz und Familie im östlichen Europa (1500–1900)*, Vienna: Böhlau.

Kaser, Karl (2008), *Patriarchy after Patriarchy: Gender Relations in Turkey and in the Balkans, 1500–2000*, Vienna: Böhlau.

Keller, Morton (1994), *Regulating a New Society: Public Policy and Social Change in America, 1900–1933*, Cambridge, MA: Harvard University Press.

Kertzer, David I. and Dennis P. Hogan (1991), "Reflections on the European Marriage Pattern: Sharecropping and Proletarization in Casalecchio, Italy, 1861–1921," *Journal of Family History*, 16 (1): 31–45.

Kett, Joseph F. (1977), *Rites of Passage: Adolescence in America 1790 to the Present*, New York: Basic Books.

King, Stephen (1999), "Chance Encounters? Paths to Household Formation in Early Modern England," *International Review of Social History*, 44 (1): 55–67.

Kioli, Felix N., Allan R. Were, and Kennedy Onkware (2012), "Traditional Perspectives and Control Mechanisms of Adolescent Sexual Behavior in Kenya," *International Journal of Sociology and Anthropology*, 4 (1): 1–7.

Klep, Paul (2004), "The Relationship between Parents and Adult Children in the Economic Culture of the Netherlands, 1880–1910," *History of the Family*, 9 (4): 385–399.

Klep, Paul (2005), "An Adult Life before Marriage: Children and the Hajnal Hypothesis," in Theo Engelen and Arthur P. Wolf (eds.), *Marriage and the Family in Eurasia: Perspectives on the Hajnal Hypothesis*, 241–270, Amsterdam: Aksant.

Klep, Paul (2011), *Gezinssolidariteit en rotten kids: schaarste, seks en het vierde gebod op het platteland in Nederland in de twintigste eeuw*, Nijmegen: Radboud University.

Knodel, John E. (1988), *Demographic Behavior in the Past: A Study of Fourteen German Village Populations in the Eighteenth and Nineteenth Centuries*, Cambridge: Cambridge University Press.

Kok, Jan (2005), "Passion, Reason and Human Weakness: The European Marriage Pattern and the Control of Adolescent Sexuality," in Theo Engelen and Arthur P. Wolf (eds.), *Marriage and the Family in Eurasia: Perspectives on the Hajnal Hypothesis*, 343–367, Amsterdam: Aksant.

Kok, Jan (2017), "Women's Agency in Historical Family Systems," in Jan Luiten van Zanden, Auke Rijpma, and Jan Kok (eds.), *Agency, Gender, and Economic Development in the World Economy 1850–2000*, 10–50, London: Taylor & Francis.

Kok, Jan and Kees Mandemakers (2010), "A Life-Course Approach to Co-Residence in the Netherlands, 1850–1940," *Continuity & Change*, 25 (2): 285–312.

Kok, Jan and Kees Mandemakers (2008), "Free Choice from a Limited Supply: The Marriage Market in Two Dutch Provinces, 1840–1940," *Romanian Journal of Population Studies*, 2 (1): 82–104.

Kok, Jan, Hilde Bras, and Paul Rotering (2016), "Courtship and Bridal Pregnancy in The Netherlands, 1870–1950," *Annales de Démographie Historique*, 132 (2): 165–191.

Kok, Jan, Wen-shan Yang, and Ying-hui Hsieh (2006), "Marital Fertility and Birth Control in Rural Netherlands and Taiwan, 19th and 20th Centuries," in Chuang Ying-chang, Theo Engelen, and Arthur P. Wolf (eds.), *Positive or Preventive: Fertility Developments in Taiwan and the Netherlands, 1850–1950*, 199–235, Amsterdam: Aksant.

Korotayev, Andrey (2000), "Parallel-Cousin (FBD) Marriage, Islamization, and Arabization," *Ethnology*, 39 (4): 395–407.

Kota, Mounica V. (2014), "Gender and Class Differences in 19th Century French Prostitution," *Oglethorpe Journal of Undergraduate Research*, 3 (1): Article 5.

Kozma, Liat (2011), "The Silence of the Pregnant Bride: Non-Marital Sex in Middle Eastern Societies," in Amy Singer, Christoph K. Neumann, and Selçuk Aksin Somel (eds.), *Untold Histories of the Middle East*, 71–88, London: Routledge.

Krishnan, Parameswara (1977), "Age at Marriage in a Nineteenth Century Indian Parish," *Annales de Démographie Historique* (1): 271–284.

Kurosu, Satomi (2007), "Remarriage in a Stem Family System in Early-Modern Japan," *Continuity and Change*, 22 (3): 429–458.

Kurosu, Satomi (2011), "Divorce in Early Modern Rural Japan: Household and Individual Life Course in Northeastern Villages, 1716–1870," *Journal of Family History*, 36 (2): 118–141.

Kurosu, Satomi, Christer Lundh, and Marco Breschi (2014), "Remarriage, Gender, and Rural Households: A Comparative Analysis of Widows and Widowers in Europe and Asia," in Christer Lundh and Satomi Kurosu, et al. (eds.), *Similarity in Difference: Marriage in Europe and Asia, 1700–1900*, 169–208, Cambridge, MA: MIT Press.

Kurosu, Satomi, Noriko O. Tsuya, and Kiyoshi Hamano (1999), "Regional Differentials in the Patterns of First Marriage in the Latter Half of Tokugawa Japan," *Keio Economic Studies*, 36 (1): 13–38.

Kuznesof, Elizabeth A. (1991), "Sexual Politics, Race and Bastard-Bearing in Nineteenth-Century Brazil: A Question of Culture or Power?," *Journal of Family History*, 16 (3): 241–260.

Laqueur, Thomas (1990), *Making Sex: Body and Gender from the Greeks to Freud*, Cambridge, MA: Harvard University Press.

Lardinois, Roland (1996a), "India: The Family, the State and Women," in A. Burguière, C. Klapisch-Zuber, M. Segalen, and F. Zonabend (eds.), *The History of the Family*, Vol. 1: *The Impact of Modernity*, 268–300, Cambridge, MA: Harvard University Press [First published 1986 in French].

Lardinois, Roland (1996b), "The World Order and the Family Institution in India," in André Burguière, Christiane Klapisch-Zuber, Martine Segalen and Françoise Zonabend (eds), *The History of the Family*, Vol. 1: *Distant Worlds, Ancient Worlds*, 566–600, Cambridge, MA: Harvard University Press (French orig. 1986).

Lardinois, Roland (1997), "Indien: Familie, Staat und Frau," in André Burguière, Christiane Klapisch-Zuber, Martine Segalen, and Françoise Zonabend (eds.), *Geschichte der Familie—Neuzeit*, 343–384, Frankfurt: Campus Verlag.

Larguèche, Dalenda (2011), "Women, Family Affairs, and Justice: Tunisia in the 19th Century," *History of the Family*, 16 (2): 142–151.

Lash, Christopher (1977), *Haven in a Heartless World: The Family Besieged*, New York: Basic Books.

Laslett, Peter (1969), "Size and Structure of the Households in England over Three Centuries: Mean Household Size in England since the Sixteenth Century," *Population Studies. A Journal of Demography*, 23 (2): 199–223.

Le Play, Frédéric (1855), *Les ouvriers Européens: L'organisation des familles* (European Laborers: The Organization of Families), Paris: Imprimerie impériale.

Le Play, Frédéric (1872), *The Organization of Labor*, Philadelphia, PA: Claxton, Remsen & Haffelfinger.

Leach, Edmund Ronald (1955), "Polyandry, Inheritance and the Definition of Marriage," *Man*, 55: 182–186.

Leckie, Barbara (1999), *Culture and Adultery: The Novel, the Newspaper, and the Law*, Philadelphia: University of Pennsylvania Press.

Leckie, Barbara (2007), "'One of the Greatest Social Revolutions of Our Time': The Matrimonial Causes Act, Divorce Court Journalism, and the Victorian Novel," in Karl Leydecker Karl and Nicholas White (eds.), *After Intimacy: The Culture of Divorce in the West since 1789*, 31–56, Frankfurt am Main: Peter Lang.

Lee, James Z. and Feng Wang (2009), *One Quarter of Humanity: Malthusian Mythology and Chinese Realities, 1700–2000*, Cambridge, MA: Harvard University Press.

Lee, James Z., Feng Wang, and Danching Ruan (2001), "Nuptiality among the Qing Nobility: 1640–1900," in Liu Ts'ui-Jung, James Z. Lee, David S. Reher, Osamu Saito, and Wang Feng (eds.), *Asian Population History*, 353–373, Oxford: Oxford University Press.

Lehmann, E. G. (1877), *Das Christliche Haus: Erbauliche Vorträge*, Leipzig: Hinrich.

Leinarte, Dalia (2017), *The Lithuanian Family in its European Context, 1800–1914: Marriage, Divorce and Flexible Communities*, Cham: Palgrave Macmillan.

Levine, David (1977), *Family Formation in an Age of Nascent Capitalism*, London: Academic Press.

Levine, David (1985), "Industrialization and the Proletarian Family in England," *Past & Present*, 107 (1): 168–203.

Levine, Nancy E. and Walter H. Sangree (1980), "Conclusion: Asian and African Systems of Polyandry," *Journal of Comparative Family Studies*, 11 (3): 385–410.

Levi-Strauss, Claude (1969), *The Elementary Structures of Kinship*, Boston, MA: Beacon.

Leydecker, Karl (1996), *Marriage and Divorce in the Plays of Hermann Sudermann*, Frankfurt am Main: Peter Lang.

Leydecker, Karl (2002), "The Drama of Divorce: Marriage Crises and their Resolution in German Drama around 1900," *Neophilologus*, 86 (1): 101–117.

Leydecker, Karl (2005), "The Politics of Divorce: Fanny Lewald's Eine Lebensfrage in the Context of Prussian Divorce Reform in the 1840s," in Rachael Langford (ed.), *Depicting Desire: Gender, Sexuality and the Family in Nineteenth-Century Europe: Literary and Artistic Perspectives*, 255–269, Frankfurt am Main: Peter Lang.

Leydecker, Karl (2007), "Divorcing Women: Divorce and the Rise of the Women's Novel in Germany, 1784–1848," in Karl Leydecker and Nicholas White (eds.), *After Intimacy: The Culture of Divorce in the West since 1789*, 11–29, Frankfurt am Main: Peter Lang.

Leydecker, Karl (2011a), "Women's Lives after Divorce in the European Novel around 1800," in Paul Bishop (ed.), *The Way of the World: A Festschrift for R.H. Stephenson*, Leeds: Maney Publishing.

Leydecker, Karl (2011b), "The Avoidance of Divorce in Goethe's die Wahlverwandtschaften," *Modern Language Review*, 106 (4): 1054–1072.

Leydecker, Karl (2013a), "'Die Scheidestunde ist da': Max Halbe's Mutter Erde (1897) and the Politics of Marriage and Divorce in German Naturalist Drama," *Forum for Modern Language Studies*, 49 (1): 60–78.

Leydecker, Karl (2013b), "'Wedekind würde sich darüber nicht wundern, denn er weiss, dass das Leben eine Rutschbahn ist': Divorce, Comedy and Endings in Arthur Schnitzler's Zwischenspiel (1905)," *Modern Austrian Studies*, 46 (3): 27–50.

Leydecker, Karl (2015), "The Economics of Divorce in the Early Twentieth Century," in Christine Kanz and Frank Krause (eds.), *Zwischen Demontage und Sakralisierung: Revisionen des Familienmodells in der Europäischen Moderne 1880–1945*, 199–214, Würzburg: Königshausen & Neumann.

Linck, Gudula (1997), "'Unter dem Schatten der Ahnen'. Die Entwicklung in China," in Michael Mitterauer and Norbert Ortmayr (eds.), *Familie im 20. Jahrhundert: Traditionen, Probleme, Perspektiven*, 105–123, Frankfurt: Brandes & Apsel.

Lind, Göran (2008), *Common Law Marriage: A Legal Institution for Cohabitation*, Oxford: Oxford University Press.

Lindholm, Charles (2002), *The Islamic Middle East: Tradition and Change*, Oxford: Blackwell Publishers.

Lindsey, Kiera (2011), "Taken: A History of Bride Theft in Nineteenth-Century Ireland and Australia," PhD thesis, Arts—School of Historical Studies, The University of Melbourne.

Lis, Catharina and Hugo Soly (1979), *Poverty and Capitalism in Pre-Industrial Europe*, Hassocks: Harvester Press.

Livi-Bacci, Massimo (2017), *A Concise History of World Population*, Malden, MA: Wiley Blackwell.

Lloyd, Sally A. (1991), "The Darkside of Courtship: Violence and Sexual Exploitation," *Family Relations*, 40 (1): 14–20.

Logan, Enid Lynette (2008), "The 1899 Cuban Marriage Law Controversy: Church, State and Empire in the Crucible of Nation," *Journal of Social History*, 42 (2): 469–494.

Loos, Tamara (2008), "A History of Sex and the State in Southeast Asia: Class, Intimacy and Invisibility," *Citizenship Studies*, 12 (1): 27–43.

Low, Bobbi S. (2000), *Why Sex Matters: A Darwinian Look at Human Behavior*, Princeton, NJ: Princeton University Press.

Lucassen, Leo (2004), "De selectiviteit van blijvers. Een reconstructive van de sociale positie van Duitse migranten in Rotterdam (1870–1885)," *Tijdschrift voor sociale en economische geschiedenis*, 1 (2): 92–115.

Lucassen, Leo (2010), "A Brave New World: The Left, Social Engineering, and Eugenics in Twentieth-Century Europe," *International Review of Social History*, 55 (2): 265–296.

Lundh, Christer (2002), "Remarriages in Sweden in the Eighteenth and Nineteenth Centuries," *History of the Family*, 7 (3): 423–449.

Lundh, Christer (2003), "Swedish Marriages, Customs, Legislation and Demography in the Eighteenth and Nineteenth Centuries," *Lund Papers in Economic History*, No. 88. Department of Economic History, Lund University.

Lundh, Christer and Satomi Kurosu (2014a), "Similarities and Differences in Pre-modern Eurasian Marriage," in Christer Lundh, Satomi Kurosu, et al. (eds.), *Similarity in Difference: Marriage in Europe and Asia, 1700–1900*, 439–460, Cambridge, MA: MIT Press.

Lundh, Christer, Satomi Kurosu, et al. (2014b), *Similarity in Difference: Marriage in Europe and Asia, 1700–1900*, Cambridge, MA: MIT Press.

Lundh, Christer and Satomi Kurosu (2014c), "Eurasian Marriage: Actors and Structures," in Christer Lundh, Satomi Kurosu, et al. (eds.), *Similarity in Difference: Marriage in Europe and Asia, 1700–1900*, 25–54, Cambridge, MA: MIT Press.

Lynch, Katherine A. (1986), "Marriage Age among French Factory Workers: An Alsation Example," *Journal of Interdisciplinary History*, 16 (3): 405–429.

Lynch, Katherine A. (1991), "The European Marriage Pattern in the Cities: Variations on a Theme by Hajnal," *Journal of Family History*, 16 (1): 79–96.

Lyon, Stephen M. (2013), "Networks and Kinship: Formal Models of Alliance, Descent and Inheritance in a Pakistani Punjabi Village," *Social Science Computer Review*, 31 (1): 45–55.

Lystra, Karen (1989), *Searching the Hearth: Women, Men and Romantic Love in Nineteenth-Century America*, New York: Oxford University Press.

Ma, Herbert H. (1987), "The Legalization of Confucianism and its Impact on Family Relationships," *Washington University Law Quarterly*, 65 (4): 667–679.

MacComb, Debra Ann (2000), *Tales of Liberation, Strategies of Containment: Divorce and the Representation of Women in American Fiction, 1880–1920*, New York: Garland.

McBride, Kim (2010), "Human Sexuality," in Felicity Crowe, Emily Hill, and Ben Hollingum (eds.), *Sex and Sexuality*, Vol. 2: *The Generations—Pill*, 384–389, New York: Marshal Cavendish Reference.

McDonald, Peter (1975), *Marriage in Australia: Age at First Marriage and Proportions Marrying, 1860–1971*, Canberra: Australian National University.

Macfarlane, Alan (1986), *Marriage and Love in England: Modes of Reproduction 1300–1840*, Oxford: Blackwell.

Macfarlane, Alan (1987), *The Culture of Capitalism*, Oxford: Blackwell.

McKinsey, Elizabeth (1984), "The Honeymoon Trail to Niagara Falls," *Prospects*, 9: 169–186.

Maines, Mary Jo (1992), "Adolescent Sexuality and Social Identity in French and German Lower-Class Autobiography," *Journal of Family History*, 17 (4): 397–418.

Mair, Jane (2014), "Belief in Marriage," *International Journal of the Jurisprudence of the Family*, 5: 63–88.

Majumdar, Rochona (2004), "Looking for Brides and Grooms: Ghataks, Matrimonials, and the Marriage Market in Colonial Calcutta, Circa 1875–1940," *Journal of Asian Studies*, 63 (4): 911–935.

Majumdar, Rochona (2009), *Marriage and Modernity: Family Values in Colonial Bengal*, Durham, NC: Duke University Press.

Malthus, Thomas ([1798] 1960), *An Essay on the Principle of Population as it Affects the Future Improvement of Society*, New York: Random House.

Mann, Kristin (1981), "Marriage Choices among the Educated African Elite in Lagos Colony, 1880–1915," *International Journal of African Historical Studies*, 14 (2): 201–228.

Mann, Susan (2005), "Women in East Asia: China, Japan and Korea," in Bonnie G. Smith (ed.), *Women's History in Global Perspective*, Vol. 2, 47–100, Urbana: University of Illinois Press.

Mann, Susan L. (2011), *Gender and Sexuality in Modern Chinese History*, Cambridge: Cambridge University Press.

Mann, Thomas ([1900] 1986), *Buddenbrooks: Verfall einer Familie*, Frankfurt am Main: Fischer.

Marchand, Wouter (2016), "Students from all Layers of Society: Study Grants, Parents and the Education of their Children, 1815–2015," *Historical Life Course Studies*, 3: 66–84.

Marcus, Steven (1966), *The Other Victorians*, London: Weidenfeld & Nicolson.

Martinez-Alier, Verena (1974), *Marriage, Class and Colour in Nineteenth-Century Cuba: A Study of Racial Attitudes and Sexual Values in a Slave Society*, Cambridge: Cambridge University Press.

Mashhour, Amira (2005), "Islamic Law and Gender Equality—Could There be a Common Ground? A Study of Divorce and Polygamy in Sharia Law and Contemporary Legislation in Tunisia and Egypt," *Human Rights Quarterly*, 27 (2): 562–596.

Masjuan, Eduard and Joan Martinez-Alier (2004), "'Conscious Procreation': Neo-Malthusianism in Southern Europe and Latin American around 1900," paper presented at the International Society for Ecological Economics, Montréal, July 11–15, 2004.

Mathur, Hari Mohan (1995), "Social and Cultural Influences on Fertility Behaviour," in Hari Mohan Mathur (ed.), *The Family Welfare Programme in India*, 146–156, New Delhi: Vikas Publishing.

Matovic, Margareta (1986), "The Stockholm Marriage: Extra-Legal Family Formation in Stockholm, 1860–1890," *Continuity & Change*, 1 (3): 385–413.

Matthijs, Koen (2002), "Mimetic Appetite for Marriage in Nineteenth-Century Flanders: Gender Disadvantage as an Incentive for Social Change," *Journal of Family History*, 27 (2): 101–127.

Matthijs, Koen (2003), "Frequency, Timing and Intensity of Remarriage in 19th Century Flanders," *History of the Family*, 8 (1): 135–162.

Matthijs, Koen (2006), "Changing Patterns of Familial Sociability: Family Members as Wittnesses to (Re)marriage in Nineteenth-Century Flanders," *Journal of Family History*, 31 (2): 115–143.

Matthijs, Koen (2008), "Determinants of Divorce in Nineteenth-Century Flanders," *Journal of Family History*, 33 (3): 239–261.

Matthijs, Koen, Anneleen Baerts, and Bart Van de Putte (2008), "Determinants of Divorce in Nineteenth-Century Flanders," *Journal of Family History*, 33 (3): 239–261.

Maubrigades, Silvana (2017), "Connections between Women's Age at Marriage and Social and Economic Development," in Maria Magdalena Camou, Silvana Maubrigades, and Rosemary Thorp (eds.), *Gender Inequalities and Development in Latin America during the Twentieth Century*, 45–66, London: Routledge.

Maupassant, Guy de (1980), "Le divorce et le théâtre," in *Chroniques*, 3 vols., Paris: UGE 10/18, 1: 408–415 [First published June 12, 1884, in *Le Figaro*].

Miller, Jane Eldridge (1994), *Rebel Women: Feminism, Modernism and the Edwardian Novel*, London: Virago.

Misra, Promode K. (1997), "'Das Mädchen ist schon in ihres Vaters Haus der Besitz von anderen'—Die Entwicklung in Indien," in Michael Mitterauer and Norbert Ortmayr (eds.), *Familie im 20. Jahrhundert: Traditionen, Probleme, Perspektiven*, 125–136, Frankfurt: Brandes & Apsel.

Mitterauer, Michael (1997), "'Das moderne Kind hat zwei Kinderzimmer und acht Großeltern'—Die Entwicklung in Europa," in Michael Mitterauer and Norbert Ortmayr (eds.), *Familie im 20. Jahrhundert: Traditionen, Probleme, Perspektiven*, 13–51, Frankfurt: Brandes & Apsel.

Mitterauer, Michael and Reinhard Sieder (1977), *Vom Patriarchat zur Partnerschaft: Zum Strukturwandel der Familie*, Munich: Beck.

Moaddel, Mansoor (1998), "Religion and Women: Islamic Modernism versus Fundamentalism," *Journal for the Scientific Study of Religion*, 37 (1): 108–130.

Mody, Perveez (2002), "Love and the Law: Love-Marriage in Delhi," *Modern Asian Studies*, 36 (1): 223–256.

Möhrmann, Renate (1977), *Die andere Frau: Emanzipationsansätze deutscher Schriftstellerinnen im Vorfeld der Achtundvierziger-Revolution*, Stuttgart: Metzler.

Monger, George P. (2004), *Marriage Customs of the World: From Henna to Honeymoons*, Santa Barbara, CA: ABC Clio.

Montemurro, Beth (2006), *Something Old, Something Bold: Bridal Showers and Bachelorette Parties as Traditions of Transition*, New Brunswick, NJ: Rutgers University Press.

Moses, Julia (2017), "Making Marriage 'Modern,'" in Julia Moses (ed.), *Marriage, Law and Modernity: Global Histories*, 1–26, London: Bloomsbury Academic.

Murdock, George P. (1959), *Africa: Its Peoples and Their Culture History*, New York: McGraw-Hill.

Naamane Guessous, S. (2007), *Au delà de toute pudeur: la sexualité féminine au Maroc*, Casablanca: A. Retnani: Eddif.

Nardinelli, Clark (1980), "Child Labor and the Factory Acts," *Journal of Economic History*, 40 (4): 739–755.

Nardinelli, Clark (1990), *Child Labor and the Industrial Revolution*, Bloomington: Indiana University Press.

Nemes, Robert (2009), "The Uncivil Origins of Civil Marriage: Hungary," in Christopher Clark and Wolfram Kaiser (eds.), *Culture Wars: Secular Catholic Conflict in Nineteenth-Century Europe*, 11–47, Cambridge: Cambridge University Press.

Neuss-Kaneko, Margret (1990), *Familie und Gesellschaft in Japan*, Munich: C. H. Beck.

Newbigin, Eleanor (2013), *The Hindu Family and the Emergence of Modern India*, Cambridge: Cambridge University Press.

Nishihara, Hiroshi (2000), "Die Trennung von Staat und Religion in der japanischen Verfassung," *Der Staat*, 39 (1): 86–109.

Novak, David (2000), "Jewish Marriage and Civil Law: A Two-Way Street," *George Washington Law Review*, 68: 1059–1078.

O'Brien, Karin (2005), "Sexual Distinctions and Prescriptions," in Sarah Knott and Barbara Taylor (eds.), *Women, Gender and Enlightenment*, 1–7, Basingstoke: Palgrave Macmillan.

O'Dowd, Anne (1994), "Women in Rural Ireland in the Nineteenth and Early Twentieth Centuries—How the Daughters, Wives and Sisters of Small Farmers and Landless Labourers Fared," *Rural History*, 5 (2): 171–183.

O'Hanlon, Rosalind (2017), "Caste and its Histories in Colonial India: A Reappraisal," *Modern Asian Studies*, 51 (2): 432–461.

Obdeijn, Herman, Paolo De Mas, and Henk Pel (2012), *Geschiedenis van Marokko*, Amsterdam: Bulaaq.

Ochiai, Emiko (2009), "Two Types of Stem Households System in Japan: The *Ie* in Global Perspective," in Antoinette Fauve-Chamoux and Emiko Ochiai (eds.), *The Stem Family in Eurasian Perspective: Revisiting House Societies, 17th–20th Centuries*, 287–324, Bern: Peter Lang.

Ochiai, Emiko (2011), "Love and Life in Southwestern Japan: The Story of a One-Hundred-Year-Old Lady," *Journal of Comparative Family Studies*, 42 (3): 399–409.

Orchardson, I. Q. (1931), "Notes on the Marriage Customs of the Kipsigis," *Journal of the East Africa and Uganda Natural History Society*, 40/41: 99–112.

Oris, Michel, George Alter, and Paul Servais (2014), "Prudence as Obstinate Resistance to Pressure: Marriage in Nineteenth-Century Rural Eastern Belgium," in Christer Lundh, Satomi Kurosu, et al. (eds.), *Similarity in Difference: Marriage in Europe and Asia, 1700–1900*, 261–269, Cambridge, MA: MIT Press.

Osterhammel, Jürgen (2014), *The Transformation of the World: A Global History of the Nineteenth Century*, Princeton, NJ: Princeton University Press.

Otake, Hideo (1977), "*Ie*" *to Onna no Rekishi* (History of Ie and Women), Tokyo: Kobundo.

Otake, Hideo (1982), *Houken-shakai no nomin kazoku* (Peasant Families in a Feudal Society), Tokyo: Sobunsha.

Oto, Osamu (1996), *Kinsei Nomin to Ie- Mura- Kokka* (Early Modern Peasants and Family, Village, Nation), Tokyo: Yoshikawa Kobunkan.

Ouwerkerk de Vries, Jan van (1795), *Korte schets der verpligtingen van eenen braaven huisvader en zulk eene huismoeder, in 't gemeen burgerlijk leven*. Verhandelingen, uitgegeeven door de Maatschappij tot Nut van 't Algemeen IV, Amsterdam: H. Keijzer, C. de Vries and H. van Munster.

Overton, Bill (1996), *The Novel of Female Adultery: Love and Gender in Continental European Fiction, 1830–1900*, Basingstoke: Macmillan.

Overton, Bill (2002), *Fictions of Female Adultery, 1684–1890: Theories and Circumtexts*, Basingstoke: Palgrave Macmillan.

Owen, Robert (1840), *Lectures on the Marriages of the Priesthood of the Old Immoral World, Delivered in the Year 1835, before the Passing of the New Marriage Act*, Leeds: J. Hobson.

Pagden, Anthony (2013), *The Enlightenment and Why It Still Matters*, Oxford: Oxford University Press.

Park, Hee-jin (2008), "Influences of the Yangban's Age at Marriage and Ban on Remarriage on Childbirth in Chosŏn Society," *Sungkyun Journal of East Asian Studies*, 8 (1): 1–15.

Parrinder, Geoffrey (2003), *Sexual Morality in the World's Religions*, London: Oneworld.

Pasco, Allan H. (2009), *Revolutionary Love in Eighteenth- and Early Nineteenth-Century France*, Farnham: Ashgate.

Peletz, Michael G. (1987), "The Exchange of Men in 19th-Century Negeri Sembilan (Malaya)," *American Ethnologist*, 14 (3): 449–469.

Perrot, Michelle (1993), "Het marginale bestaan van ongehuwden en alleenstaanden," in George Duby and Phippe Ariès (eds.), *Geschiedenis van het persoonlijke leven*, 248–263, Amsterdam: Uitgeversmaatschappij Agon BV.

Phillips, Roderick (1988), *Putting Asunder: A History of Divorce in Western Society*, Cambridge: Cambridge University Press.

Phillips, Roderick (1991), *Untying the Knot: A Short History of Divorce*, Cambridge: Cambridge University Press.

Pieris, Ralph (1956), *Sinhalese Social Organization: The Kandyan Period*, Colombo: Ceylon University Press Board.

Pomeranz, Kenneth (2000), *The Great Divergence: China, Europe, and the Making of the Modern World Economy*, Princeton, NJ: Princeton University Press.

Poovey, Mary (1988), *Uneven Developments: The Ideological Work of Gender in Mid-Victorian England*, Chicago: University of Chicago Press.

Potthast-Jutkeit, Barbara (1997), "'Jetzt denk ich nicht ans Heiraten': Die Entwicklung in Lateinamerika," in Michael Mitterauer and Norbert Ortmayr (eds.), *Familie im 20. Jahrhundert: Traditionen, Probleme, Perspektiven*, 65–85, Frankfurt: Brandes & Apsel.

Potthast-Jutkeit, Barbara (1997), "The History of Family and Colonialism: Examples from Africa, Latin America, and the Caribbean," *History of the Family*, 2 (2): 115–121.

Prince Peter of Greece and Denmark (1955), "Polyandry and the Kinship Group," *Man*, 55: 179–181.

Probert, Rebecca (2008), "R v Millis Reconsidered: Binding Contracts and Bigamous Marriages," *Legal Studies*, 28 (3): 337–355.

Probert, Rebecca (2009), *Marriage Law and Practice in the Long Eighteenth-Century: A Reassessment*, Cambridge: Cambridge University Press.

Probert, Rebecca (2017), "English Exports: Invoking the Common Law of Marriage across the Empire in the Nineteenth Century," in Julia Moses (ed.), *Marriage, Law and Modernity: Global Histories*, 168–186, London: Bloomsbury Academic.

Puschmann, Paul (2011), *Casablanca: A Demographic Miracle on Moroccan Soil?* Leuven: Acco Academic.

Puschmann, Paul (2015), "Social Inclusion and Exclusion of Urban In-Migrants in Northwestern European Port Cities. Antwerp, Rotterdam & Stockholm, ca. 1850–1930," PhD thesis, Leuven University.

Puschmann, Paul and Koen Matthijs (2015), "The Demographic Transition in the Arab World: The Dual Role of Marriage in Family Dynamics and Population Growth," in Koenraad Matthijs, Karel Neels, Christiane Timmerman, Jacques Haers, and Sara Mels (eds.), *Beyond the Demographic Divide: Population Change in Europe, the Middle East and North Africa*, 119–165, Farnham: Ashgate.

Puschmann, Paul and Arne Solli (2014), "Household and Family during Urbanization and industrialization: Efforts to Shed New Light on an Old Debate INTRODUCTION," *History of the Family*, 19 (1), 1–12.

Puschmann, Paul, Nina Van den Driessche, Per-Olof Grönberg, Bart Van de Putte, and Koen Matthijs (2015), "From Outsiders to Insiders? Partner Choice and Marriage among Internal

Migrants in Antwerp, Rotterdam & Stockholm, 1850–1930," *Historical Social Research/Historische Sozialforschung*, 40 (2): 319–358.

Puschmann, Paul, Per-Olof Grönberg, Reto Schumacher, and Koen Matthijs (2014), "Access to Marriage and Reproduction among Migrants in Antwerp and Stockholm: A Longitudinal Approach to Processes of Social inclusion and Exclusion, 1846–1926," *History of the Family*, 19 (1): 29–52.

Puschmann, Paul, Richard Paping and Koen Matthijs, eds. (2016), *Familie en levenskansen in het verleden*, Leuven: Acco.

Putnam, Robert (2015), *Our Kids: The American Dream in Crisis*. New York: Simon & Schuster Paperbacks.

Radcliffe-Brown, Alfred R. (1950), "Introduction," in Alfred R. Radcliffe-Brown and Daryll Forde (eds.), *African Systems of Kinship and Marriage*, 1–85, London: Oxford University Press.

Raghuvanshi, V. P. S. (1969), *Indian Society in the Eighteenth Century*, New Delhi: Associated Publishing House.

Ramien, T. [Magnus Hirschfeld] (1896), *Sappho und Sokrates*, Leipzig: Verlag Max Spohr.

Regt, Ali de (1984), *Arbeidersgezinnen en beschavingsarbeid: Ontwikkelingen in Nederland 1870–1940*, Meppel: Boom.

Reher, David S. (1991), "Marriage Patterns in Spain, 1887–1930," *Journal of Family History*, 16 (1): 7–30.

Reher, David S. (1998), "Family Ties in Western Europe: Persistent Contrasts," *Population and Development Review*, 24 (2): 203–234.

Reid, Anthony (1987), "Low Population Growth and its Causes in Pre-Colonial Southeast Asia," in Norman G. Owen (ed.), *Death and Disease in Southeast Asia: Explorations in Social, Medical and Demographic History*, 33–47, Singapore: Oxford University Press.

Reid, Anthony (1988), *Southeast Asia in the Age of Commerce, 1450–1680*, Vol. 1: *The Lands below the Wind*, New Haven, CT: Yale University Press.

Reid, Anthony (2014), "Urban Respectability and the Maleness of (Southeast) Asian Modernity," *Asian Review of World Histories*, 2 (2): 147–167.

Rheinstein, Max (1953), "Trends in Marriage and Divorce Law of Western Countries," *Law and Contemporary Problems*, 18 (1): 3–19.

Riesebrodt, Martin (2013), "Religion als analytisches Konzept und seine universale Anwendbarkeit," in Peter Schalk (ed.), *Religion in Asien? Studien zur Anwendbarkeit des Religionsbegriffes*, 1–12, Acta Universitatis Upsaliensis, *Historia Religionum* 32, Uppsala: Uppsala Universitet.

Rodriguez, Maria Sara (2014), "Marriage is a Basic Good, Discernable through Reason, and Is Entitled to Recognition and Protection by the State," *International Journal of the Jurisprudence of the Family*, 5: 111–144.

Rose, Sonya O. (1992), "Introduction," in Sonya O. Rose (ed.), *Limited Livelihoods: Gender and Class in Nineteenth-Century England*, 1–21, Berkeley: University of California Press.

Ross, Andrew Israel (2015), "Serving Sex: Playing with Prostitution in the Brasseries à Femmes of Late Nineteenth-Century Paris," *Journal of the History of Sexuality*, 24 (2): 288–313.

Roulston, Chris (2010), *Narrating Marriage in Eighteenth-Century England and France*, Farnham: Ashgate.

Rowntree, Benjamin S. (1901), *Poverty: A Study of Town Life*, London: Macmillan.

Ruggles, Steven (1987), *Prolonged Connections: The Rise of the Extended Family in Nineteenth-Century England and America*, Madison: University of Wisconsin Press.

Ryan, Bryce (1952), "Institutional Factors in Sinhalese Fertility," *Milbank Memorial Fund Quarterly*, 30 (4): 359–381.

Sa, Sophie (1985), "Marriage among the Taiwanese of Pre-1945 Taipei," in Susan B. Hanley and Arthur P. Wolf (eds.), *Family and Population in East Asian History*, 277–308, Stanford, CA: Stanford University Press.

Sabean, David (1997), *Property, Production, and Family in Neckarhausen, 1700–1870*, Cambridge: Cambridge University Press.

Sachsen-Gessaphe, Karl August Prinz von (1989), "Concubinage in Mexico," *International Journal of Law and the Family*, 3 (1): 40–57.

Safa, Helen I. (1995), *The Myth of the Male Breadwinner: Women and Industrialization in the Caribbean*, Boulder, CO: Westview Press.

Saito, Osamu (1998), "Two Kinds of Stem-Family System? Traditional Japan and Europe Compared," *Continuity and Change*, 13 (1): 167–186.

Saito, Osamu (2000), "Marriage, Family Labour and the Stem Family Household: Traditional Japan in a Comparative Perspective," *Continuity and Change*, 15 (1): 17–45.

Saito, Osamu (2001), "Children's Work, Industrialism and the Family Economy in Japan, 1872–1926," in Hugh Cunningham and Pier Paolo Viazzo (eds.), *Child Labour in Historical Perspective, 1800–1985*, 73–90, Florence: UNICEF.

Saito, Osamu (2005), "The Third Pattern of Marriage and Remarriage: Japan in Eurasian Comparative Perspectives," in Theo Engelen and Arthur P. Wolf (eds.), *Marriage and the Family in Eurasia: Perspectives on the Hajnal Hypothesis*, Amsterdam: Aksant.

Saito, Osamu (2014), "Demographic Regimes in the Asian Past," paper at Conference to Celebrate the 50th Anniversary of the Founding of the Cambridge Group, Cambridge: Downing College.

Sanciñena-Asurmend, Camino (2014), "The Pattern of Marriages under Spanish Law," *International Journal of the Jurisprudence of the Family*, 5: 37–61.

Sarkar, Tanika (1993), "A Book of Her Own: A Life of Her Own: Autobiography of a Nineteenth Century Woman," *History Workshop Journal*, 36: 35–64.

Schapera, Isaac (1933), "Premarital Pregnancy and Native Opinion: A Note on Social Change," *Africa*, 6 (1): 59–89.

Scharffs Brett G. and Suzanne Disparte (2010), "Comparative Models for Transitioning from Religious to Civil Marriage Systems," *Journal of Law & Family Studies*, 12: 409–430.

Schieth, Lydia (1990), "Elisa oder das Weib wie es seyn sollte: Zur Analyse eines Frauen-Bestsellers," in Helga Gallas and Magdalene Heuser (eds.), *Untersuchungen zum Roman von Frauen um 1800*, 114–131, Tübingen: Niemeyer.

Schlegel, Alice (1991), "Status, Property, and the Value on Virginity," *American Ethnologist*, 18 (4): 719–734.

Schoonheim, Marloes (2005), *Mixing Ovaries and Rosaries: Catholic Religion and Reproduction in the Netherlands, 1870–1970*, Amsterdam: Aksant.

Schwarzkopf, Jutta (2007), "Bringing Babies into Line with Mother's Jobs: Lancashire Cotton Weavers' Fertility Regime," in Angélique Janssens (ed.), *Gendering the Fertility Decline in the Western World*, 309–334, Bern: Peter Lang.

Scott, Joan W. and Louise Tilly (1975), "Women's Work and the Family in Nineteenth-Century Europe," *Comparative Studies in Society and History*, 17 (1): 36–64.

Seccombe, Wally (1993), *Weathering the Storm: Working-Class Families from the Industrial Revolution to the Fertility Decline*, London: Verso.

Segal, Naomi (1992), *The Adulteress's Child*, Cambridge: Polity.

Sellers, Charles (1991), *The Market Revolution: Jacksonian America, 1815–1846*, Oxford: Oxford University Press.

Sen, Samita (1998), "Gendered Exclusion: Domesticity and Dependence in Bengal," in Angélique Janssens (ed.), *The Rise and Decline of the Male Breadwinner Family?*, *International Review of Social History: Supplement 5*, 65–86, Cambridge: Cambridge University Press.

Seuffert, Nan (2003), "Shaping the Modern Nation: Colonial Marriage Law, Polygamy and Concubinage in Aotearoa New Zealand," *Law Text Culture*, 7 (1): 186–220.

Sewell, William (2009), *Structure and Mobility: The Men and Women of Marseille, 1820–1870*, Cambridge: Cambridge University Press.

Seymour, Mark (2006), *Debating Divorce in Italy: Marriage and the Making of Modern Italians, 1860–1974*, Basingstoke: Macmillan.

Shang, Geling (2003), "Excess, Lack and Harmony: Some Confucian and Taoist Approaches to Family Planning and Population Management—Tradition and the Modern Challenge," in Daniel C. Maguire (ed.), *Sacred Rights: The Case for Contraception and Abortion in World Religions*, 217–235, Oxford: Oxford University Press.

Shaw, Alison and Aviad Raz, eds. (2015), *Cousin Marriages: Between Tradition, Genetic Risk and Cultural Change*, New York: Berghahn Books.

Sholkamy, Hania (2003), "Rationalities for Kin Marriages in Rural Upper Egypt," in Nicholas S. Hopkins (ed.), *The New Arab Family*, 62–79, Cairo: American University of Cairo Press.

Shorter, Edward (1971), "Illegitimacy, Sexual Revolution and Social Change in Modern Europe," *Journal of Interdisciplinary History*, 2 (2): 237–272.

Shorter, Edward (1973), "Female Emancipation, Birth Control and Fertility in European History", The American Historical Review 78(3), 605–640.

Shorter, Edward (1975), *The Making of the Modern Family*, New York: Basic books.

Showalter, Elaine (1990), *Sexual Anarchy: Gender and Culture at the Fin de Siècle*, Harmondsworth: Penguin.

Shumway, Jeffrey M. (2001), "'The Purity of My Blood Cannot Put Food on My Table': Changing Attitudes towards Interracial Marriage in Nineteenth-Century Buenos Aires," *Americas*, 58 (2): 201–220.

Simotta, Daphne-Ariane (1995), "Marriage and Divorce Regulation and Recognition in Austria," *Family Law Quarterly*, 29 (3): 525–540.

Sinclair, Alison (1993), *The Deceived Husband*, Oxford: Oxford University Press.

Siu, Helen F. (1990), "Where Were the Women? Rethinking Marriage Resistance and Regional Culture in South China," *Late Imperial China*, 11 (2): 32–62.

Skinner, G. William (1997), "Family Systems and Demographic Processes," in David I. Kertzer and Tom Fricke (eds.), *Anthropological Demography: Toward a New Synthesis*, 53–95, Chicago: University of Chicago Press.

Sloterdijk, Peter (1983), *Kritik der zynischen Vernunft*, 2 vols., Frankfurt am Main: Suhrkamp.

Socolow, Susan Migden (2000), *The Women of Colonial Latin America*, Cambridge: Cambridge University Press.

Sommer, Matthew (2000), *Sex, Law and Society in Late Imperial China*, Stanford, CA: Stanford University Press.

Son, Byunggiu (2010), "The Effects of Man's Remarriage and Adoption on Family Succession in the 17th to the 19th Century Rural Korea: Based on the Andong Kwo˘n Clan Genealogy," *Sungkyun Journal of East Asian Studies*, 10 (1): 9–31.

Sörgjerd, Caroline (2012), *Reconstructing Marriage: The Legal Status of Relationships in a Changing Society*, Antwerp: Intersentia.

Spagnoli, Paul G. (1983), "Industrialization, Proletarianization, and Marriage: A Reconsideration," *Journal of Family History*, 8 (3): 230–247.

Springhall, John (1986), *Coming of Age: Adolescence in Britain 1860–1960*, Dublin: Gill and Macmillan.

Staël, Germaine de ([1802] 1995), *Delphine*, trans. with an introduction by Avriel H. Goldberger, DeKalb: Northern Illinois University Press.

Stan, Lavinia (2010). "Eastern Orthodox Views on Sexuality and the Body," *Women's Studies International Forum*, 33: 38–46.

Stockard, Janice E. (1989), *Daughters of the Canton Delta: Marriage Patterns and Economic Strategies in South China, 1860–1930*, Stanford, CA: Stanford University Press.

Stone, Lawrence (1990), *Road to Divorce: England 1530–1997*, Oxford: Oxford University Press.

Stone, Lawrence (1993), *Broken Lives: Separation and Divorce in England 1660–1857*, Oxford: Oxford University Press.

Störmer, Charlotte, Corry Gellatly, Anita Boele, and Tine De Moor (2018), "Long-Term Trends in Marriage Timing and the Impact of Migration, the Netherlands (1650–1899)," *Historical Life Course Studies*, 6 (Special Issue 1): 40–68.

Sundt, Eilert ([1857] 1993), *Sexual Customs in Rural* Norway Andong Kwo˘n Clan' *A Nineteenth Century Study*, Ames: Iowa State University Press [Translation from *Sædeligheds-Tilstanden i Norge*].

Szołtysek, Mikołaj (2012), "The Genealogy of Eastern European Difference: An Insider's View," *Journal of Comparative Family Studies*, 23 (3): 335–371.

Szołtysek, Mikołaj (2015), *Rethinking East-Central Europe: Family Systems and Co-residence in the Polish-Lithuanian Commonwealth*, Bern: Peter Lang.

Szołtysek, Mikołaj, Sebastian Klüsener, Radosław Poniat and Siegfried Gruber (2017), "The Patriarchy Index: A New Measure of Gender and Generational Inequalities in the Past," *Cross-Cultural Research*, 51 (3): 228–262.

Szreter, Simon and Kate Fisher (2010), *Sex Before the Sexual Revolution: Intimate Life in England 1918–1963*, Cambridge: Cambridge University Press.

Tadmouri, Gazi O., Pratibha Nair, Tasneem Obeid, Mahmous T. Al Ali, Najib Al Khaja, and Hanan A. Hamamy (2009), "Consanguinity and Reproductive Health among Arabs," *Reproductive Health*, 6 (17): 1–8.

Takagi, Tadashi (1987), *Mikudarihan: Edo no Rikon to Joseitachi* (Three-lines-and-a-half: Divorce and Women in Edo), Tokyo: Heibonsha.

Tambiah, Stanley J. (1979), "A Performative Approach to Ritual," *Proceedings of the British Academy*, 65: 113–169 [Radcliffe-Brown Lecture in Social Anthropology].

Tambiah, Stanley J. (1989), "The Position of Women in Sub-Saharan Africa and North India," *Current Anthropology*, 30 (4): 413–427.

Tanner, Tony (1979), *Adultery in the Novel: Contract and Transgression*, Baltimore, MD: Johns Hopkins University Press.

Taylor, Barbara (2005), "Feminists versus Gallants: Manners and Morals in Enlightenment Britain," in Sarah Knott and Barbara Taylor (eds.), *Women, Gender and Enlightenment*, 31–52, Basingstoke: Palgrave Macmillan.

Terian, Sara Kärkkäinen (2004), "Marriage Rituals," in Frank A. Salamone (ed.), *Encyclopedia of Religious Rites, Rituals and Festivals*, 230–235, London: Routledge.

Thackeray, William Makepeace ([1847–48] 1968), *Vanity Fair*, Harmondsworth: Penguin.

Therborn, Göran (2004), *Between Sex and Power: Family in the World, 1900–2000*, London: Routledge.

Therborn, Göran (2011), *The World: A Beginner's Guide*, Cambridge: Polity Press.

Thompson, E. P. (1963), *The Making of the English Working Class*, New York: Vintage Books.

Thornton, Arland (2005), *Reading History Sideways: The Fallacy and Enduring Impact of the Developmental Paradigm on Family Life*, Chicago, IL: University of Chicago Press.

Thornton, Arland and Hui-Sheng Lin (1994), *Social Change & the Family in Taiwan*, Chicago, IL: University of Chicago Press.

Tilburg, Marja van (1998), *Hoe hoorde het? Seksualiteit en partnerkeuze in de Nederlandse adviesliteratuur 1780–1890*, Amsterdam: Het Spinhuis.

Tilly, Louise A., Joan W. Scott, and Miriam Cohen (1976), "Women's Work and European Fertility Patterns," *Journal of Interdisciplinary History*, 6 (3): 447–476.

Timm, Annette and Joshua Sanborn (2016), *Gender, Sex and the Shaping of Modern Europe: A History from the French Revolution to the Present Day*, London: Bloomsbury Academic.

Todd, Emmanuel (2011), *L'Origine des Systèmes Familiaux*, Paris: Gallimard.

Todorova, Velina (2000), "Family Law in Bulgaria: Legal Norms and Social Norms," *International Journal of Law, Policy and the Family*, 14 (2): 148–181.

Tönnies, Ferdinand (1887), *Gemeinschaft und Gesellschaft. Abhandlung des Communismus und des Socialismus als Empirischer Culturformen*, Leipzig: Fues's Verlag.

Topley, Marjorie (1975), "Marriage Resistance in Rural Kwantung," in Margery Wolf and Roxane Witke (eds.), *Women in Chinese Society*, 67–88, Stanford, CA: Stanford University Press.

Torfs, Rik (2005), "The Permissible Scope of Legal Limitations on the Freedom of Religion or Belief in Belgium," *Emory International Law Review*, 19 (2): 637–684.

Tsuya, Noriko O. and Satomi Kurosu (2010), "Family, Household, and Reproduction in Northeastern Japan, 1716 to 1870," in Noriko O. Tsuya, Wang Feng, George Alter, James Z. Lee, et al. (eds.), *Prudence and Pressure: Reproduction and Human Agency in Europe and Asia, 1700–1900*, 249–285, Cambridge, MA: MIT Press.

Tsuya, Noriko O. and Satomi Kurosu (2014), "Economic and Household Factors of First Marriage in Two Northeastern Japanese Villages, 1716–1870," in Christer Lundh and Satomi Kurosu, et al. (eds.), *Similarity in Difference: Marriage in Europe and Asia, 1700–1900*, 349–391, Cambridge, MA: MIT Press.

Tsuya, Noriko O., Wang Feng, George Alter, James Z. Lee, et al. (2010), *Prudence and Pressure: Reproduction and Human Agency in Europe and Asia, 1700–1900*, Cambridge, MA: MIT Press.

Tucker, Judith E. (2008), *Women, Family, and Gender in Islamic Law*, Cambridge: Cambridge University Press.

Turner, C. J. G. (1987) "Divorce and Anna Karenina," *Forum for Modern Language Studies*, 23 (2): 97–116.

Van Bavel, Jan (2004), "Deliberate Birth Spacing before the Fertility Transition in Europe: Evidence from Nineteenth-Century Belgium," *Population Studies*, 58 (1): 95–107.

Van Campen, W. J. (1866), *Het huwelijk: Handboek voor Christelijke echtgenooten*, Amsterdam: A. van den Hoeven.

Van Cruyningen, Piet (2000), "Behoudend maar buigzaam: Boeren in West-Zeeuws-Vlaanderen, 1650–1850," PhD thesis, Wageningen University.

Van de Putte, Bart (2003), "Homogamy by Geographical Origin: Segregation in Nineteenth-Century Flemish Cities," *Journal of Family History*, 28 (3): 364–390.

Van de Putte, Bart, Frans Van Poppel, Sofie Vanassche, Maria Sanchez, Svetlana Jidkova, Mieke Eeckhout, Michel Oris, and Koen Matthijs (2009), "The Rise of Age-Homogamy in 19th century Western Europe," *Journal of Marriage and Family*, 71 (5): 1234–1253.

Van den Boomen, Nynke and Paul Puschmann (2018), "Born Out of Wedlock at the River Waal. Illegitimacy in the City of Nijmegen, the Netherlands, 1811–1850," in Paul Puschmann and Tim Riswick (eds.), *Building Bridges: Scholars, History and Historical Demography. A Festschrift in Honor of Professor Theo Engelen*, 539–569, Nijmegen: Valkhof Pers.

Van den Eeckhout, Patricia (1993), "Family Income of Ghent Working-Class Families ca. 1900," *Journal of Family History*, 18 (2): 87–110.

Van Leeuwen, Marco and Ineke Maas (2002), "Partner Choice and Homogamy in the Nineteenth Century: Was There a Sexual Revolution in Europe?" *Journal of Social History*, 36 (1): 101–123.

Van Leeuwen, Marco H. D., and Ineke Maas (2010), "Historical Studies of Social Mobility and Stratification," *Annual Review of Sociology*, 36: 429–451.

Van Leeuwen, Marco H. D., Ineke Maas, and Andrew Miles, eds. (2005), *Marriage Choices and Class Boundaries: Social Endogamy in History*, Cambridge: Cambridge University Press.

Van Nederveen Meerkerk, Elise (2017), "Challenging the De-Industrialization Thesis: Gender and Indigenous Textile Production in Java under Dutch Colonial Rule, c. 1830–1920," *Economic History Review*, 70 (4): 1219–1243.

Van Poppel, Frans (1992), "Trouwen in Nederland. Een historisch-demografische studie de 19ᵉ en vroeg-20ᵉ eeuw," PhD thesis, Wageningen University.

Van Poppel, Frans (1995), "Seasonality of Work, Religion and Popular Customs: The Seasonality of Marriage in the Nineteenth- and Twentieth-Century Netherlands," *Continuity and Change*, 10 (2): 215–256.

Van Poppel, Frans (1997), "Family Breakdown in Nineteenth-Century Netherlands: Divorcing Couples in the Hague," *History of the Family*, 2 (1): 49–72.

Van Poppel, Frans and Renzo Derosas (2006), "Introduction," in Renzo Derosas and Frans van Poppel (eds.), *Religion and the Decline of Fertility in the Western World*, 1–19, Dordrecht: Springer.

Van Wijk, Anya (1986), *Marokkaanse impressies*, The Hague: Nederlands Bibliotheek en Lektuur Centrum.

Vickery, Amanda (2009), *Behind Closed Doors: At Home in Georgian England*, New Haven, CT: Yale University Press.

Vikström, Lotta, Frans van Poppel, and Bart van de Putte (2011), "New Light on the Divorce Transition," *Journal of Family History*, 36 (2): 107–117.

Vlaardingerbroek, Paul (1995–96), "Marriage, Divorce, and Living Arrangements in the Netherlands," *Family Law Quarterly*, 29 (3): 635–644.

Voigt, C. F. T. (1821), *Hausbedarf für Verlobte und Neuverehelichte und solche, die es noch werden wollen*, Leipzig: Seeger.

Vries, Sophie (2018), "Een zoektocht naar geluk. Een verkennend onderzoek naar de wensen bij partnerselectie in de periode 1920–1995 aan de hand van Nederlandse contactadvertenties," Nijmegen: Unpublished paper at Radboud University.

Waddington, Mark and Mark van Hoecke (1998), "Legal Cultures, Legal Paradigms and Legal Doctrine: Towards a New Model for Comparative Law," *International and Comparative Law Quarterly*, 47 (3): 495–536.

Wang, Feng, Cameron Campbell, and James Lee (2010), "Agency, Hierarchies, and Reproduction in Northeastern Chinese Populations, 1789–1840," in Noriko O. Tsuya, Wang Feng, George Alter, James Z. Lee, et al. (eds.), *Prudence and Pressure: Reproduction and Human Agency in Europe and Asia, 1700–1900*, 287–316, Cambridge, MA: MIT Press.

Wanhalla, Angela (2014), *Matters of the Heart: A History of Interracial Marriage in New Zealand*, Auckland: Auckland University Press.

Ward, Peter (1990), *Courtship, Love, and Marriage in Nineteenth-Century English Canada*, Montreal and Kingson: McGill-Queen's University Press.

Wassermann, Jakob (1987), *Laudin und die Seinen*, Munich: dtv.

Watkins, Susan (1981), "Regional Patterns of Nuptiality in Europe, 1870–1960," *Population Studies. A Journal of Demography*, 35 (2): 199–215.

Watt, Ian (2001), *The Rise of the Novel*, Berkeley: University of California Press.

Weeks, Jeffrey (1981), *Sex, Politics and Society: The Regulation of Sexuality since 1800*, London: Longman.

Weinzierl, Michael (1997), "Kein First Amendment und wenig Laicite," in Michael Weinzierl (ed.), *Individualisierung, Rationalisierung, Säkularisierung. Neue Wege der Religionsgeschichte*, 246–258. Wiener Beiträge zur Geschichte der Neuzeit 22, Munich: R. Oldenbourg Verlag.

Weitbrecht, Mrs. (1875), *The Women of India and Christian Work in the Zenana*, London: James Nisbet.

Welchman, Lynn (2007), *Women and Muslim Family Laws in Arab States: A Comparative Overview of Textual Development and Advocacy*, Amsterdam: University of Amsterdam Press.

Westermarck, Edward (1891), *The History of Human Marriage*, London: Macmillan.

Wharton, Edith ([1907] 1996), "Madame de Treymes," in *Three European Novels*, 1–52, Harmondsworth: Penguin.

Wharton, Edith ([1913] 2000), *The Custom of the Country*, Oxford: Oxford University Press.

Wharton, Edith ([1922] 2006), *Glimpses of the Moon*, London: Pushkin Press.

White, Nicholas (1999), *The Family in Crisis in Late Nineteenth-Century French Fiction*, Cambridge: Cambridge University Press.

White, Nicholas (2013), *French Divorce Fiction from the Revolution to the First World War*, London: Legenda.

White, Nicholas and Naomi Segal, eds. (1997), *Scarlet Letters: Fictions of Adultery from Antiquity to the 1990s*, Basingstoke: Macmillan.

Wienholts, Karin (2018), "'Liefst eenigzins gefortuneerd'. Een verkennend onderzoek naar voorwaarden in huwelijksadvertenties in de periode 1800—1950," Nijmegen: Unpublished Paper at Radboud University.

Wikander, Ulla (1998), *Von der Magd zur Angestellten. Macht, Geschlecht und Arbeitsteilung 1789–1950*, Frankfurt: Fischer Verlag.

Wikman, K. Rob W. (1937), *Die Einleitung der Ehe, eine vergleichend ethno-soziologische Untersuchung über die Vorstufe der Ehe in den Sitten des Schwedischen Volkstums*, Åbo: Åbo akademi.

Witte, John Jr. (2012), *From Sacrament to Contract: Marriage, Religion, and Law in the Western Tradition*, Louisville, KY: Westminster John Knox Press.

Witte, John Jr. and Joel A. Nichols (2005), "Introduction," in John Witte Jr. and Eliza Ellison (eds.), *Covenant Marriage in Comparative Perspective*, Grand Rapids, MI: Eerdmans Publishing Co.

Wolf, Arthur (1995), *Sexual Attraction and Childhood Association: A Chinese Brief for Edward Westermarck*, Stanford, CA: Stanford University Press.

Wolf, Arthur (2005), "Europe and China: Two Kinds of Patriarchy," in Theo Engelen and Arthur Wolf (eds.), *Marriage and the Family in Eurasia: Perspectives on the Hajnal Hypothesis*, 215–240, Amsterdam: Aksant.

Wolf, Arthur P. and Chieh-shan Huang (1980), *Marriage and Adoption in China, 1845–1945*, Stanford, CA: Stanford University Press.

Wolf, Arthur P. and Theo Engelen (2008), "Fertility and Fertility Control in Pre-Revolutionary China," *Journal of Interdisciplinary History*, 38 (3): 345–375.

Wollstonecraft, Mary ([1798] 1975), *Maria or the Wrongs of Woman*, ed. Moira Ferguson, New York: Norton.

Wollstonecraft, Mary ([1798] 2005), *Maria or The Wrongs of Woman*, New York: Dover.

Wood Hill, Marilynn (1993), *Their Sisters' Keepers: Prostitution in New York City, 1830–1870*, Berkeley: University of California Press.

Worthman, Carol M., and John W. M. Whiting (1987), "Social Change in Adolescent Sexual Behavior, Mate Selection, and Premarital Pregnancy Rates in a Kikuyu Community," *Ethos*, 15 (2): 145–165.

Yagi, Toru (2001), *Kon'in to Kazoku no Minzokuteki Kozo* (Ethnographic Structure of Marriage and Family), Tokyo: Yoshikawa Kobunkan.

Yan, Yunxiang (2002), "Courtship, Love and Premarital Sex in a North China Village," *China Journal*, 48: 29–53.

Ze'evi, Dror (2006), *Producing Desire: Changing Sexual Discourse in the Ottoman Middle East, 1500–1900*, Berkeley: University of California Press.

Zhao, Zhongwei (1997), "Deliberate Birth Control under a High-Fertility Regime: Reproductive Behavior in China before 1970," *Population and Development Review*, 23 (4): 729–767.

Zisowitz Stearns, Carol and Peter N. Stearns (1985), "Victorian Sexuality: Can Historians Do it Better?," *Journal of Social History*, 18 (4): 625–634.

Zola, Emile ([1881] 1966–69), "Le divorce et la littérature," in *Oeuvres complètes*, 15 vols., 543–547, Paris: Cercle du livre précieux. XIV [First published February 14, 1881, in *Le Figaro*].

INDEX